THE HOUSE THAT JAM BUILT

Llewellyn S. Smith

with
Phyllis Cowan

Baby Boomer Press
Markham, Ontario, Canada

1995

Published by:
Baby Boomer Press*
P.O. Box 525
Markham, Ontario.
L3P 3R1
(905) 472-0546

Design and illustrations by Deborah Larson
Electronically Typeset by Fine Impressions, 416-487-1106
Old photographs from E.D. Smith* archives
New photographs by R. Fuller Cator*
Title of book comes from Canadian Business, September 1977

ISBN 0-9694574-5-6

Bound to stay Open

This book has been bound using the patented Otabind process. You can open this book at any page, gently run your finger down the spine and the pages will lie flat. Otabind combines improved bookbinding adhesive technology with a unique free floating cover to produce a reader friendly book.

Printed by
WEBCOM Limited*
3480 Pharmacy Ave.
Scarborough, Ontario
Canada, M1W 3G3

In addition to being more enjoyable to read or work with than books that won't stay open, Otabind books are uncommonly durable.

Printed on Recycled Paper

* Denotes a Canadian Association of
  Family Enterprise (CAFE) member

Dear Friends,

The idea of writing this book was introduced to me by our lawyer, Paul Milne of Simpson, Wigle in Hamilton, Ontario. Paul has a keen interest in the evolution and direction of family owned companies. He felt that the E.D. Smith story should be shared. In fact, when I started this project with Phyllis Cowan of Markham, Ontario, my basic intention was to record both our history and current affairs for the benefit of my children, Gerard who is 16, Graham age 9 and 6 year old Claire.

But as we started combing the archives and talking with former and existing staff, relatives, friends and associates, the book took on a life of its own and I was encouraged to broaden the audience. So here we are today, with a substantial story to tell. It is an historical, military, political, psychological and business minded adventure. Now our loyal customers will have an idea what is behind our name. I am hoping readers can share some excitement, tears and fears, learn from our mistakes and above all, fathom the vision of the Smiths through the years.

For myself, the research has helped identify the key values in our family that have made the past a success and will guide us in the future.

Our company, which is now North American with a factory in both Canada and the United States, wouldn't be where it is today without the support of our customers and suppliers and the loyalty, intelligence and commitment of our staff, both past and present. On behalf of the Smith family, a big THANK YOU!

Special thanks to my parents who were approached on many occasions to sell the business yet held on. In doing so, they gave me the opportunity to take the firm to the fifth generation. I appreciate their unqualified support.

I hope you enjoy our book.

Llewellyn S. Smith

Table of Contents

Dear Friends   i

Prologue   iv

Smith Family Tree   vi

The First Generation—The Beginning   1
Silas Smith—United Empire Loyalists Arrive—Settling In—
Hearth and Home—The Hungry Years—Early A.B.C.s

The Second Generation—War And Independence   13
Ananias Smith—War of 1812—The Battle of Stoney Creek—
Who was this Brave Billy Green?—A New Business—Growth
and Development—Lasting Influence

The Third Generation—Back To The Land   25
Sylvester Smith—A Woman Ahead of Her Time—The Pioneer
Wife—Saltrisin' Bread—An Outspoken Woman—The Proud
Parents—The Scene is Set

The Fourth Generation—The House That Jam Built   51
Ernest D'Israeli Smith—The Young E.D.—E.D.'s Diaries—The
Fruit King—The Senator—Cecil Smith—The Great
Depression—The Senator's Predictions—The Senator
Retires—Letters of Tribute—Christina Ann Armstrong, Mrs.
E.D.—The Women's Institute—Verna Smith Conant—
Elizabeth Smith—Virtuous Energy—E.D.'s Three Other
Sisters—Leon Smith—The Rose King—Helderleigh
Nurseries—York Nurseries—Treetops—Money and Power
Cause Problems

**The Fifth Generation—Not Just Jams And Jellies
Any More**   119
Armand—The Military—Armand Meets W.W.I.—Somewhere
in France—Major Kimmins—Brigadier Armand Smith Goes

Back to War—Evelyn in England—A Grave Decision—The
Accident—E.D. Smith Company Visits HP Sauce—A Dismal
Sight—The Hip is Very Bad—The Brigadier Sails Home—
Leon Fights His Own War—The Major, E. Llewellyn G.
Smith—War Memorial—Armand Carries On—Minimum
Wage Threat—Company Houses—Armand has his Hands
Full—Expansion in Food Processing—The Brigadier Retires—
The Sauces and Their Secrets—Discovery of HP Sauce—Lea
and Perrins—E.D. Smith and HP Sauce—E.L.G. Visits HP—
Alastair Visits HP—The Secret Ingredient—The Sauces and
Me—Enter the French

The Sixth Generation—Harvest Of Values　　　　173
E. Llewellyn G. Smith—75th Anniversary—Fire and Water—
E.L.G. at the Helm—"A" for Achievement—Maple Leaf
Mills—A Tiger By the Tail—Tomato Season—Garden
Cocktail—The Great Share Scare—Clifford Sifton—CAFE—
100th Anniversary

The Seventh Generation—Back To Basics　　　　201
Llewellyn Sifton Smith—At School—Learning the Ropes—
CAFE and Me—Acquisition—Free Trade—Sale of Garden
Cocktail—David Nichol and Private Label—Byhalia—Winona

The Eighth Generation—A Canadian Survivor　　　229
As We Approach the Millennium—Looking Back—Now—
Looking Forward to 2000

Epilogue　　　　245

Recipes　　　　251

Current Employees In Winona And Byhalia　　　256

25-Year Employees In Winona And Byhalia　　　260

Prologue

Roast chicken, green beans, rice and salad. I surveyed the dinner table with pleasure and called to my children.

"Dinner's ready. Please come to the table."

Gerard, Graham and Claire brought their respective sized appetites with them. The year, 1995 and a lot was happening in their lives: good things, busy times, some worrisome moments and confusing days.

Dinner time offered an opportunity to talk.

Helping himself, Gerard started off with, "Dad, there were these people talking to me. They weren't even born here but they want the government to give them things. Shouldn't they go back to where they came from?

"Do you know why they left?"

"I don't know, but isn't Canada for Canadians?"

"I can't agree more. But tell me, what's a Canadian?"

"Someone who lives and works here," said Graham.

"That's true," I answered, "but the Smiths didn't always live and work here. We came from the United States, in New Jersey and before that, from England. Everybody in Canada came from somewhere else except maybe our Native People and even they came from somewhere."

"How long have we been here?" asked Claire.

"Well, as a family we've been living here since July 1787."

"Why didn't the Smiths stay in the States?" asked Gerard. All three pairs of eyes focused on me for an answer.

I had been waiting for this question for a long time.

I was ready.

From the company archives and personal papers of family members, I had been compiling a family history. Some of this information had survived fire, flood and all manner of dislocations. I had it put in order and arranged in the form of a story.

I decided to call it simply:

THE HOUSE THAT JAM BUILT—For my children

With the kids settled quietly around me, we started going through what I had put together.

Our journey would cover more than 200 years and follow the life and times of eight generations of Smiths in Canada.

I wanted to explain how, why and when the first direct descendent of our family, **Silas**, came to this country.

We needed to see how his son **Ananias** carried on through war and adversity.

Sylvester, the third generation, suffered with disease most of his adult life but rejoiced in his five children and strong wife.

One of his boys was **ERNEST D'ISRAELI**. We see him grow from farmer, to businessman to Senator.

His son **Armand**, fought in two wars and managed to pull the company through the Depression and keep it on the leading edge of its time.

Next, **Llewellyn**, their grandfather grew the business from that point in a changing world and marketplace.

Now it is my turn.

Smith Family Tree

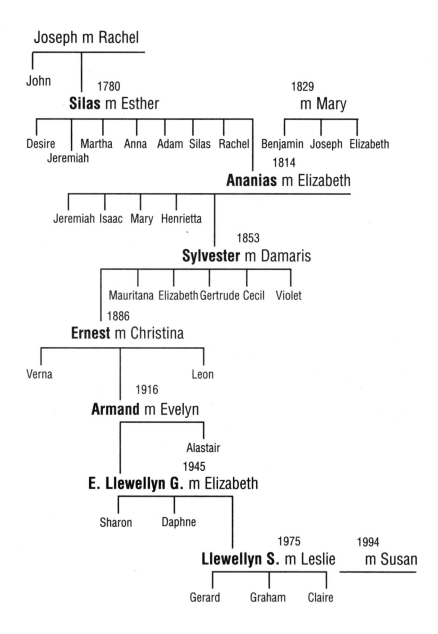

THE FIRST GENERATION

THE BEGINNING

Silas Smith 1756–1844

The First Generation

The Smith Family	World Events
	1620 Mayflower lands at Plymouth, Mass.
	1666 Great Fire of London
	1670 Hudson's Bay Company founded
	1706 Benjamin Franklin born
	1727 Sir Isaac Newton dies
	1732 George Washington born
1756 **Silas** and his wife Ester born	1756 Beginning of Seven Years' War
	1769 Napoleon born
	1773 Boston Tea Party
	1775 Famous ride of Paul Revere American War of Independence
1780 **Silas** and Ester married	
1781 Desire born	
	1782 First census in Niagara recorded 16 families, 83 people
1783 Jeremiah born	
1784 Martha born	
1785 Anna born	
1787 **Silas**, family and friends reach Niagara frontier—Adam born	
1788 Silas Jr. born	1788 The Hungry Years
	1789 French Revolution
	1791 Canada Act (upper and lower Canada formed)
1792 Rachel born	
1794 **Ananias** born	
1795 Elizabeth Showers Smith born (wife of **Ananias**)	
	1796 Rise of Napoleon Bonaparte John McIntosh transplants wild apple trees
	1799 George Washington dies
1802 Crown Deed issued to **Silas**	
	1803 Design for refrigerator patented
	1807 Chief Joseph Brant dies

THE FIRST GENERATION

THE BEGINNING

There is something heroic in the self-sacrifice of these our forefathers who gave up their farms, their homes and all the ties of neighbouring associations, and came here to battle with nature in her rudest state, with poverty, age, even starvation staring them in the face, and all for the love of the old flag. Is there so much devotion now? Would we give up our farms and homes and flee to some savage wilderness, if revolutionists were to gain the upper hand?

Ernest D'Israeli Smith, February 1, 1880
(fourth generation)

Silas Smith 1756–1844

He crouched down low to the ground, dug his hand deep into the soft, warm earth, scooped it up and then let the rich soil sift through his thick fingers. Patting it gently where it lay was his way of saying good-bye. The success of the Americans in the War of Independence meant Silas and his family could not remain in America.

It was in his blood to resist imposed compromises. His ancestors had left England to be able to practice their Puritanical beliefs without fear. His father and mother, Joseph and Rachel had settled in this district, called "Pahuckquapath" by the Indians, to escape such tyranny themselves.

Here, in the Blue Mountains is a pass, truly, one of the most curious freaks of nature, and perhaps nowhere is there a similar disturbance on the orderly face of nature. This pass is known as the Water Gap by the whole country. Below these rapids on the east side of the river about 5 miles from the shore was the home of the Smiths many of whom emigrated to this country in 1776 and the following years, among them Silas Smith my great grandfather, who often in the winter of their early settlement had to subsist upon roots and buds to a great extent before they had land enough cleared to raise a subsistence upon.

E.D. Smith 1875

The First Generation

United Empire Loyalists Arrive

Silas and his family knew they were leaving a wonderful and exciting land. Both he and his wife Esther were 31 years old, had been married just seven years and had five children, Desire, Jeremiah, Martha, Anna and baby Adam. They arrived in Canada on one of their three horses, or safely tucked into a saddle bag but most walked. When they reached Fort Niagara, Silas took his oath of allegiance and gained approval to cross the Niagara River along with two cows and 46 other families in July, 1787. They were probably met by military bateaux to carry them across, however some were not so lucky.

> Upon reaching the Niagara River the men effected a crossing above the Falls by lashing a pole across an old flat-bottomed boat, fastening an ox by the head to each end of the pole, and forcing the animals to swim across, thus propelling the scow and its passengers and baggage.
>
> *Early Life in Upper Canada*

These people were some of Canada's first immigrants. They came here to escape problems and worries and to find a new life just as many new Canadians do today.

The journey included several neighbours, friends and Silas' brother John. It must have been a fearfully gruesome trip buoyed up by the thoughts of freedom and hope in a new land.

Imagine the cold, dark nights, the rain, the fear of predators. Hear the crying, hungry children and the loud, raised voices of desperate men. Watch the women, strong and caring, constantly moving and protecting their families.

How did they eat? What did they eat? Well, if you think about it, the very first activity when a group of pioneers stopped to rest, was to build a fire. It gave warmth, protection and boiling water to cook fish or rabbits, along with roots and plants they gathered. Then they would move on.

What motivated these people to endure such hardships? Were they just headstrong zealots? It is strongly felt by some today that these Loyalists were united more in spirit and reason than in their blind allegiance to the British. In any case, it was the culmination of many factors that set them on their journey. Because they travelled as a large cohesive group and many settled close to one another, they quickly developed a sense of community and caring that has endured to this day in places like Winona.

Two of the destinations these pioneers were headed for, The Forty and The Fifty refer to the supposed distance from the border in miles. Silas and his family settled at the Fifty Mile Creek on a spot about 190 meters west of the present Fifty United Church.

The area was covered with dense forests of oak, maple, beech, hickory, elm and other hard wood trees as well as evergreens. The surface of the lake swarmed with wild fowl, huge flocks of wild pigeons darkened the sky and there was abundance of fish not only in the lake but in the streams. Most communication was made by canoes along the lake shore but there were Indian trails—the most important being the one that is now number 8 highway.

Armand Smith (fifth generation)

Settling In

The British government needed and wanted loyal, strong pioneers and indeed encouraged the Loyalists to travel north with the offer of grain, tools, land and "love of the flag."

As a usual rule each family was supplied with clothes for three years. Indian blankets were used for making coats and a coarse cloth was supplied for making trousers. Then each family was given an axe, and a hand saw. The axe was short-handled like a hatchet and was very little use for cutting the huge trees in the forest. Each of two families was given a whip-saw and a cross-cut saw. Each of five families received a chest of tools with chisels, augers etc. For shooting game for food each group of five families was given a fire-lock. The families who settled in Nova Scotia were given bricks to build chimneys but the Saltfleet Loyalists were forced to use wood and clay for their chimneys until one of their own enterprising citizens built a brick kiln at Fruitland. Sir Frederick Haldimand the Governor at the time tried to find seed grain for the settlers by sending agents to the Mohawk Valley to buy all they could. The Governor also bought cattle and sheep to help the loyalists stock their farms.

Saltfleet Then and Now

Such an enticement was easy to accept in the face of unrest and unwelcome conditions. It was a matter of submitting a petition for land and when Silas Smith did so he mentioned he was a well-established man both in land and person and that he was willing to leave all this behind to live under the British flag and enjoy British law and customs. He was granted 600 acres of land, 200 acres for himself and 200 acres for each of his two sons. At first he was given merely Squatter's Rights but when all the land was bought from the Indians in 1789, the Land Board at Niagara was established and his settler's "location ticket" was replaced by a Certificate and the deed for this land was finally issued on May 17, 1802. The northwest part of Lot 2, Concession II, Saltfleet township (100 acres), Lot 2, Concession III (100 acres), Lot 2, Concession IV (300 acres) and Lot 2, Concession V (100 acres) became home.

From the soil came their food and livelihood. How could they have known that this soil would provide increased prosperity for their descendants right into the 21st century?

Hearth and Home

Their first log dwelling could have been as large as 20' x 15' but probably smaller. Many were about 10' long, 8' wide and 6' high, sloping to a back wall of 4'. The logs of pine or basswood were notched to help them fit tightly together. Moss, clay and small bits of wood chinked the holes. Windows with glass were a luxury to come later so an opening to let in light and fresh air might just have been covered with a heavy fabric. During the winter they would hew down the logs on the inside to get a flat, finished look.

With the assured protection of a roof over their heads, they started to make it home. A chair, a table, a shelf, a bed, even a thing as simple as a peg for clothing all added to the comfort.

Even under ideal circumstances it was difficult to endure these pioneer conditions. Building a shelter, clearing land, planting a few grains to establish a crop, all took second priority to just staying alive. Summers in this part of the world are generally favourable and the Smiths and others managed to

EARLY RECIPES CONTAIN NO REFERENCES TO EGGS BECAUSE THERE WERE NO CHICKENS.

Hearth and Home

become well enough entrenched to make it through the first winter. The fall wheat they had planted was actually joyfully harvested. What a feeling of accomplishment!!

But, little Jeremiah, who had arrived in the new land an infant, died, as did many others, young and not so young. Life was hard and about to become harder.

The Hungry Years 1788–1789

The government appreciated the sacrifices of the settlers and the idea was that the provisions given them were to last long enough for them to become independent.

But in their second summer, 1788, before they were really established, the Hungry Years hit them—"the years of famine," the scarce years," "the starved years," a horrendous time.

There was a terrible drought—no blade of green grass could be seen. The three horses and one of the cows died. The following spring a new settler arrived with an ox which, with the remaining cow was yoked and together they plowed the small clearing which had been made. In the fall great joy was experienced when they could gather in ripe ears of wheat and corn. During those hungry years

Typical, basic one room of a pioneer log home. Could be warm and cozy or damp and dark. The large fireplace was used for cooking and warmth and did not always have a chimney.

The First Generation

Silas Smith travelled on foot to the Indian settlement on the Grand River to purchase a bag of corn and returned carrying it on his back. He also walked from The Fifty to Niagara with a bushel of wheat to have it ground at Samuel Street's mill. The family lived chiefly on black squirrels, wild ducks and other wild fowl and animals but at last their ammunition ran out and even this source of food was denied them.

> The survival rate of some settlers would have been much lower if it weren't for Pumpkins! Plentiful, nutritious, long lasting.

Gertrude Smith (fourth generation)

Children were taught to follow the squirrels to see where they hid their nuts and collect them; seed potatoes that had been planted were dug up and eaten; a beef bone was passed from house to house and boiled to try to glean a little bit of nutritional stock. The deer starved and the wolves grew fat.

Living near Lake Ontario assured them of fish to eat, water to drink (but the viciously cold winter made the ice unusually thick and difficult to cut through), and the government supplied them with certain articles of food and supplies so that most did not starve.

However in the summer of 1789 things became so severe that a letter of appeal from the settlers of the district was sent to the British command at Niagara, namely, 'His Excellency John Graves Simcoe Esq. Governor and Commander-in-Chief in and over His Majesty's Province of Upper Canada.' Silas, a prominent man in the community already, was a major force in the application of this letter.

Silas Smith.

Crown Deed with Great Seal

The Hungry Years

In response, they were loaned "a quantity of pork, peas, and rice" from the government stores that were themselves becoming more and more depleted. Still five years later they were unable to repay this loan and another petition asked if they could repay it in wheat or grain, for they had absolutely no money. The government had no choice but to accept this alternative because they needed to sustain the lives and loyalty of these valuable settlers. Actually, most records show that these loans were eventually forgiven, and life went on.

In the midst of these antagonistic times babies were born. Silas Junior arrived September 30, 1788, Rachel was born June 14, 1792 and Ananias April 22, 1794. Silas' wife Esther bore eight children, fed, clothed, nursed and taught them. The pioneer wife was a woman of exceptional stamina, strength and resource. The men worked hard but life could not have been quite so trying for them as it was for the women. The birthing and rearing of children took their toll. Just to wander the cemeteries of southern Ontario, the Burial Ground at The Fifty, for

The Hungry Years

Corn failed, and fruit and herb. The tender grass
Fell into dust. Trees died like sentient things,
And stood wrapped in their shrouds of withered
leaves,
That rustled weirdly round them sear and dead.
From springs and brooks no morning mist arose;
The water vanished; and a brazen sky
Glowed hot and sullen through the pall of smoke
That rose from burning forests, far and near.

Slowly the months rolled round on fiery wheels;
The savage year relented not, nor shut
Its glaring eye, till all things perished,—food
For present, seed for future use were gone.
'All swallowed up,' the starving Indians said,
'By the great serpent of the Chenonda
That underlies the ground and sucks it dry.'

William Kirby

example, is to see how many men married two or three times. So too was the case for Silas and Esther. She died in 1828. At the age of 72 he was married again to Mary McGee and they had three children! Silas died in 1844 when he was 88 years old and is buried in St. Andrew's churchyard, Grimsby with his two wives.

Early A.B.C.s

The hardworking pioneers were so caught up with the daily task of keeping mind and body together, it is a wonder they had time to even consider such spiritual and academic issues as church and school. They did. Silas centred his religious zeal right in his home with church and Sunday School every week for the community while Monday to Friday the local school took place under his roof until a real school opened in 1816.

It was a matter of priorities and vision. Even though he lived in a time when survival depended mainly on muscles and brawn, he knew that to be successful farmers and citizens, his children would need to know how to calculate profit and loss, how to read and how to think.

Their sense of law, order and diligence set high standards for their descendants to follow.

Armand Smith
(fifth generation)

Silas Smith

A desperate man in desperate times. He lived by the courage of his convictions and followed a path he believed in, even though it was considered by many to be an unpopular one.

Politically a British subject, with no intention of changing or adapting to imposed regimes, he was prepared to give up a settled, prosperous life and risk everything to start over, to be independent.

He had a pioneer mentality without which he could never have succeeded.

Along with his cohesive family unit his community of friends shared a common goal. With an eye to the future, he prospered.

THE SECOND GENERATION

WAR AND INDEPENDENCE

Ananias Smith 1794–1874

The Second Generation

The Smith Family	World Events
	1802 Process discovered of preserving food by canning
	1807 Chief Joseph Brant dies
	1809 Abraham Lincoln born
	1812 War of 1812; population of Canada 90,000
	1813 Battle of Stoney Creek;
1814 **Ananias** marries Elizabeth	1814 Congress of Vienna
1815 Jeremiah born	1815 Battle of Waterloo (Wellington defeats Napoleon)
	1816 School established in Saltfleet by Common School Act
1817 Isaac Brock born	1817 Road between York (Toronto) and Montreal completed
	1819 Queen Victoria born
1820 Mary Eliza born	1820 Church built at The Fifty; Florence Nightingale born
1822 Henrietta born	1821 Napoleon dies
1823 **Sylvester** born	1823 Louis Pasteur born
1825 Hester Ann born	(pasteurization)
1827 Catharine born	
1828 Ester dies	1828 York (Toronto) General Hospital opened
1829 **Silas** remarries to Mary McGee (they had three children, Benjamin 1833, Joseph 1835, Elizabeth 1837)	1829 The John Bly steamer starts to sail between Hamilton and York; Welland Canal opened
Ananias adds to his house; Martha Jane born	1830 First sulphur matches in Canada, made in Hamilton
1831 Damaris Isabella McGee (E.D.'s mother) born	1831 Upper Canada College founded
1832 Caroline born	1832 Cholera epidemic; fire in Hamilton
	1833 Slavery abolished in British Empire
1834 Amanda born	1834 York becomes Toronto, incorporated as a city
1836 Ransom born	

THE SECOND GENERATION

WAR AND INDEPENDENCE

To know the history of Canada in general and southern Ontario in particular is to study the story of the Smith family.

E. Llewellyn G. Smith
(sixth generation)

Ananias Smith 1794–1874

It could not have been easy to be the fourth boy and eighth child in a pioneer family. Born April 22, 1794 to Silas and Esther, into a household that was by that time quite well established, Ananias would have been expected to work in the fields, fish, and carry on the pioneer spirit of taming the wilderness. His parents had brought many skills with them and were not content to merely eke out a living. They wanted more than that and probably pushed their children very hard.

Ananias too, was a man of strong will and purpose and evidently disagreed with his father regularly. Did Silas rule with an iron hand? Did Ananias rebel? It seems he did. He never followed his father's Methodist faith. This alone was bound to cause trouble, but he did become a member of the Anglican church. Thus his religious attitude remained intact but the tradition of following in his family's church did not.

The War of 1812

Silas had faced the challenge of settling in a new land and now Ananias faced the challenge of fighting to keep it independent. At just 18 years of age, he found himself serving with the 4th and 5th Lincoln Regiments and fighting in the War of

The Second Generation

1812 along with three of his brothers, local boys and relatives. This might well have been one of the most exciting periods of his life. Against incredible odds, the landowners of thinly-populated Upper Canada managed to repel the American advances. In spite of having far less troops, incredibly bad roads (in some places non-existent or merely Indian trails), and an overall desire not to be forced to fight, they had a few distinct advantages over the Americans: a determination not to be chased out and lose their land again; some training; and a great leader—General Isaac Brock, who gave his life in this war.

What a war it was. It had everything: trickery, gallantry, atrocities; Indians, redcoats, battleships, cavalry charges; cowards, heroes and bunglers. It was probably the crucial war in our history. For the first and only important time, Canada's two founding races stood together to drive an invader from their soil. Had they failed there'd be no centennial to celebrate. But they won and, united as never before, went on to build a country.

The Formative Years

The Battle of Stoney Creek

The most decisive battle was fought June 6, 1813 at Stoney Creek and was the turning point of the war. The Americans were defeated here but had it been otherwise, the E.D. Smith company would never have been Canadian.

The enemy moving up through the Niagara Peninsula were 3,500 strong. Their supplies followed them along the lakeshore in row-boats. On June 5th, they lay camped at the Gage farm where the homestead was commandeered for the use of the staff and the women and children were locked up in the cellar.

At the time of the battle James Gage was thirty-nine years old, a prosperous farmer and merchant, for he kept a general store and for many years this was the only store and stopping-place between Ancaster and Niagara. He was locked up in a building nearby and guarded by a sentry. The surrounding settlers were imprisoned so that no one

DURING THE WAR OF 1812, THERE WAS A BIG DEMAND FOR SALT FOR GUNPOWDER FROM THE SALTFLEET SPRINGS.

The Battle of Stoney Creek

could carry a message out to a General Vincent who was camped at Burlington Heights.

Isaac Corman got inside the enemy lines and learned important secrets he then told to a local nineteen-year-old, Billy Green, who ran until he reached Vincent and poured the story into his ears. With this information, Vincent lead a surprise attack against the Americans by night with 700 men down through the glade that ends at Stoney Creek. They gave Billy Green 'the scout' a corporal's sword and told him to lead, for he knew every inch of the way.

The Americans were asleep, oblivious to danger. The settlers attacked, and the affair developed into a hand-to-hand fight. The Americans could not find their generals and no doubt thought the number of the enemy much greater than it was because the settlers along the mountain top made a great deal of forbidding noise. The Americans retreated until they reached the Forty Mile Creek.

On June 6, 1913, Her Majesty Queen Mary of England, pressed a button in Buckingham Palace and unveiled a statue in Stoney Creek in memory of the Battle of Stoney Creek, to commemorate 100 years of peace with the United States.

The preservation of the Niagara district may, with the strictest justice, be fairly attributed to the attack upon the enemy at Stoney Creek. The nature of the war seems to have changed after that most manly and energetic affair and the campaign on that frontier terminated in the capture of the American stronghold, Fort Niagara.

The Battle of Stoney Creek 1813
The Story of Hamilton

Some of the advantages Ananias, Billy Green, the Indians and local farmers had over the Americans demonstrate the mentality of these settlers at the time. They had a fierce pride in the ownership of their land; they had allies scattered throughout the countryside and all along the border; they were in superb physical condition from their daily toil; and they knew the local geography. These young men had scampered over the hills all their lives chasing and hunting rabbits, birds, deer; collecting berries and roots; and generally exploring as nature bade them. The Americans outnumbered the local folk to a great extent but they totally underestimated their training, knowledge and skill.

Who was this brave Billy Green?

Billy's family, like the Smiths, had torn themselves away from the prosperity of New Jersey soil to settle in the wilds of Upper Canada. Their fear of Americans became well entrenched in the mind of young Billy. Being the eleventh child in his family (and apparently the first white baby born in the area), he often found himself on his own and came to be at home in the woods of the escarpment. When he joined the militia during the war, he put both his love for his family's new home and his scouting ability to good use.

He is our own Paul Revere. In 1875 the government acknowledged his bravery by giving him $20.00. He should be as famous as Laura Secord. Perhaps we should name a candy bar after him.

A New Business

In 1814, Ananias married Elizabeth Smith of West Flamborough and settled at "The Fifty." They built their one-story home at the corner of The Fifty Road and what is now Number 8 Highway. Modern for the times, it was constructed of siding, shingles, with two fireplaces and windows. (E.D. as a young boy lived on top of the escarpment and would often stay with Ananias, his grandfather, in this house during the long, cold winter because it was closer to school.)

Because he did not share the excitement of being a recently-landed United Empire Loyalist, because he was overshadowed by the war of 1812 and because no one in his immediate family kept any written records that remain, we can only speculate on much of Ananias' life. At the time, apparently, older sons were often granted land by the government and Ananias assumed he would inherit the family farm. But when his father married Mary McGee in 1829 after the death of his mother the year before, and had three more children, two of them sons, he probably realized he would not receive the land.

FOR ONE DOCTOR , THE MINIMUM COST OF DELIVERING A BABY WAS A CHICKEN.

A New Business

The picture I get is of a fellow who had most of his schooling in the home and his "on the job training" was the farm. He had never developed a saleable trade. Since he would have to fend for himself, he went into business catering to travellers. He set about this by building a stable for horses, adding to his house, extending the front with a verandah and generally turning himself into one of the many tavern/innkeepers that were to emerge in Upper Canada.

I have often heard him tell how the Americans used to stop overnight with him on their way to Michigan from New York. His Inn was just one day's march from the river Niagara. I have heard grandmother tell of these travellers who remarked to another, 'See the Canadian, why! these people are just like our folks.'

E.D. Smith 1870

He supplied lodging, fresh horses and some rumours persist that liquor was also available. This would have indeed brought him some revenue but would also have alienated him in the eyes of his father and perhaps other neighbours and friends. These were hard, strict times but he did what he thought he had to do. There was another tavern that Ananias built (yes, E.D. used the word tavern to describe it) just across the road from the first one, that was still in business when E.D. was seven years old, so it proves that he went into this business in a big way.

All sorts of travellers came by: farmers, Americans, rustic labourers, soldiers and Indians. The fact that everyone sat at the same table, irrespective of social position was of great annoyance to the Englishmen who were not yet ready to accept the American influence of democracy and equality of all.

Ananias Smith 1794–1874

The Second Generation

I would love to have been there on one particularly dark, cold winter night, observing an assortment of people drinking birch beer and eating fried bread, when a half-frozen stranger fell through the door and told his awesome story.

> I have just travelled from the Niagara River and I saw it with my own eyes! The famous Niagara River had ceased to flow! No water fell over the falls! Local fellows told me that apparently strange winds and massive ice build-up above the falls had caused such a giant plug, that the waters were stopped. Stopped, I tell you! Here, let me prove it.

To attest to this strange story, he pulled from his pocket a hunk of dark, oily, heavily grained wood and claimed it was a piece from an old wreck he found when he walked on the exposed rocks at the base of the falls. Rocks no one had ever seen before.

Strategically located, this tavern became a meeting place, a destination of its own and the local watering hole. It helped become part of the fabric that made Winona eventually a town of importance for it helped encourage settlement.

Niagara Falls—Then and Now

Then

1829—Attract tourists by setting a full-rigged schooner on fire, at night, about one mile upstream from the falls. Watch the spectacle of it plummeting to its fiery, watery demise.

Now

1995—Tourists come to see the Skylon Tower, bright lights and wax museum.

It must have been a hard life, but in this way, Ananias was able to support a family and on September 20, 1823, his son Sylvester was born (the father of E.D. Smith). He and all other 10 children of Ananias and Elizabeth lived to be married which was quite remarkable because so many died at a young age during these times.

He made money at his tavern because he had cash enough to give my father $900 to help buy his land on the mountain. He gave each of his seven daughters $100 as a dowry and a proper setting out in housekeeping equipment and a cow.

E.D. Smith

Growth and Development

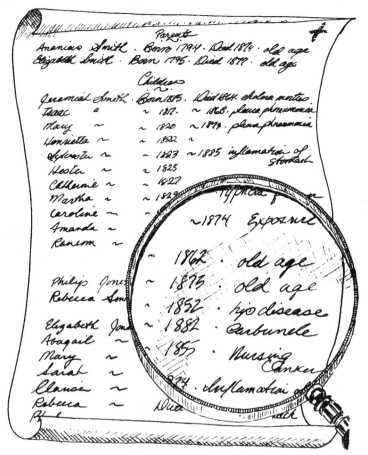

Some causes of death

Growth and Development

Upper Canada was basically settled by farmers, who built the homes and soldiers who built the forts, which became the towns. The soldiers became the customers for the farmers' produce and the people of the land who moved to town became customers as well. What did these new city dwellers do for a living? They developed skills such as bricklaying, plastering and lathing, for the next generation of homes were more than just log structures. These tradespeople in turn needed merchants, lawyers, tinsmiths, general stores, offices, printing

The Second Generation

shops and farmers to supply them with necessary goods and services.

It often happened that a farmer would have difficulty paying for supplies; so many of them bargained to repay debts with services. They became blacksmiths, auctioneers, bakers, tailors, innkeepers and butchers. At first these skills were used in a barter system but quickly turned into actual professions that were in demand.

Lasting Influence

Ananias and his family are a perfect example of this stepping stone generation between the truly pioneer, sod-breaking settlers and us. When he died in 1874, little did he realize that the war he fought, the family he put together, the values he instilled, the land that he farmed, the food he produced, the houses he built, the schools and churches he supported would all help pave the way for future generations. At times he must have felt it was merely a matter of survival, because life even then was unbearably difficult.

But looking at his achievements from where we are today, we see that he not only survived but improved his lot in life as well as that of the community around him. He was tough. His family was tough. Life was tough. With the unquestioning support of his wife, he gave his children the tools of living.

Their efforts allowed their son to get back to the land; their grandson would become a prominent fruit grower, Canadian politician and Senator; their great-grandson would fight in "the war to end all wars" and walk with kings; and their great-great grandson would build the family assets into a multi-million dollar company. Now it is up to me, their great-great-great grandson, and my family, to continue the legacy.

Most men who acquire a competence do not start out to make themselves wealthy—they have an ambition to succeed in life and take pride in doing well whatever is their task.

E.D. Smith

Ananias Smith

As a young man, his defiant attitude came to the fore fighting for his country and presumably against his father. Status quo did not suit him.

He too chose an unpopular route—livelihood from his tavern. He struck out on his own so that he could maintain his independence.

Being an astute businessman in his own way, he earned enough money to set each of his children up in the world.

The family unit was strong enough to keep the family together and the morals and values of a worthy generation were firmly in place.

THE THIRD GENERATION

BACK TO THE LAND

Sylvester Smith 1823–1885

The Third Generation

The Smith Family	World Events
	1837 Morse Code devised
	1838 Settler population of Upper Canada 400,000
	1840 Death penalty for stealing cows abolished
1844 **Silas** dies	1844 First edition of Globe newspaper
	1845 Potato famine in Ireland; Franklin expedition sets out to find Northwest Passage
	1846 Hamilton incorporated as a city
	1847 Thomas Edison born; John Deere invents steel plowshare
	1849 California gold rush
	1852 First Canadian postage stamp issued
1853 **Sylvester** and Damaris marry; **Ernest D'Israeli** born	
	1854 Great Western Railway opens line Hamilton to Windsor
1856 **Sylvester** gets malaria; Mauritana born	1856 Saltfleet swamp burns; malaria
1859 Elizabeth born	
1861 Gertrude born; Christina Armstrong Smith born (E.D.'s wife)	1861 start of American Civil War
	1863 Gettysburg Address; Henry Ford born
1865 Cecil born	1865 Abraham Lincoln shot; slavery abolished
	1866 Fenian Uprisings
	1867 New Brunswick, Ontario, Nova Scotia, Quebec enter Confederation; town of Ontario changes its name to Winona
	1869 Mahatma Gandhi born; Suez Canal opens
	1870 Manitoba enters Confederation
1872 Violet born	1871 British Columbia enters Confederation
1873 **E.D.'s** eyes fail	
1874 **Ananias** dies	1874 Winston Churchill born; Toronto Argonaut Football team founded
1875 **E.D.** sets out first grape vines	

THE THIRD GENERATION

BACK TO THE LAND

Depend upon it, these Smiths knew exactly what they were about, and just where they intended to go. They didn't fool and woe to any attempting to thwart them from their immediate purpose.

Varley V. Smith, Chatham, Ontario

Sylvester Smith 1823–1885

The fifth child of Ananias and Elizabeth, he was interested in agriculture (which is not surprising) and when old enough to start out on his own, his father gave him $900 as a down payment on a farm on the top of the Escarpment. This was the old 170-acre Michael Laughty place, with about 70 acres cleared and stumped.

Perhaps it is melodramatic to say Sylvester was an "unsung hero" of his time but the impression I have is just that. Here is a man who endured hard physical labour running his farm, fighting the elements, raising his children and for much of his life suffering the after-effects of a dreaded disease. His mind does not seem to have been geared to question or challenge life, but just live.

In 1853 he married Damaris Isabella McGee, who had come from the Maritimes to teach in a Wentworth County school.

She proceeded to become what some consider the pivotal person in the Smith saga.

Without her strength, convictions and intellect, the Smiths might well have continued just in the local farming tradition as did most of their neighbours. This would have been fine and commendable but she made the family exceptional.

The Third Generation

Sylvester Smith 1823–1885, Damaris Smith 1831–1913

A Woman Ahead of Her Time

As we approach the year 2000 it is interesting to note that there is a surge of interest in the life of the women of the last 200 years and not just in how they relate to the men in their lives but to themselves.

Damaris Isabella McGee Smith, (E.D.'s mother) is one of these pioneer women. Thanks to her copious letters, remarks to local newspaper editors and personal diaries with vivid descriptions, we have a marvellous insight into the sometimes very exciting times of her generation.

Well preserved in our archives are copies of these diaries which she called *The Pioneer Wife*. But the real treasure was to find the original copy of this manuscript in Muskoka, in Douglas Conant's dry, tidy garage. Douglas is a grandson of E.D. and therefore a great-grandson of Damaris and he has carefully preserved many precious writings and pictures. I was thrilled to be able to actually hold and touch and see the paper she wrote on, the words she wrote and feel her strength come through the pages.

We will see the life and times of Damaris, Sylvester (whom she constantly refers to as Conrad), and family through her eyes, in her words.

A Woman Ahead of Her Time

The Pioneer Wife

To what destiny I propose in these pages to show you, with the hope that my experience will not in vain have been recounted if I can help one soul struggling in the dim present to take courage, and trust in God that all will come right if we do our duty to the best of our ability.

When I married Conrad, and settled down to farm life in Ontario those who knew me best were not more surprised than myself, as I had been brought up "down East" where farming had ever been secondary to lumbering, and therefore in disrepute as a means of making money or assuring any solid foundation for success in life.

Whether it was the romance of the new life, the wealth of delicious fruit, which was uncommonly abundant that first year of my visit here, the opportunities my dear relatives gave me to become acquainted with a certain young farmer, or all combined, certainly before many months I was in a fair way to forget all my unconscious prejudices against a farmer's life, and before a year I had taken the irrevocable step.

Our house—how shall I describe it? When Conrad's father bought the farm for him, and put him in a way to pay for it in time, there was in legal phrase an encumbrance on it. The widow of the former owner held possession of her thirds, and lived in the "Manor House" so that we were compelled to occupy a log house that had been built for a tenant, servants or poor relation as was often the custom in those days.

This house was unique in many ways. It was a square structure of logs with each log projecting at the corners—so handy to hang or lay things on as I afterwards discovered. It stood in the very centre of a square meadow covered with snow when I first saw it. It had a legend connected with it, and when I tell you it was to the effect that a former tenant, a wood chopper, had told his friends that he never felt like himself of a morning until he had gone outside and lifted one corner of it, you will be able to judge of its size, or the truth of the legend.

The Third Generation

****

When I look back and compare our beginning in housekeeping with the style that the young people of the present day expect (about 1893), I cannot think but that Conrad and I were both very much under the influence of a happy dream, to be content and see an assured future before us. Looking back too for motives and causes for my complacency at least, under the self denials of my early married life I recognize another factor, the duty of, I will not say penance, but endurance; this was a part of my nature inherited from my father.

Hinges and locks of doors and windows were made of wood. The wooden latch of the door was on the inside, and could be lifted from outside by a leather latch-string passing through a hole a few inches above; this string might be left in at night, but as a general rule it was left out, and the old saying, "the latch-string is always out," signified the hospitality of our pioneer settlers.

I busied myself in trying to make the home as attractive as possible with the materials we had gathered. Conrad had inherited a mechanical talent and during our honeymoon had made a cupboard—it is true it was innocent of carving and not very smoothly planed, and was painted the orthodox color—blue-gray. But it was a marvel of skill in my estimation—and it was capacious.

****

An addition to the livestock was a great event for it meant to me a new experience—buttermaking. No one can believe for a moment that there was any commercial advantage in feeding and caring for cows from which to make butter to sell for 10 cents a pound. But we did not keep account then and were sanguine of success in farming, like our ancestors.

The Pioneer Wife

It was enchanting to skim the cream off the milk, and make it into rolls of fragrant butter all my own and in a tray that Conrad had made from wood that grew on the farm. The equal of that tray I have never seen; it was made oblong and large; a ten pound roll in the bottom would look like a jewel in its very best setting. Ten pound rolls innumerable have been moulded and set in that old familiar tray; now, after 40 years, it bids fair to descend to the coming generation as an heirloom of great significance.

First and foremost the arrangement of spring work on a farm of one hundred acres, then as now, included a "hired man," and our hired man, when selected from the odds and ends of the population, proved to be an exceedingly faithful colored boy of 17 for whom we made a bed in the attic.

I could see from the first year that we needed more help on the farm, but no one then thought of chartering a ship and going after a load of Chinese; no, not even to this day; rather do we throw all manner of obstacles in the way of that enterprising, industrious, and economical race when they try to gain an entrance to this country as best they can. But then, the farmers have very little to say about these things; they just work away and let politicians manage for them.

You will not be surprised to learn that her son E.D. had an interest in politics. He learned it was another avenue he could use to help the farmers. He also went overseas to recruit people to come to work for him, just as his mother suggests. It is almost uncanny to see how many of her ideas and suggestions actually came to be.

****

In our trips over the farm Conrad had told me how he was going to move this fence to such a place; clear up such a bit of land where it appeared a dozen or so rotten logs had encumbered six or eight acres for years and nothing had been produced from it but scanty pasturage; plant this field to barley, that to something else; how many tons of hay this field would grow and how much wheat per acre that one was capable of raising. I think it was those excursions with their lessons in farm economy that gave me the insight into and the subsequent enthusiasm I felt in our occupation, and *the firm faith I had that life could be made a success on the farm*. In spite of many mistakes and discouragements I always held to this faith.

As summer advanced the butter product was a failure so also was the garden. Of course Conrad sympathized with me and tried to lessen my chagrin by taking a good share of the failure upon his own broad shoulders. Nevertheless it was an experience of value to me in later life.

We had the sunshine in our hearts and we improved the opportunities as they presented themselves. What cared we that we had no carriage. Had we not our horses, and many and delightful were the tête-a-têtes while riding across country or to the village church on Sundays. And what delightful excursions into the big deep woods where we could lose ourselves among the gigantic trees and speculate what the primeval forest was like when Indian tribes roamed through it.

Earth is crammed with heaven.

Damaris Smith

Having been brought up in comparative luxury with all my wants supplied as from an invisible agency which I afterwards recognized as an indulgent father, it was a new and curious experience to study ways and means. We did not often go to town for supplies as Conrad had laid in a supply when we moved into our new home in March, but as time passed and they began to diminish and new wants arose I would jot down on a memorandum what I intended to purchase on our next trip to town. By the time we went I would have a long list. But before leaving Conrad advised me to try and reduce the list as much as possible. I would strike out the things I thought I could get along without.

The Pioneer Wife

The final revision would take place in town. We would find that our money was going too fast to hold out until the next crop was sold and would come home without many things we had intended to get and thought we could hardly get along without. Yet we did get along—very well—no doubt well enough. I well remember that those lessons were most useful to me and helped to lay the foundation of many good qualities in my children.

****

In the autumn we were able to move into the farmhouse which had an addition—a lean-to which was divided into two rooms, a bedroom and a kitchen. When cold weather came, in addition to our stove we built fires in the great fireplace and in this room we received our friends and had many happy evenings. Here for the first time we read novels. No doubt some who read this narrative will elevate their nose when I record that Conrad had read but one book in his life, before this winter—a biography of Lord Nelson, who was his hero up to this period. One is led to wonder how young men employed their leisure in those days. I cannot imagine. I have a conviction that most of them when not fishing, sat on the fence and whittled and swapped jack knives. As for Conrad who loved music I am convinced that his violin and flute filled any aching void caused by a scarcity of literature.

We had got a frame house built in the location where we wanted it. It was built in such shape that a front could be added as soon as our circumstances would warrant; and it was planned for health and convenience.

In the house most of the bedrooms and the dining room and kitchen had east windows, and great stress was laid on an easy method of ventilation, through the top sash of the windows and yet to have them burglar proof. The windows were never closed at the top except during an east storm, or a particularly cold spell in mid-winter. The kitchen had three windows and were never darkened except by the merest excuse for a curtain. The fresh air and consequent cheerfulness enjoyed from those east windows cannot be reckoned.

I wanted as good a house as soon as possible for my children because I had no intention to sacrifice my children beyond redemption to pioneer habits.

By this time they had a son, Ernest D'Israeli and a daughter Mauritana.

****

There was one plan of the utmost significance to the success of a farmer, namely the plan of the rotation of crops, with which, I soon learned no farmer, old or young, was supposed to brook any suggestion relative thereto. He alone was responsible for the ultimate profits, so he alone took upon himself all the responsibility for the plans each year. Often during the winter I noticed Conrad in an abstracted mood, head bent, gazing into some unknown depth. When I would ask him what he was thinking so hard about he would say, "I was thinking where I would plant the second field of oats or barley."

Evening Hours, Then and Now
Then
Light the smokey lamp, sit on your wobbly homemade chair to read a treasured classic.
Now
Find the T.V. remote control and sit on upholstered comfort from Sofa World.

I felt sure he understood his business and to a great extent the nature of his soil. There was one field that had been lying comparatively idle for three or four years on which the neighbors predicted he would not raise enough to pay for the ploughing. Conrad had a mental reservation that he would disappoint them and he did.

There did not appear to be any place according to his showing even on a two-hundred-acre farm, for a few vegetables and flowers. But I did not give up the cherished idea. There had been a plum tree—the only one on the place. It had been blown over, but ripened several quarts of delicious plums. I took this for what was a sample of what could be produced and kept fast hold of determination to

The Pioneer Wife

raise plenty of similar ones when Conrad once got his fields and yards arranged. There was also under the apple trees and in sly and covert places, ruins of currant bushes, from which I hoped to make new plantations.

We had got a garden laid out and it was my garden, and I could experiment in it and arrange it to my heart's desire. I was successful in some things: strawberries, tomatoes and plums.

I had a project already evolved and hidden away in one corner of my brain. I had once driven past a whole field of fruit trees all in rows and cleanly cultivated. One of my mottoes has always been, whatever anyone else can do, I can do. I made some borders for flowers on either side in front of the house and I took great pleasure in doing it. My flowers were of the old fashioned hardy sorts, at first, such as marigolds, asters, pinks, primroses, nasturtiums, sweet rocket and loves lies bleeding. They were a beginning and a pleasure.

I had to dig these borders at odd times; it would have been rank treason to expect the menfolk to do it. Even while doing it myself I felt doubtful of my warrant to spend any time or labor on anything so unprofitable. However no one enjoyed the flowers and shrubbery more than Conrad. It was part of our daily life to pay the flowers a visit and comment on their beauties and from them many a text was taken for many a lesson from the Divine power. Looking back I see that my few flowers had their influence. The next and succeeding years I often had as many as forty kinds of flowers including roses.

One of her grandchildren, Leon, became known as "The Rose King of Canada"—another example of how she helped pave the way for future generations. This is definitely the foreshadowing of the fruit business. It seems Conrad was against any vines or trees or shrubs being planted. His heart was very much set on being a farmer who plowed sod, mowed hay and stooked grain. Damaris had a knowing sense of what the land was really best suited for but it would take the continued efforts of her son Ernest, to fully realize its potential, and he became known as "The Fruit King."

The Third Generation

I cherish the thought of this lady as an economist, a philosopher, an educator and a gardener. She came to know herself and her capabilities which is a rare talent indeed.

If there is a lesson to be learned from reading Damaris' diaries, it is to see how wonderful and powerful it is when a husband and wife support one another.

I had become acquainted with my best interests, so to speak; had got an insight into the current ways of making and saving money, with the express object of first paying for the farm. Conrad had assured me it could be done (i.e. pay for the farm) and I was only too willing to help so far as lay in my power.

******

The price and demand for wheat rose and they were able to pay off the farm more quickly than anticipated. They were able to make improvements and even add a few more sheep and cattle.

Damaris was, like most ladies of the time, against the evils of alcohol. This attitude, augmented by the same opinion of Mrs. E.D. her daughter-in-law, may well be the reason the Smiths never considered using their grapes in the wine making business.

When the local carpenter is drunk one week out of five, at those times my reflections on the weakness of human nature would have been very unpleasant reading.

When I first heard the following story, I found it hard to believe! But it's true. Old surveyors tell such horror stories of tramping through similar disease-infested Ontario swamps many years ago.

Hardships fell upon us in the summer of 1854. For several miles along the rear end of the farm lay a swamp. That summer it was very dry, and some settler wishing to clear up a bit of land along the border, set out a fire and let it get into the standing timber—when it got beyond control and swept over hundreds of acres, in a few days, nearly all the

The Pioneer Wife

trees falling over with their roots. Every farm for miles was in danger and all the population turned out to arrest the destruction. It only ceased its fury when the wind fell, and then the air for miles was filled with smoke so dense that for days we could scarcely see a foot in advance. People walking along the highway were obliged to follow the fences in order to know when they had arrived at their own homes. Long after the fire had abated its fury, it continued to crawl and burn in favourable places and was never finally under control until the heavy fall rains. In fact it was Christmas before we saw the last stray puffs of smoke. The following two summers were very wet, the fallen trees lay soaking in pools and low places, the bark falling off as it rotted.

Towards autumn, first one and then another fell sick with ague, or some form of malarial fever until finally, nearly every family for miles around was prostrated with the pestilential breath of that Gehenna (a place of torment— hell). There were scarcely enough left to care for the sick; even those who did not succumb were but walking invalids kept going by force of circumstances and will power.

Conrad was down with fever and lay for weeks helpless and suffering, sometimes delirious and at all times hopeless. Of all diseases this must be the worst to take away or deaden all feeling of hope, ambition and will power.

About the time Conrad was out of danger, my turn came and it left a woeful effect on the constitutions of all the children born about that time. (E.D. was two or three years old.)

****

About 1880 the crisis came. The two previous summers had been very dry, but this summer the drougth was unprecedented. Not only for weeks but months the sun glared down upon the poor helpless stricken earth; with unwonted power day after day the heat became more intense, the air seemed all a-tremble with waves of heat which nearly blinded one. All the streams and shallow

COFFEE WAS SOMETIMES HARD TO COME BY SO THEY DRANK A BURNED CORN BREW.

wells had long since gone dry; for miles in extent the cattle had to be driven to the lakes for one drink a day and water for house use had to be carried in barrels from the same source. Our neighbor's well which we depended on in ordinary drouths gave out too, except a little for the owner's use. Something had to be done.

Parties organized to bore out old wells hoping to strike a vein deeper down. Some were successful, and our turn came; boring commenced in a well near the barn for convenience. Day after day in the glaring heat and in clouds of dust, the horse travelled around in the circle, pulling the power for the drill with a dogged perseverance and patience which could only have been born of his utter subjugation to his master, man.

I shall always remember the last day of the experiment. The company had gone to the depth of the drill; they could get an addition to it at considerable expense, but there was a doubt of getting water at even a much greater depth; a consultation was held when it was decided to abandon the project. As a last and final effort however, it was thought advisable to try another well in a lower strata, and in the centre of the farm.

With the faintest of hopes they arranged the machinery, when after boring for two hours the procession came back with flags flying, and music in the air, so to speak. Water was running over the top of the well, was the report. What this means on a farm no one can estimate except those who have experienced a scarcity of water for their stock. It meant much for me and the children as well as the men folk. Life took on a roseate hue immediately; the mercury went down several degrees; when I visited the scene of the first well-boring experiment, the following day, and saw the earth trodden into dust to the depth of a foot or more, where the poor horse had gone round and round for several days and in such an atmosphere of heat and dust, my pity was tinctured with profound respect for the persistency with which man and beast will punish themselves to attain an object, lawful or otherwise.

****

The Pioneer Wife

Ransom Smith's monument, found in the Stoney Creek Cemetery. Here it highlights some wonderful names of Smith children born in the 1800s.

The Third Generation

Though I am convinced that many families have no organized plans for the future, I know we had. From the time our eldest child opened its eyes to the lights and shadows of this beautiful world, we never ceased to plan for its future.

Aside from being a means toward earning a living, I could understand that education makes people more tolerant; that it dispels prejudice as the morning sun dispels a mist; and above all it helps us to enjoy life; to appreciate the beauties of the earth, the sky and all nature.

I am able to work hard because I have a constitution uncontaminated by inter-marriage, tight corsets, high heels, or any description of false living.

If I got time to read the family newspaper before ten o'clock I considered myself fortunate. I read it not only as a diversion but as a duty. I considered I owed it to my family, to keep up to some extent with the movements of the times, and as a means of helping to form a taste for reading, and literary research in the children.

Even the young girls in our family were taught to drive a team, and harrow but were never kept out of school a day, no matter what the emergency.

The hardest life has its compensations. One of our greatest pleasures was to gather in the sitting room, evenings, and listen to the children reading tales written by the immortal Scott, or any sound literature we could get hold of. It cultivates similar tastes and sentiments, and strengthens and spiritualizes the family ties—*the family bond; what possibilities it implies; what tender sentiments are nourished under its aegis.*

****

The invention and addition of a mowing machine relieved men of their greatest burden; so they had more time to do extras and we had 'got things snug' as Conrad was wont to say. We had a two-seated carriage in which we annually, in June, after the crops were in, visited our friends in the west. Altogether, we had got to be quite well-to-do farmers.

The Pioneer Wife

In spite of this comment, Damaris remembered Conrad's lessons in economy and still would not pay the three dollars necessary to buy a pair of boots to wear in the muddy barnyard and contented herself with the old castoffs from the men. Her thriftiness filtered down to her children and future generations.

Life is made up of events each adding to our experience, and to reach the goal, with a clear conscience is the best we finite creatures can do.

Damaris Smith

She realized there could be some merit in being selective in which cows they raised but Sylvester could not believe that some were better than others and chose to ignore her. She even independently experimented with various fertilizers and studied drainage problems. The opinion of women of the day did not carry much weight. She did persevere in her beliefs through the written word and it must have given her much satisfaction.

However I arrived at a belief later on that it was one thing to be a good grain farmer and another to be a good stock farmer and grain farmer as well, and that both qualifications are rarely found in one and the same person. The more is the pity for both are necessary to any great degree of success on land.

****

In those days we knew naught of self-sealers, and what fruit we did not preserve, we dried. We had an abundance of pears thanks to the old New Jersey settlers and the drying of them each year made plenty of work. I can see them now spread out on platters, boards, and every available flat utensil and they had to be toted from the oven to the roofs of outbuildings, or any safe place where the sun shone until by the time, what the bees had left of them, they were dry enough to put away. They were in a state that required plenty of washings before cooking. If no other discovery had been made during this century except how to hermetically seal, it would pass down the ages as the woman's.

In addition to cattle and fruit, I tried goose farming also. The third spring I had a fine lot of goslings hatched, and was congratulating myself that I would soon have plenty of feathers when a neighbour's hog broke in and ate them all up in a few minutes.

My turkey farming ended disastrously too. I had about twenty old enough for market and they would bring many dollars. When I found their remains scattered over many fields, I said that I would raise no more turkeys while there were foxes adjacent.

****

I read a story once with the line in it: '...she stood in the Hall in which her ancestors had stood before her, and gazed upon the wide domain of which she was the fair proprietress.' I would recall this line often and it made me appreciate and feel pride in our dearly earned acres.

According to Gertrude Smith, she and her brothers and sisters called Damaris "the Spartan mother" because she carried so much on her own shoulders and always "hewed the line."

An Outspoken Woman

I hope that quoting directly from her diaries helps to give the full impact of the force and resourcefulness of my great-great-grandmother. No one could say things just quite the way she could. One of her contemporaries said, "She is a particularly intelligent woman who has a mind like a man." I'm not sure just how that would be interpreted today but I am sure that back then it was the highest compliment.

Bill Reekie, having over 40 years with the E.D. Smith company, writes, "I have been told by the family that all of the Smith brains came from Sylvester's wife, Damaris."

It might be fair to say not just the brains but the interest in politics, women's issues, fruit farming and business stemmed from her. This lady saw the whole picture. She did not allow

An Outspoken Woman

herself to be just a farmer's wife which would have been easy enough to do considering the fact that it alone was a huge job. She found the time to explore many other avenues, to have a great deal of initiative to write voluminous pages of diaries (as we have just seen here), letters to the local editors and newspaper articles with her own byline. Neighbours and older folks probably branded her a rebel, and commented on her ideas as the scourge of the new generation. Some of her opinions are so scathing that one would really not want to be on the receiving end of her wrath.

One great curse for women's weakness is her dress, to which she is slave: the weight of her skirts and the inconvenience of them would soon debilitate a strong man, while tight sleeves and boots paralyze the muscles; the high heels injure the spine. Who could expect a woman to vote intelligently when her toes are aching from compression?

****

Oh foolish women! Who hath bewitched you that you should sacrifice the finer instincts of your nature on what altar? Womankind, apparently intelligent, through fear of being considered too awfully old-fashioned, have with many qualms of conscience fastened about their persons a foundation for a hump on their backs, commonly referred to as a bustle, which, had they been born with, they would have sought the aid of the most skillful surgeon to remove.

****

While in the bush searching for a lost cow I got so sweltered inside my bonnet that I took it off and carried it under my arm and I lost it; for had I not to carry my skirts besides? My thoughts soared beyond such trifling things (I always hated them, sunbonnets) and I never got another. Besides they are dangerous as they shut out both sight and sound. In later years my little girls were not made to do penance by wearing such head gear.

Story of Saltrisin' Bread

My own powers of endurance helped me through many emergencies. One such emergency arose very often in the first two months of our life in this square house in the square meadow. It was about the bread that I was making in those two months when the earth was ice bound and old Boreas was busy adjusting the winds. In that year of Grace there were no bakers travelling the country with flaky delicate looking loaves of an indigestible boneless compound as at present. Farmers' wives made their own "saltrisin'." For miles and miles I don't suppose any other kind was made or even heard of.

Now it is with "saltrisin'" bread as with all other concerns of life; it has to be learned to make it a success.

It befell me to learn by experience, but till my dying day I shall believe that some knowledge of chemistry is worth much experience in compounding and cooking food. Experience is as unsatisfactory as the old woman's answer when asked how she made certain cakes.

"You just take so much shortening and so much sour milk, soda, salt, and mix them."

"But how much, Aunty? In what proportion?"

"Why, *just enough* honey, just about the right quantity."

Saltrisin' Bread

Recipe for Saltrisin' Bread

Early in the morning stir some flour and warm water with a pinch of salt into a batter, and set the dish containing it into another filled with water just high enough to come to the top of the batter in the inside vessel, and keep it at a certain temperature—say about blood heat, until after six hours the batter will begin to rise. Then as you have been obliged to watch it from the first to make sure that it did not get too hot or too cold, so now you must be on the alert or it will foam over.

This is the end of her saltrisin' instructions. It must be presumed we would know the rest. Actually, this is one recipe that is best just read and not attempted!

No matter whether the baby needs attending or paterfamilias has a cut finger to tie up, or whatever else may befall—that rising must be made into dough or worse consequences will follow, one of the consequences being a most disagreeable smell, the first one of which I shall *never* forget. It was at my Aunt's house the previous summer. When the bread was being mixed I saw her smiling. Presently she remarked,

"I daresay you wonder what that smell is?"

"Yes," I said.

"That is the yeast," she said, "a sign we are to have good bread."

The Pioneer Wife

The Third Generation

****

The most hateful task of all my farm life was to keep the bottom of my skirts clean. They had to be the regulation length to appease Mrs. Grundy and that was a few inches too long for cleanliness.

How I fretted and fumed or more figuratively beat my wings against the bars, for my skirts had first and foremost to be held, so that I was nearly always handicapped by them. I have hoped against hope that the next generation would shake themselves free from this incubus. But I have hoped in vain so far, for in this year of 1893 at any hour of the day if I look out of my window I see the genus woman passing by in skirts that sweep the pavement.

Ostensibly they are out airing their children but really they are stirring up germs on the side walk for the children to breathe, and thus hasten the innocents on the never ending train, cemetery-ward. I often see a second little toddler by the side of his mother, breathing from the cloud of dust stirred up by her petticoats.

She has made her presence felt historically through her strong opinions, Christian morals, animated writings and above all—her children.
What an example for us!

The Proud Parents

What parents wouldn't be pleased to be able to say, "my son, the senator," or "my daughter, one of the first woman doctors in Canada," or "my son the civil engineer," or "my daughter, the historian"? Sylvester and Damaris could. They must have been proud.

Sitting here in the 1990s, parents continue to want their children to do well, to excel, to learn, to be successful, to be happy, all the superlatives we can think of. What were the attitudes, visions and circumstances that Sylvester and Damaris instilled in their children?

Confidence   Even today, when status quo is questioned or challenged it is often interpreted as wrong or at the very least ill-advised. Some of us Smiths have, over the years, managed to

The Proud Parents

confront popular opinion, and indeed convince the public of the merit of our ideals. We must have had a confidence of spirit to have the courage to forge ahead even against the tide. Such confidence probably came from: education; faith; and the sincere search for right over wrong, good over evil, common sense over silliness.

Organization   One of the reasons families like ours managed so well was because they were incredibly well organized. Consider the intensity of the daily work load, the lack of modern conveniences, the remoteness of country life, the independence necessary for survival. Every hour of every day was accounted for because they had so very much to do.

Hard Work   This feature of success may seem obvious but how often today do we hear, "I can't do that, it's *hard!*"

Love of Family Life   This is a tough one. Cars, planes, subways, great highways, make it easy for people today to go places, get away, leave. Not that that means less love of family, but it has led to less family life—together. Damaris made it clear they had family meetings, would talk around the dinner table, all members knew what one another was doing. It gave the family a focus, a common understanding of what was expected and how to get it. I hope we can be as successful.

Philosophy of Life—Religion   Back then, organized religion was accepted as a part of our family's routine. Elizabeth, Damaris' second daughter, had an intense religious faith.

> Her Anglicanism was essential to her sense of well-being. This association of high, almost unobtainable, spiritual ideals with a sense of superiority vis-a-vis other religions made Anglo-Saxon Victorians like Elizabeth earnest and energetic in the pursuit of the excellence which would dispel doubt and confirm superiority. It also made it very difficult for them to accept mediocrity, real or imagined, in others or themselves.
>
> Veronica Strong-Boag, *Woman With a Purpose*

Religion gave them a strength, a conviction, a focus. Does this exist today? In our family we spend less time in church, but when we do go it is enjoyable. It feels warm and we feel part of a larger family. Our spiritual strength I believe, is expressed more in a set of well thought-out values and operating principles. By sticking to our values, there is a belief that life will treat us well, both on earth and beyond.

****

Each generation of Smiths has seen a remarkable change in the world around them during their lifetime. Damaris was no exception. She went from living in a dirt-floor, one-room, log cabin to being driven by her son's chauffeur.

Jack Davies, the chauffeur, joined the company in 1913, the year she died. He and his wife Anne lived in the Stone House at the front of the property for 50 years! He drove four generations of our family to work, to school, wherever necessary. Imagine how much he could have helped in the writing of this book!

****

The Scene is Set

Follow now with me, the lives and times of Ernest, Mauritana, Elizabeth, Gertrude, Cecil and Violet, the six children of Sylvester and Damaris, and we will see how they all put good values to good use.

These six children were born during an incredible period of history between 1853 and 1872. Railways were opening up the huge continent providing freedom and travel opportunities never dreamt of before. American unrest spawned the Civil War, Lincoln was assassinated, slavery abolished, the Suez Canal opened, making the world even smaller. In 1858 Gail Borden founded the New York Condensed Milk Company, in 1869 Joseph Campbell, Henry John Heinz (The Pickle King) and Timothy Eaton, all discovered the sudden craze for consumer goods, pre-packaged and processed foods.

The time was right for great things to happen.

She had plans for her children's future and persevered in her task to the end, that they would do themselves and their parents credit in the world.

Gertrude Smith

Sylvester Smith

A strong man married to a strong woman, they produced six strong-minded children.

Resigned to a life as a farmer, we get no indication that he aspired to be other than that. He was content with what the land had to offer.

He did however have a great resolve to continue to improve his and his family's condition in life in spite of suffering from the aftermath of malaria most of his adult life. He instilled in his family a strong work ethic, a determination to succeed under difficult circumstances and the belief that to strive for something will make it so.

Damaris realized the importance of the potential of the soil and knew that it was capable of producing more than just grain. She was an experimenter and a risk taker. She understood the power of the land and knew that if properly utilized, it could unleash boundless rewards. She lived to see her son E.D. make this happen.

THE FOURTH GENERATION

THE HOUSE THAT JAM BUILT

Ernest D'Israeli Smith 1853–1948

HELDERLEIGH

The Fourth Generation

The Smith Family	World Events
1875 E.D. sets out first grape vines	1876 General Custer's Battle of the Little Bighorn
1877 Elizabeth (**Ananias'** wife) dies	
1878 Elizabeth (**E.D.'s** sister) fails medical school entrance	1878 John A. MacDonald becomes Prime Minister of Canada; secret ballot now the way to vote
1880 E.D. sells fruit for first time	1880 Dr. Emily Stowe, first woman doctor, allowed to practice
1881 "everything subsidiary to fruit"	1881 Canadian population over 4 million
1882 E.D. Smith Company founded	1883 start of Toronto Women's Suffrage
1885 **Sylvester** dies	1885 last spike of C.P.R. driven; Louis Riel executed
1886 E.D. marries Christina; Elizabeth marries Adam Shortt	1887 Welland Canal open
1888 Verna born	1889 Adolph Hitler born
1889 E.D. moves down from the escarpment and buys Bedell property; starts nursery business	1890 first electric street car in Toronto
1891 **Armand** born	1891 Canadian James Naismith invents basketball
1895 Evelyn Hannah Gibson born (wife of Armand)	1892 women allowed to study and practice law
1900 E.D. elected to Federal Government; Leon born; Cecil taps Niagara Falls	1893 U.S. stock market crash; Algonquin Park established
1901 Saltfleet census lists E.D. as "fruit grower"	1896 start of Toronto, Hamilton, Beamsville railroad
1903 Roberta Thurston born	1897 Women's Institute founded; Yukon, Klondike goldrush
1904 beginning of jam factory	1899 start of Boer War
1906 E.D. starts Beamsville Preserving Company	1901 Queen Victoria dies; Toronto Symphony gives first performance
1909 E.D. president of Fruit Growers Association	1903 Wright brothers fly at Kittyhawk
1910 E.D. does not run for re-election; builds home named Helderleigh	1905 daily C.P.R. service to Vancouver begins; Einstein proposes theory of relativity
1911 company now E.D. Smith & Son when **Armand** joins	1908 Oshawa starts automobile production line; Anne of Green Gables published
1913 Damaris dies; E.D. appointed Senator; **Armand** in England to make jam	1911 Casa Loma completed
1914 E.D. sick; **Armand** returns home	1914 start of World War I
1916 **Armand** marries Evelyn Hannah Gibson	1915 Canadian troops land in France
	1916 Houses of Parliament in Ottawa destroyed by fire
1918 **Ernest Llewellyn Gibson** born	1917 Russian Revolution; all women of Canada allowed to vote

THE FOURTH GENERATION

THE HOUSE THAT JAM BUILT

No man is more largely engaged in, or has a better knowledge of the fruit growing industry than E.D. Smith.

Newspaper article 1901

Ernest D'Israeli Smith 1853–1948

You are going to become acquainted with several Ernest D'Israeli Smiths. The first one is the "Young E.D," whose early environment we saw through the eyes of Damaris his mother, and the rest we will see through his diaries.

The second stage takes place over the next 30 years when he was called "The Fruit King." Finally, during his last 30 years, he was E.D. "The Senator," a pioneer in the building of Canada "who fell into the role of politician like a type-cast actor."

The Young E.D.

Like his mother, he was a diarist.

He wrote at first to document his daily activities but quickly saw that his diaries were becoming a signpost to show him where he should be headed. He noted seasons, weather and soil conditions. He documented what he planted where and how well it grew. These works became his personal reference books that furnished him with a vision. By studying the past, he could plan for the future. The following excerpts are full of fascinating details, stories, disappointments, successes and poignant learning all selected to give us a picture of the man and his life. They explain why he continued to live in the country when it was popular to move to the big city; we watch him change from grain and livestock farmer into a fruit farmer and then businessman and politician; we come to understand his value system; and we develop a profound respect for a man who "did things right."

Diary of Events Great and Small

1866-67 Father and mother busy and full of care working hard and making plans for the future of their family, hoping and striving to place them in a position to acquire distinction. Time alone will show whether or not these fond hopes are to be realized. God has blessed us with no mean amount of ability, if we improve these with care and prudence trusting ever in the mercy of God we may become worthy of applause.

1869 Sick most of the year.

1873 If by any chance a boy or girl does receive a tolerable education they almost invariably quit the farm and employ their talents or industry in some other profession, deeming the farmer's life slavish and degrading. But here they ere, for there is no life that can be made so free, so noble and so honorable as a farmer's. *There is no doubt but that if skill and thought are applied, mines of wealth can be drawn from the earth, this having been accomplished, what class of people possess more advantage for social, moral and intellectual culture than the farmer?* He is surrounded by the poetry of nature; after laboring with the body it is a relaxation to sit down in the library and pore over the vast volumes of thought, his mind is clearer than the professional man's, if he trains it and while he obtains a luxurious living by the toil of the day he is free to do whatsoever he will when night comes on. His sleep is not the troubled nap of the man who exercises only his mind but the fatigues of the day induce a sound slumber refreshing and invigorating.

A Dr. Bethune tried to cure E.D.'s eyes by putting leeches on them!

1873 My eyes hurt terribly.

Diary of Events

1874 Eyes so bad I had to stay in a dark room for three weeks. I thought I should lose my sight altogether. When I commenced bathing them in warm water and milk they recovered strength rapidly. Now I can read half a day at a time, if careful.

Looking back on this part of his life, he admitted that he was "lucky" enough to have been deprived of the chance to achieve his life's ambition to be a civil engineer because of failing eyesight. His eyes were so bad he couldn't study or read for any length of time. His sister Elizabeth wrote about the pain he suffered.

Ma and Ernest were to see Dr. Roseburgs and he gave him no hope, but said that the eyes would get worse. He would get him a pair of spectacles at Toronto for about ten dollars.

March 8, 1877

Out last night to the Grange and coming home upset and the horse ran away and broke the cutter badly. I might have caught them when they first started if I had been very quick, but owing to a lame leg caused by a kick from Chiquita a week before, I could not spring quick enough to catch the trailing lines. We walked about 1/2 mile and found the horses broken loose from the cutter about 1/3 of a mile from home. The exertion has made my leg worse today. The kick was upon the right thigh and seems to have injured the bone. I do not know whether to go for the doctor or not. The mare kicked my head at the same time fortunately however did not injure it further than a skin bruise.

Sylvester, E.D.'s father, was so sick by this time that E.D. took over the management of the farm and with the enthusiasm of youth *tried to find a more remunerative way of farming*.

June 10 Diary of events as they seem, that I have time or inclination to inscribe, some, which will quite probably be less important than many I shall not note, either from neglect or ignorance. Events mostly in connection with everyday farm life and consequently not likely to be very interesting to a casual reader, although there is undoubtedly plenty of room both for poetry and eloquence in a description of the growing crops and ripened fields of grain, the hurricane-rent air, or the balmy breeze, the green luxuriance of a favorable year or the arid drouth of an unfavorable one, the baseball, the Grange or the Church.

June 12–July 26 Hauled in 2690 sheaves, 11 loads of wheat, William, Cecil and I.

July 28 Finished hauling the wheat, 4660 sheaves altogether, so large that we could only haul about 240 at a time, from 10 1/4 acres—grain so plump I anticipate at least 300 bushels.

July 29 Sunday, went to church and nearly to sleep. It is too hot & I have to work too hard to enjoy anything but rest & sleep on Sunday.

Aug. 3 I am very much behind, my man William being sick this week.

Aug. 11 Cut 4 acres oats east of grapes, too ripe & short to pay to bind; in some places very poor, scarcely anything; I think it would pay best to get ground ploughed as early in the spring as weather will permit when the ground will not bake but not to sow at least before May.

We should watch how he is teaching himself.

Aug. 18 The thickest manure I ever saw on this farm. Let us see the result; the land certainly needs it.

Aug. 28 We hauled in 10 acres oats which were partially wet under the band after a week's bright sun upon them which will learn me a lesson never to bind up oats wet— better to bind them dry and haul them in immediately than bind them wet and let them stand out in two weeks of drying weather.

Sept. 14 Grange picnic. Speeches mostly upon that now much disputed question Protection versus Free Trade, or rather Protection to our farmers versus the present one-

CLEARED ABOUT $300 IN 1877 WHICH WAS QUITE AN IMPROVEMENT.

sided policy of Free Trade on our part Protection for our neighbors over the border. The staple argument of the Free Traders is that the consumer pays the duty, consequently the Americans are deliberately injuring themselves with their Protective Tariff & hurting no one else. It looks not like it when from being a large importing country of manufactured goods a few years ago, she now not only supplies her own people but is pushing her goods into competition abroad with the goods of almost every country, and again Free Traders say "to sell you must buy." Whereas the United States have almost ceast buying from England whilst her exports thither are every day increasing and increasing in price as well. But the consumer does not pay the duty except in case of something the importing people cannot produce as cheaply. For instance take the case of a man who owns a farm on the boundary line between the U.S. & Canada; suppose he raises a quantity of barley upon each side of the line, that upon the American side he sells for 75 cents a bushel. How is it possible for him to realize 75 cents for that raised upon the Canadian side for he, to sell in the same market must pay a duty of 15 cents per bushel no doubt, therefore the producer & not the consumer pays the duty in this case.

The number of bushels that each acre produces should never come as a surprise to any farmer and the child would be very young in our family who would not make an early effort to know this number.

Damaris McGee Smith

Sept. 19 Grange tonight & heard Spohn, VanWagner & Kitchen talk that old Protection talk & never a chance did they give your humble servant to say a word sure.

Oct. 17 A grand picnic in Hamilton in honor of Sir John A MacDonald. I was up a little while but owing to the immense crowd could not hear anything, so came back to Stoney Creek.

The Fourth Generation

Oct. 28 Got 15 acres ploughed in the swamp, grapes ploughed & 1 1/2 acres in corn field, timothy seed is up in swamp thick about an inch high. How one ought to cherish home companions; for their thoughts are our thoughts, their aspirations our aspirations, they delight in our success, sympathize with our misfortunes, mourn with us in our distresses, whilst the reverse is almost always the case with this cold selfish world outside the immediate family circle, for one's relations seem to be eaten up with envy, if anything fortunate happens to us, instead of exulting in our success, as they should do. The only way to be respected & at the same time popular is to lead an exemplary life so *manage your private affairs as to prosper financially*. To become popular one must push push ever forward and play a dexterous hand; for, if he steps back and gives others his place, he loses one round in the ladder which it will take considerable time to recover, if ever. Boldness and plenty of general intelligence to back it up is indispensable.

I find that through the summer when one is constantly engaged in manual labor one gets stupid at literary feats, loses all control of language and words and barely recuperates during the winter; but alas! there is no help for it, if one is not independently rich. All one can do is his best, run a bold course, gain a local name, die, be buried, have a long line of mourners & onlookers at the funeral, in a year, or ten at most, which is but a minute in the long Eternity, be forgotten. And thus this world goes spinning on, this one takes it easy, enjoys life, indulges his appetite and passions, dies and leaves not a trace behind, fades does his memory into the dim past so quickly. The one that runs the gallant course straining every nerve to outstrip his fellows, dies and leaves but a trace, his memory too, soon fades away, but is the trace not worth striving for? Do not these traces make the world what it is, instead of what it might be, a den of veritable wild hearts and human gorillas? Each one exerting his utmost to leave a brighter & broader trace, brightens and broadens the world.

He seems to be hungry for intellectual conversation and deep thinking. Here he is, a young man, living quite remotely

Saltfleet Township

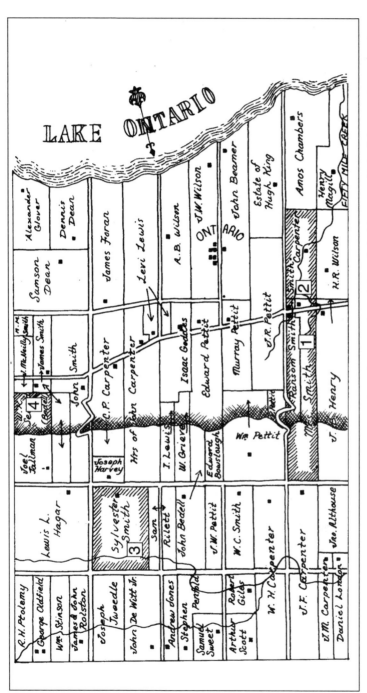

Saltfleet Township in the mid 1850s. Note the Fifty Mile Creek and Smith holdings. 1/Silas' home 2/Ananias' home 3/On top of the escarpment Sylvester's homestead where E.D. was born. 4/The land bought by E.D. in 1889 when he moved below the mountain. The town of Ontario changed its name to Winona in 1867.

in the country, trying to put together the pieces of the world he has been given, in such a way that they will make sense and make a difference. We know he did it.

These words also reflect the thoughts of a man getting ready for a public and political life.

> Dec. 31 Was nominated for Councillor today. Intend to run & try it. Commenced to freeze up today. A cooper is building a cistern in the cellar out of two inch pine. Put up tin eavestroughs on south shed and wooden troughs on east side of barn.

1878

> Jan. 7 Coldest day we have had yet, a little sleighing but the ground is rough. Was elected today by a handsome majority mostly owing to the Grange & the Church, or at least to friends acquired at those places for I would have been little known otherwise, being away to school so long & never until these last two or three years having mingled much with the world. As it was I did not know 1/4 of the voters personally.

In his political capacity, he became heavily involved in local school issues. He was quite disgusted with a committee's lack of action concerning the building of new schoolhouses.

> Feb. 21 This school issue is causing a lot of problems but all is not lost yet & we will continue to battle on. We intend to hold another Musical & Literary Entertainment tomorrow evening at Stoney Creek. These entertainments learn one confidence & how to affect different characters but the literature is of so poor a quality that please the "canaille" (riffraff—he uses wonderful words, L.S.S.) that it does not elevate one's ideas much, and I guess I had better not waste my time much more with them. I had better prepare speeches for occasions that are likely to turn up, & write original essays with care & thought.

> Mar. 13 Which is better to sell, milk or butter?

1878 Diary

I like farming and believe that if I owned this
or any good farm with 120 acres cleared & 50 acres
of bush, I could make it pay as follows, now
let us see how near I will come, on say, 5 years
from this time, as it will take that long to get
the thing running, full blast with our limited means

20	acres	in fall wheat—10 fallow, all manured @25 per acre	$500.00
20	"	to keep 5 horses 15 hay 5 oats or roots	00000
10	"	of tilled land & the bush to keep 25 ewes	175.00
10	"	fallow	00000
3	"	grapes	450.00
1	"	waste around the buildings	00.00
1	"	strawberries	150.00
1	"	raspberries	100.00
1	"	onions	200.00
3	"	keep 100 hens	100.00
50	"	" 20 cows & 5 young animals & bull	
120		cows to average $40 for butter	800.00
	10	hogs at $10	100.00
	20	strips of bees at $10 profit	200.00
		plums & sundries	25.00
		Total product $2800.00	

Mar. 21 Have a man quarrying stone out of the mountain by the side of the road at $1.00 per cord. They are beautiful stone so far.

May 5 *Here is beauty of fruit—a dependence upon other sources of income than spring grain. The more I farm the more I am convinced of the necessity of as great a diversity of crops as possible consistent with economy, then if one fails, another may succeed.*

May 14 Heavy frost killed all the young shoots on the grape vines except a few short ones or buds $200 more gone. Oh its discouraging fearful uphill work, but it's "never say surrender."

The Fourth Generation

May 18 Ma was to town with butter today & only got 15 cents per pound for most beautiful butter & cheated on weight besides. One of the women folks teaching school one week would make as much as the six cows do in two weeks.

This must have upset him a great deal. He knew how very hard his mother worked to make the butter and how proud she was of her efforts. It might have been a time for him to vow to always be honest in his dealings both as a politician and businessman.

May 28 Drilled in 5 acres of oats in swamp by the bridge, number 7 wheel on 11 square shaft which sowed 2 1/2 bushels to the acre. Up to council & put in a very busy day, issuing roadwarrants etc. Sheared the sheep today. 144 pounds from 26 sheep. Wool opens at 20 cents per pound.

May 30 Sold the old cow called Dink for $32.00.

June 5 I was up to the County Council and succeeded in getting a committee appointed to investigate our school difficulty. The problem being, the report of the Committee on Education recommended that the power of County School Inspectors be curtailed as regards putting in force the law relating to the building of schoolhouses. The said power was to be vested in the hands of rural school Trustees. A deadly blow at the grandest institutions of this young country. Who ever heard tell of the power to put a law in force being taken out of the hands of a disinterested party and placed in the hands of those selfishly interested. We might as well have no law with regard to the erection of schoolhouses if Trustees are to be sole custodians of them. The only consolation about the recommendation is that it is so remarkably stupid, the authorities will give no heed to it.

Has much changed in the last 100 years?

July 29 An eclipse of the sun today.

Aug. 10 Building granary.

Sept. 24 The elections resulted in a decisive victory for the Conservative party. The great question was Protection

1878 Diary

versus Free Trade or a revenue tariff only. The truth is, if the duty was removed the price of American barley would fall a little but the price of Canadian would rise the most of the 15 cents.

E.D. was obviously a Protectionist, with good reason. I am a Free Trader and I believe that if E.D. were here today, he would see and support the global market advantages. Clearly times have changed and with the changing markets and changing economic structures, Free Trade makes much more sense. I think E.D. was right for his time and I think I am right for these times. Others might disagree.

Oct. 12 A third of the apples are bored with the codlin moth. Systematic and united effort is necessary to combat this scourge. Sir John A. MacDonald was called on to form a ministry.

Oct. 16 I believe 15 acres of corn & 5 acres of roots will make 20 cows give more milk for 7 months than ordinary pasture.

Nov. 10 The threshers have been here three days. We took the first ride in the new buggy today. Mauritana & I went to Stoney Creek to church.

I expect the masons tomorrow to build the root cellar. *This has been the most disagreeable year to work since I have been home & we have got the least return for our labor.* The most labor, the most straw, the least grain per acre and the lowest prices that I have yet seen & in spite of all this, *by the exercise of frugality we will be able to show a balance at the end of the year,* after buying a new buggy & keeping up a house in town & two of the family at school in the city (Cecil and Elizabeth) during the winter.

Nov. 13 Masons commenced the cellar today. School problem settled.

Nov. 23–28 Carpenters working.

1879

Jan. 11 Over a month since last entry and it has witnessed my nomination for councillor and my defeat at the polls, about the first time I was ever beaten for anything of importance that I tried for. My defeat was owing to various causes:

1. To there being five candidates on the mountain so that I did not receive a large support.

2. To the odium of being in the Council during a year in which the taxes were increased even though the increase was less than the extraordinary expense incurred by the erection of large bridges which were swept away by the floods in the autumn: the bridge over Big Creek on Barton Street cost about $534 and the one over Stoney Creek on Barton Street cost about $126 plus numerous smaller ones.

3. To a malicious slander originated by my enemies and circulated among those not acquainted with me, the effect that I had said to John Wilson a year ago that I was the smartest man in the township. A remark which I am sure I did not make and which my friends all gave me credit for having too much common sense to make; nevertheless it did its work like all petty scandals. The old saying that one enemy can do more injury than ten friends can undo, being again illustrated. The only fault I have to find with my friends is that they did not tell me of the scandal in time for me to stop its evil results partially at least.

4. To my not canvassing as H.P. VanWagner did.

Jan. 26 Entries in my little diary seem to get farther separated the more leisure I have, though the leisure is a delusion, for it seems I am fully occupied with things that are not paying me.

Twenty-five years have now passed over my head and though never idle I have spent enough time in frivolous undertaking and things of no import to have given, if well spent, enough of additional knowledge to make me much wiser, better, richer and healthier than I am, as would indicate the difference between energy and sloth.

1879 Diary

Twenty-five years later he had not changed his mind.

May 30, 1904 Spare time can usually be better spent reading. There is so much to learn; there is no end to it and the one who knows the most gets on best if he is able to make use of his knowledge either in business or conversation.

Even though we all "waste" time, I feel that the Smiths might waste less than many. My father and grandfather always seemed busy at one thing or another and I certainly don't seem to have any spare time. This is definitely a Smith trait. However I should add that leisure is healthy for self-renewal activities.

Mar. 18 Took the contract of hauling the sand & brick for our new schoolhouse.

Mar. 27 I cannot get out of debt for as soon as I get money it goes for something that I need or that I think will return a handsome profit, for example last week I bought a cow fresh. Though we do not waste a cent needlessly & we live very economically so far as dress & luxuries go, laying out everything in improvements of the mind of the rising youth of the family & improvements of the farm so that we ought, if we do not miscalculate get ample returns sometime.

Investing time and money in education and business upgrading has been an on-going interest of my family from day one. In both cases it is considered a good way to spend money but it also means that usually there is a debt somewhere.

Apr. 21 Talk of building a stone road.

He is referring to #8 highway, just an Indian trail, which was owned by Albert Carpenter. As early as 1838, stagecoaches were travelling along it from Niagara to Hamilton and may well have stopped at Ananias' tavern. It became a toll road to pay for road improvements.
I wonder what E.D. would have to say about "user fees." I believe this is the way to go. Somewhere along the path we have got ourselves into a big government build-up with little accountability as to the value of services offered.

The Fourth Generation

May 10 Set out an apple called the Ontario procured from the fruit growers association—2nd tree from bottom on the 10th row from the east.

May 13 Set seedling plum trees in the west row at the top in the hen yard; onions are up. Early cherry trees are out in blossom, grape buds are just showing their colours.

May 16 Washed 30 sheep drawing the water with a pail and adding some hot. A hard day's work.

June 8 Hived the first swarm of bees.

Aug. 23 Plucked the first bunch of ripe grapes today, Champions. *Grapes will pay here I believe*, under careful management.

Sept. 17 Shipped 803 pounds of grapes today to Robert Murray in Guelph.

This is the first transaction of selling grapes and therefore the very beginning of his fruit selling business. It must have been incredibly exciting for him! His dream was coming true.

Sept. 30 Finished cutting corn and pulling beans. Farmers have mostly good barns but poor houses. No doubt the next decade will be largely devoted to housebuilding. (One of his many predictions.)

He described in great detail his sales trip around Ontario, selling grapes in various towns, such as Walkerton, Paisley, Port Elgin, Southampton, Listowel and Clifford. Because he was about a week late compared to the other growers, he learned that the next year he must start selling much earlier.

In his travels he studied the soil, the architecture, the geography, and learned where the next rail line would go, realizing that such access would mean another customer.

His diaries become preoccupied with the discussion of fruit and his successes with it. His trust in the value of the produce from the soil is paying off.

UNTIL THE MIDDLE OF THE 19TH CENTURY, TOMATOES WERE BELIEVED TO BE POISONOUS BUT ITS BEAUTY LED TO ITS BEING HUNG UP IN A HOUSE AND CALLED A "LOVE APPLE."

1880

Jan. 6 The roads are bad, very muddy. The frost is nearly out, unusually warm. Will lose about 200 bushels of carrots, rotten from being frozen and scarcely fit for hogs.

Jan. 20 Northeast snow storm with no frost in the ground, the roads are in a fearful state. I went to town with beef, butter, cheese and forgot to get pay for a sheepskin that I sold to the same man I sold the beef hide to. I don't see how it is but I nearly always make some such blunder in a large day's transactions. It is most provoking, the skin was to be a dollar and I don't know the man's name, only know him by sight.

Follow with me here, the thoughts E.D. had about hoarding, profit and loss and the overall business scene. He ended his career with a reputation that implied he never operated with a profit motive in mind and I am sure he did not glorify the "almighty buck" but he *was* an astute businessman who *did* wish to make a profit and worked very hard at doing so. His famous and sincere altruistic motives overshadowed his desire for money and success.

March 4 Notes on the result of the hard times we have just lived through, ought to be taken by every careful observer & remembered for another crisis will almost be sure to come in 20 or 30 years. One of the causes of the hard times was the overstock of goods by merchants, so that when other causes started houses breaking down & large quantities of goods were thrown upon the market, other struggling houses had to sell at a loss or not sell at all & as they were obliged to have money were forced to sell these in turn affected others & so on. Prices had to fall and & kept falling. Manufacturers were obliged to close their factories until all this old stock got sold, which took about 5 years. The consequences were, that raw material was not wanted to any great extent & prices fell lower & lower until they reached almost starvation prices. Steel rails fell from $70 per ton to $20 when Sir Charles Tupper bought 50,000 tons. But what I wish to note is things which could be of benefit to a farmer at the next crisis. Wool went down

The Fourth Generation

gradually from 35 cents per pound to 20. We sold two years', 1878 & 79 for 23 1/2 cents. Now wool is 35 cents again & perhaps good wool might bring more. The interest at 7 per cent would have been only about 1 1/2 cents per pound per year & as wool does not shrink in weight, money could not have been made easier than in holding wool over until the crisis had passed. Likewise whatever iron goods a farmer needed should have been bought during the hard times.

March 21 Not enough snow for sleighing and too much for wheeling.

May 4 Sowed oats east of grapes and 1 1/3 acres in orchard, peas & oats mixed. Set out cherries & pears & peaches, ground in beautiful order.

May 6 Put out a lot of grape cuttings north of henyard and set out grapes. Sowed 3 acres oats.

May 11 Fine weather, everything growing well. Wheat about a foot high, cherries, peaches & plums have been out in bloom for 3 or 4 days, apples will be out soon. Sowed lower field summer fallow, with rape, about a bushel upon the field, ground in beautiful order. Finished setting the four rows of grapes about a hundred first class two year old vines, the first 18 in the 1st row etc. The remainder of the Rogers are good roots but only one year old from cutting. The Isabellas were miserable old things that appear to have been heeled in the nursery for two or three years in bunches, coarse roots, little fibre & very little or no sap. I fear they will not amount to much.

May 29 Grapes are growing splendid. If they continue through the season as they have begun and I intend they shall if work will do it. Tomorrow to council.

June 7 *First mess of strawberries yesterday.*

Could he possibly have known that in a few years these strawberry plantings would be the source of his most popular jam ever?

June 10 I guess we can drive the work ahead of us now. Have hired a third hand for about 20 days who did all the spading and hoeing and nothing else, and a boy about 10 days to drive a team and a team hired about 8 days. It is a great satisfaction to be up with the work and it does not cost any more in the long run. A dollar paid out for wages in the spring when the work is needed is better than more money paid afterwards.

June 19 Least a good swarm of bees yesterday and soon must clip the wings of the queen.

Aug. 19 I did a hard half day's work shocking oats. Set up 3100 from 1:30 to 8 o'clock (half!! a day's work) and a person would have to stir themselves to do more. Shipped ten baskets of plums to Montreal today.

He is very much in the fruit shipping business by this time and realized he did not like wholesalers or others shipping his fruit.

Oct. 14 Been to London, Ontario for six weeks selling fruit. Made my expenses out of 10% commission on fruit sold for others and sold my own grapes to a good advantage. I let Ransom fill order for peaches to my Listowel customers and they have left me for him. I find one has to be sharp in business.

Husked 42 bushels corn and quit at 5:30 for rain, could have husked 45 easy. The last generation should cease puffing, they could not do more.

There must have been some rivalry between E.D. and Sylvester judging by this last remark. Is it possible that E.D. had heard his father say, "Why when I was your age I used to etc etc etc"?

Heeling in nursery stock about 1890

Nov. 27, 1880 Unusually cold. I learned a good deal in my trip to London this fall but lost a good deal in being away from home. I find it does not do to be away from home at any time longer than a few days. Trusty men can be had occasionally but they do not understand how to carry on anything of importance without a directing head. *I intend to go into fruit now extensively as I believe there will be an almost unlimited market for the next generations*. The country is growing so fast. The population of Toronto has increased in 18 years from 44 to 80 thousand & many other town and cities in like ratio, at the same rate (and present prospects indicate a faster increase) the consumers of fruit will double in the next twenty years easily and moreover better facilities for shipping will be found & consequently other markets will be opened up & also hundreds of towns of from 500 to 1000 pop. now who consume little or none of the choice fruits shipped from the fruit district now will not only become better able to buy said fruits but will also acquire a taste for them & when they do will be determined to have them, so that taking these & other things into consideration *I believe those who go into fruit at once will reap the largest rewards of anyone engaged in farming*. My present plan is to set out 8 acres in berries & currants other than strawberries also 2 1/2 of the latter as well as 4 acres of peaches near the walnut & pine plantation, all to be set out in the fall of '81 and spring of '82. Then in the spring of '83, 4 acres of plums & a henhouse for 500 hens. These will eat about 500 bushels of corn or other grain & 300 or 400 bushels of carrots or other vegetables & leave a net profit over feed of about 500 dollars besides keeping down the curculio (grain weevil, that injures fruit such as plums) when the trees get into bearing, then as to cattle I intend to raise about 2500 bushels of roots, keep on stable in north shed holding 8 head for young cattle & cows & feed them entirely upon roots & straw or cornstalks & the other stable at the barn for steers feeding them hay roots & cornmeal so that I will need to plant annually about 15 acres corn, 3 or 4 acres roots, have 40 tons of hay & balance of farm in grain, wheat above oats below, here then is summary of supposed proceeds and expenditures *10 years from now*.

```
hens . . . . . . . . . . . . . . . . . . . . . . . .$500
small fruits  . . . . . . . . . . . . . . . . . .1000
apples  . . . . . . . . . . . . . . . . . . . . . .500
peaches  . . . . . . . . . . . . . . . . . . . . .500
plums  . . . . . . . . . . . . . . . . . . . . .1,000
farm  . . . . . . . . . . . . . . . . . . . . . .1,000
grapes . . . . . . . . . . . . . . . . . . . . .1,500
bees . . . . . . . . . . . . . . . . . . . . . . .1,000
labor  . . . . . . . . . . . . . . . . . . . . . .2,000
farm  . . . . . . . . . . . . . . . . . . . . . .1,000
house  . . . . . . . . . . . . . . . . . . . . .1,000
total . . . . . . . . . . . . . . . . . . . . . . .7,000
Expenses  . . . . . . . . . . . . . . . . . .(4,000)
```
Interest and profit per annum . .$3,000

The Fourth Generation

E.D. is inspired. He is envisioning the future and planning for it. Holding the original of this, written in his own hand, while drinking a cup of coffee and eating a piece of toast heaped with E.D. Smith strawberry jam, gave me goosebumps. Words written by a person who has never heard of me but I know who he is—eerie—and I know an incredible amount about him and his successes.

We set our own limitations in life. My move into the United States, unleashing the creativity of our people, going back to building brands, sharing information as stakeholders, becoming the driver of the organization—these are the dreams of today that compare.

1881

April 26 Most people are ploughing and sowing. (But he is not. They are farming grain but he is deeply into fruit.) Set out 31 grape vines today 9 concords finishing up first long row between Delawares. These Concords were *of my own raising* & the best vines I have handled this year all fibrous roots.

April 27 Set out 157 grape vines today. Vines *of my own raising* and splendid ones too!

These words are a great inspiration. He is becoming more and more independent, raising his own vines. This shows me I need to get back into the test kitchen with our staff and create my own products and packaging—*of my own raising*.

April 28 Set out 114 vines. I have two cold frames of tomatoes or rather hotbeds with cotton covers instead of glass. (FIRST MENTION OF TOMATOES! This means we have been in the tomato business since 1881!) One of them has plants starting their second pairs of leaves, the other was just sowed.

April 29 Set out 107 Concord vines among the Delawares, 77 of them vines of my own raising.

May 4 Put ashes around some plants, hen manure around others. Have set out 865 vines this year so far 250 of them of my own raising.

1881 Diary

May 11 Set out a row of grape vines from henyard to road as follows. Dug a trench 3 ft wide & about 20 inches deep. In the bottom put rotten sugar beets about 5 inches deep then a thin layer of clay, then about 2 or 3 bushels of poudrette (a dried deodorized night soil mixed with various substances and used for fertilizer) for 5 vines at south & 2 bushels ashes and bones partly dissolved under. Then a thin layer of clay, then a layer of cow manure, then clay, then cow manure, then clay then about 3 or 4 inches of very rich topsoil, manured heavily last year, then planted vines and covered with top soil also filled trench with top soil then put balance of clay on top as it will settle probably 3 inches. Set vines about 3 inches below level of ground or having about six inches of earth over them. Cherry trees are partially out in bloom, grape buds are pink.

At first E.D. did all the work but gradually he hired men and orchestrated most of it, planned continually, always with an eye to the future.

May 28 Planted about 3,000 tomato plants today. (Obviously planning to go into tomatoes in a big way.) The rows were set by Ma, Wm. Ready, Wesley Harvey, Oscar, Cecil and Victor.

May 30 Watered all the tomato plants that lived, about one half. Set out 4,000 tomato plants. Have about 6,000 alive now, 3,000 more to plant.

The next diary entry is without a doubt the most significant in his evolution as a fruit farmer and in the history of the Company.

Cultivation is the sure road to success, let not a weed show its head and keep the ground ridged up over winter and spring, plenty of drains and manure & *farming will pay, no doubt of it*. I guess I will have to drop the bee business, it requires such close attention that *I cannot spare the time from the fruit* to devote to it. I will however keep a few if I can without too much bother. I have two hives now which ought to be attended to preparatory for winter. *So I will have to make a new list of future operations in the mind's*

eye, and I may as well here remark that everything will be
subsidiary to the fruit business.

500 apple trees when full grown ought to produce	$500
500 hens " " " " " "	500
19 acres of grapes " " " " " "	4000
4 " plums " " " " " "	1000
20 " small fruits " " " " " "	2000
Farm proper	1000
	9000

There ought to be a good margin of profit
from such an income if properly attended
to and I intend it-shall

**There ought to be a good margin of profit from such an
income if properly attended to and I intend it <u>shall</u>.**

This is another inspirational passage with calculations. I
wonder if he just wrote it down or did he think and pause and
pace.

Dec. 16 Bought ten head of cattle. Roads fearfully rough.
Elizabeth and Gerti coming home.

1882 The Year the E.D. Smith company was founded.

March 12 No snow this winter. Very unfavourable for me
as I had 100 cords of wood to haul.

March 20 Mud mud everywhere. Have about 6000
Concord cuttings put away in boxes of lake sand in the
cellar.

April 12 Sowed my tomato seed. Finished planting 4800
currants. Sold steers and lost $2.

May 8 Have 10,000 strawberry plants set, 6,000 more to
plant.

May 12 This had been a disastrous 6 months for me. $120 loss most likely on fruit, $200 loss in not being able to haul my wood up owing to the mud roads all winter, now the loss of the oat crop in the swamp and the probable partial failure of corn. It is indeed very discouraging. It seems hard work to make anything farming. Wheat was all froze out about & hay also *so the only hope is in the grapes* which have a fine lot of wood to start with. It is a good year to make my plants grow of which I set so many but I can't stand the strain, as I will have about $600 to pay next fall for wages and $600 more for Elizabeth and Cecil, besides the running expenses which are heavy.

It is once again the fruit, the grapes in particular that are going to pull him through. He said before all would be subsidiary to fruit so, the fruit is definitely uppermost in his mind. Although Sylvester did not die until 1885, he was very sick in his last few years and was probably no help on the farm at all. Ernest seems to have taken over the role of provider and father.

1883

In the winter there is less work, for his comments are mostly about the temperature and the condition of the roads. They obviously go to Hamilton sometimes by sleigh.

March 18 We have had an awful truly alarming loss in fruit trees. A month ago there came an ice storm following a heavy fall of loose snow and made an uncommon thick crust 7/8 to one inch thick upon which the boys skated all over. Under this crust the mice swarmed from adjacent sod fields in crowds. I lost about 25 apple trees, 9 peach trees and perhaps 200 grape vines 4 or more years old. And about half the maple trees along the roadside now about 4 years old. Others have lost much heavier.

May 2 The wheat is almost all killed. Clover in the swamp killed from standing too long in water.

June 29 It has rained more this year than in three ordinary years. As for getting in the swamp it is out of the question. We have been laying tile part of the time and find an immense benefit.

The Fourth Generation

Aug. 15 Expect to finish hauling in the poorest crop of wheat ever. Grapes are injured bad in some places with mildew, or with something that we can't name yet—the berry turns brown or in some cases mouldy, stops growing & finally drops off. Biggar's, Carpenter's and Ransom's all bad.

Nov. 21 Bad frosts meant low price for grapes but still better than anything else on the farm.

Dec. 8 Thirty years old and no sign of matrimony.

1884

Sept 14 Been a magnificent year thus far for things to grow, vines and bushes never looked so fine. I have the grandest show for strawberries I ever saw. Roots promise a magnificent crop, even corn. Have the tenant house nearly done.

1885

Mar. 1 So cold that cellars froze up.

May 10 Lost 16 colonies of bees out of 21.

Aug. 30 It is safe to say that if no strawberries had been wasted the yield of Crescents would have reached 10,000 boxes per acre. All were badly wasted owing to not having pickers enough at the proper time.

He compares sandy soil, his soil, soil with ashes, soil with manure, soil without. He is learning about the land he believes in so strongly and is writing solely about business, not a lot of chitchat. What was planted where, when. A real reference work. Much crossing out and adding, things are changed, blanks were obviously left and then filled in. As traditional crops fail, fruit succeeds.

Each page of accounts, meticulously kept over several years, shows how the fruit had successes where the grain did not.

He was now into roses and shrubs, plums, apricots, peaches and pears. "Glover Vineyard planted in three days, May 12 to 14."

Cattle and Horse Accounts go back to 1877.

"AN ORDER IN ONE HAND AND A SPADE IN THE OTHER, HIS FROCKTAILS FLYING IN THE WIND," IS THE WAY HIS DAUGHTER REMEMBERS E.D.

1885 Diary

Wheat Account started 1875 with great detail each year, dutifully put in columns. Remarks include "frozen out," "frozen out—very bad," "a perfect season for wheat," "wet last fall & could not get it in early enough," "badly winter killed," "wheat did not fill well," and the entry for 1887 "none sown." The rest of the page is blank.

Barley Account started 1876—wonderful detail for 4 years and then "none sown." The rest of the page is full of information on roses, roses, roses.

Oats Account started 1877 with the same denouement: "all drowned out in May," "swamp put in very late and ground rough," "failure owing to drouth."

Peas account which he started in 1877, lasted only until 1878 because "no rain after they were sown and too late"; "something seemed to kill the young plants so they were thin."

Corn Account from 1877 to 1887 lasted longest. Did better with corn.

Millet Account recorded: "did not come up," "too dry."

He started his Bee Account in spring of 1879 with great detail on swarms, hives, artificial swarms, queen bees, larva surviving the winter covered in just the right amount of chaff. These bees were extremely important for the pollination of all the fruit trees and plants. Every major orchard used to have a skilled beekeeper.

April 29, 1881 Plum trees planted. The bottom tree in each row has a spade full of fresh hen manure about a foot from the tree spread around after the roots were covered. Will probably be too far off to do any good first year but I want to see the result. Also the top tree on middle row has a cat buried near it on north side.

Fall 1881 Planted Red Raspberries. Set out 5120 on two acres below the grapes set in the spring.

Dec. 14, 1886 Planned the route for draining the swamp. Cecil ran a line from the swamp to the mountain along the ditch running through the grape yard and bending east over the high hill to strike the lowest area. (Cecil was an engineer.)

The Fourth Generation

Cost of Tenant House including hauling sand, mason, nails, shingles, barn, well, fence, land, total cost of lot and building $450.

Set out grapes on top of the mountain in 1874.

Set out grapes and planted plum trees below the mountain in 1887.

Set out cherries below the mountain in 1889.

Vineyard Account—On the mountain 1889 crop a total failure from frost May 29th.

1889 Moved

These heavy frosts, harsh climate and unsuitable soil were too hard on his tender fruit. He knew that in the shelter of the escarpment, below the mountain, the soil was better suited and the climate a little softer. His faith in the success of his fruit growing was based on research, planning, hope and determination. He had already firmly decided not to remain a general farmer, so he had to find conditions that would best suit him as a fruit farmer. He wanted the best return possible for his invest-

E.D. Smith homestead, bought in 1889 when they moved below the mountain. Later used as a boarding house.

ment of time and money and this was the place to get it. So he moved below the escarpment and bought a farm that had been owned by the Bedells, relatives of Laura Secord.

Where he settled is our present farm and business. The two stone houses on the property, built in 1832 are still standing. E.D. would be pleased to know we are still here.

Other Interests

So, the young grain farmer evolved into a fruit grower, fruit seller and politician. Soon his neighbours were calling him "Honest E.D." and starting to depend on him for advice and leadership. When he spoke, he made sense. People knew the truth when they heard it and they heard it from him.

Even as a young man he was a progressive entrepreneur and probed into established farm customs in order to find more productive ways of doing things. In 1876 a Grange was formed in Stoney Creek (an organization founded to promote agricultural interests) and E.D. was secretary for many years. He wrote articles about the work of the Grange for the Hamilton and Toronto papers under such headings as "Co-Operation," "Market Fees," "Road Tolls," "Protection versus Free Trade," "Farm Labour" and others on the growing of small fruits, grapes, plums and peaches.

Through his involvement in organizations such as this, E.D. was in a position to help make things happen. In 1883 for example, and for several years afterwards, he sat as secretary for the Grape Growers Club and recorded many odd entries.

Moved by Murray Pettit and seconded by George Slingerland, that it is advisable that every grower of cherries, berries and grapes shall kill all robins and destroy all nests and eggs possible from their first appearance in the spring until the grape crop is gathered. At the same time sincerely regretting that the old friend of our early youth has become one of our most formidable enemies.

That was how they decided to deal with the bird problem then. Today, when the grapes are ripe, great loud blasts of sound every few minutes scare the birds away.

The Fourth Generation

The Fruit King

By 1883 fruit was being sold through a commissioned agent in Hamilton. Realizing that he could do without this middleman, he became his own agent and proceeded to become the agent for all farmers around because using a commissioned agent "did not by any means return the grower the full share of profit that he was entitled to receive." Without the middlemen, the farmer had a greater profit. (So did E.D.) It was not until he began to buy and sell fruit that he got a suitable return for his labour. So he initiated the system of selling fruit direct to the retail merchants. To him this was just good, plain, business sense.

Makes First Pure Jam in Canada

By the turn of the century, E.D.'s neighbours had bought from him and successfully planted so much fruit stock which had grown so well, that there was a glut of fruit on the market. He was the shipper but he couldn't sell it all and it was going to go to waste. Once again, he turned a potential loss into profit by using this fruit to begin the production of the first pure jams ever made in Canada. (Until then, it had all been imported from England.)

We tend to think of E.D. as an altruistic man who started the jam business because there was a surplus of fruit. Fruit spoiling on the vine, tree or shipping dock was loathsome to him. In the best interests of conservation and because of his thrifty, puritan upbringing he could not stand to see it wasted. Making it into jam would preserve it and be beneficial to all.

Take off the rose-coloured glasses and realize, as Armand (E.D.'s son) did looking back, that because of this glut of fruit, prices were too low and E.D. wanted to make more money. A refreshing thought to those of us today who are worried about being too materialistic.

And make more money he did. Those were the boom days. They would send out carloads of five-pound green jam pails and the storekeepers would not have enough room to put them in their stores. They would just set them outside and the farmers would come in with their buckboards and buy this jam. "In those days," says Armand, "we didn't have the competition and we were making considerable money."

BY 1886 E.D. CONSIDERED HIS ENTIRE WEALTH
TO BE $12,000.

Makes First Pure Jam

On top of all this, in 1900 E.D. was elected as a Member of Parliament for his riding of Wentworth. And we think we are busy!

Invention of "Blower Cars"

In this same year, over 1,000 tons or 142,000 baskets of small fruits were shipped express from Smith's alone, via rail. He based the success of his fruit shipping business on this form of transportation. As an M.P. on March 15, 1901 in a budget speech to Parliament, he showed the losses fruit growers sustained because government regulations on shipping fruit via rail were lax.

It devolves upon the Minister of Agriculture (Hon. Mr. Fisher) to do something to compel the railway companies to carry these apples and other perishable products of the farm in ventilated cars. It is the duty of the government to see that these railway companies provide suitable cars.

E.D. is the gentleman with his foot up on the the wagon bringing produce to be shipped in the blower cars. His wife Christina and son Armand are in the pony cart. About 1900.

The Fourth Generation

The fruit sometimes became more than 10 degrees hotter inside the car than out. It spoiled. Thus the farmers suffered losses. The fruit had to be kept cool during transport and he knew how to do it.

What we do today of course, is put it in a refrigerator car but they didn't have them in those days. By going into the ice farming business, he solved the problem. During the winter, he cut ice from his pond and stored it. Then, he found a way to place it in rail cars where the air flowing over the ice would cool the fruit and in effect create what were called "blower cars." Ingenious.

In government as well as his business, he was always looking for a straightforward line of action. If he saw a problem, he fixed it.

As early as 1901, wearing his businessman's hat, he had plans to ship fruit to England. But wearing his farmer's hat he was tilling 450 acres altogether, had 125 acres in fruit and a large lot in nursery stock. In this one year alone he had 150 tons of grapes and 250 tons of other fruit, aside from apples. He knew that when his 6,000 plum trees reached maturity he would have up to 60,000 baskets of plums to ship every season.

In the midst of all this work and hurly-burly, E.D. married Christina in 1886 and by 1900 had three children: Verna, born April 23, 1888, Armand, born April 12, 1891 and Leon, born September 10, 1900. Christina managed most of the family affairs and in his writings, there is no mention of his domestic life.

The First Jam Factory

The jam was no longer imported but the man to make it was! E.D. found Mr. A.M. Cocks, an experienced jam maker, in England. He paid his way out to Canada to start the jam business here. (This is an early example of hiring an outside professional.) They set up some cooking apparatus in the basement of the fruit house and in early 1904, the first jam kettles were put up on the second floor. Later that year the first complete jam factory was begun and completed in 1905.

Mr. Cocks made our first commercial jam in that year in this new factory. It was no longer made in the store room of the old fruit house alongside the reservoir for block ice. We

The First Jam Factory

Early jam was cooked and stirred in open kettles.

used to bring the ice in on an overhead track for our
refrigerating rooms and this block ice was stored in what is
now the garage. We cut the ice from a pond which is now
the factory yard and we used it for both cooling our rooms
for fruit and icing fruit railway cars. Cars would come in
from the main line of the H.G. & B., which ran alongside of
the fruit house.

Armand Smith 1949 (at the unveiling of E.D.'s portrait)

A wonderful story goes along with this famous piece of railway track, that highlights the determination and strength of
E.D.

Because the fruit shipping business depended on the H.G. & B. electric railway as a life line, when the tracks were being laid it was vital that they run close-by the plant. There was a dispute with the village of Stoney Creek on a technical point. E.D. and a number of his men and residents (most likely employees of the company who had a vested interest in its success) and even employees of the H.G. & B. crept out one dark night when all the village of Stoney Creek had gone to sleep and laid down those tracks, right where he wanted them, which pretty well solved the question.

The growth of the rail lines in Canada was in direct relation to the success of the distribution of the fresh fruit. E.D. did quite a bit of lobbying in Ottawa to promote these rail lines for his own business but also for the farmers of the "Garden of Canada."

We have a most excellent system. Our fruit grown in the Niagara District is put on board a passenger train at Toronto or Hamilton the evening of the day it is loaded on which it was mostly picked and is rushed to destinations at the same rate of speed as passengers landing in Montreal, Ottawa and other points equidistant, which covers all of Ontario east of the lakes, at daylight next morning and on the following day at noon or soon after reaching such distant points as St. Johns N.B. and Winnipeg and by the following morning three days after the fruit was on the tree, landed in Saskatchewan in the west and Sydney and Halifax on the east. Surely that is a good system and I do not know any country in the world that has a better one.

Speech to the Commons 1904

By 1907 he had the Martindale Farms in St. Catharines, three farms at Jordan, two farms at Beamsville and four farms at Winona, and the York Nurseries in Toronto. He learned through experimenting and researching which were the best

The First Jam Factory

House of Commons Debates

FOURTH SESSION—NINTH PARLIAMENT

SPEECH

OF

MR. E. D. SMITH, M.P.

ON

SUPPLY - - TRANSPORTATION OF PERISHABLE PRODUCTS

OTTAWA, FRIDAY, JULY 29, 1904.

---

trees and would not sell a tree until he himself knew it was the best for the area.

The fruit he grew included plums, cherries, grapes, peaches, apples, tomatoes, raspberries, strawberries, black currants, red currants and pears. (In the 1960s we were still growing cherries, plums and grapes.)

****

By now we were making catsup (ketchup) from whole tomatoes and Smith made such a high-quality product it trampled the imported product from the United States. It was badly needed in Canada and was so successful that not only did they use all the tomatoes from the E.D. Smith farms, but could buy tomatoes from all their neighbours. It came to the point that the local economy revolved around tomato season.

E.D. Resigns and Builds Helderleigh

In 1908 he resigned as MP. He wasn't feeling well and it took several years before he felt better. How he had the energy to mastermind the building of his huge landmark of a home, Helderleigh, I'll never know. This magnificent building, constructed from stone quarried right out of the mountain, stood within a peaches throw of the present office. By today's standards it was big and drafty, hard to heat and perhaps not practical but back then it was the perfect residence for a company president, a political gentleman and his family.

The Fourth Generation

Douglas Conant, a grandson of E.D. remembers vividly the massive front entrance; the wonderful dining room and long Christmas dinner table with a goose on a platter at one end and a turkey at the other. His grandmother would carve while the maids served the vegetables. Then the guests would go out hunting or hiking on the escarpment and return cold and hungry to the warm parlour with its potpourri, grand piano, huge bear rug and elaborate, warm fireplace with brass fittings, to open their stockings.

After E.D. died, Verna and Armand were the executors and they sold Helderleigh to a Roman Catholic order. It burned down in 1992. It must still be a shock to the local people passing by not to see it standing there in all its glory.

The First Office Building

Back to business.

E.D.'s first office was located in the "Home Farm" stone house, still standing at the front of the property, where Mr. A.E. Kimmins and Mr. J.W. Hewitson were his able assistants. In 1911 they built their first formal office building.

> It stands in spacious grounds tastefully laid out with rose beds and perennial borders, specimen trees and shrubs of various kinds. There is accommodation for a staff of about thirty, with private offices for executives of departments. J.D. Lamont is office manager and chief accountant and W.N. Langdon is cashier.
>
> The Grimsby Independent

Never content with status quo, unfermented grape juice joined his product line in 1912 along with tomato purée, maraschino cherries, apple and cherry pie filling.

To help further augment sales, E.D. and son Armand went to England in 1912 and 1913 to set up their own jam manufacturing plant to supply the hungry market at home. Why England? From the beginning, the Smiths have felt a strong attachment to the country and its people. Also it was a place already set up with expertise and machinery to make jam.

> I rented an old building and had to get to know the tricks of the trade. In those days we used gooseberry juice to help

The First Office Building

set the jam. My manager was a young Scotsman who didn't know much but at least he was honest. My head cook proved to be a jailbird and eventually we had to put him in jail.

Armand Smith in a letter home 1913

With the outbreak of war, Armand wanted to return home for several reasons: to join his First Contingent unit; the plant needed managing for E.D. was not well; no exports were allowed out of England anyway, so his job there was finished. He had a huge supply of jam to get rid of and the story goes that E.D. "threw his hat as high as the office" when he heard that his son had sold the whole lot to a Major who was buying up goods for the Navy.

Not only was E.D. not well, it was feared he would die. The problem lay in his stomach and for two years he had apparently scarcely digested anything. Doctors discovered that he was lacking in a certain acid so he took hydrochloric acid for years and said, "just thirty-three cents of medicine a day keeps me alive!"

Ironically, he never found food very interesting. Perhaps because of his problem he was unable to enjoy it as most people do or maybe he was just too busy to eat.

Left to right, Armand, Christina, Verna, Ernest and Leon

The Fourth Generation

Christina, his wife, was constantly after him to eat and would even chase after him around the farm to try to get some food into him. After dinner, if he were asked what he had just eaten, chances were that he had no idea at all.

E.D. The Senator

In 1913, he was appointed to the Senate by Sir Robert Borden and he felt it such an honour to now be able to reach out and serve his country even more than before. Armand was well involved in the business by this time and it freed up E.D. to further pursue these political interests. He travelled to Ottawa by train and maintained an apartment where his daughter Verna presided as "Chatelaine." Christina really did not care for the social limelight associated with this senatorial position but Verna apparently cut quite a swath through the Ottawa scene on her father's arm.

He was always very proud to be able to say that he paid his own train fare to Ottawa, that the people of Canada did not have to; he paid for his own lodging when there; in his capacity as Senator he had access to passes for many events but he would not let his family use them giving the reason, that they would be using the money of Ontario people for their own gratification; most notable of all, *he was the very first Senator to ever resign* because he felt he could not honestly be paid for a job he felt he was becoming too tired to do. You have to know that by this time he was 92 years old!! In Canada, Senators are given a job for life, but integrity was too big a part of his life to accept money for something he couldn't do. Is there a lesson here somewhere?

Parliamentary records throughout the years show that he had the keenest interest in the country's welfare and progress.

Sketch of lapel pin done by Cady McKay who designed the old maple leaf label. He was the night watchman and was found shot to death in the factory in 1922. This pin belonged to James Reekie and was donated to the archives by his son William.

A Mind of His Own

We have given the Daylight Saving act a fair trial since its inception and are heartily sick of it. On Monday we went back to the old time. The act has caused us many hundreds of dollars of financial loss, and our workmen will no longer tolerate it. For them it means colds, rheumatism and extreme discomfort. Nearly every morning the trees and vegetables amongst which they work are wet with dew, so that their feet and legs, if working in tomatoes, as well as their arms, if picking either fruit or vegetables, are soaking wet and this is not conducive to either health or comfort, besides a great detriment to the value of the fruit. Even the factory hands object to working by electric light in the morning which they will have to do after this and they prefer the old time. In fact we have never heard a man or woman in the country say a good word for this act. We will be greatly inconvenienced on account of the city and villages having the new time, but of the two evils we are going to choose the least and after this stick to the old-established time and trust that at another session of parliament this foolish legislation which is of infinite injury to the health of a vast number of people in the city as well as the country, will change.

E.D. Smith letter to the editor, September 7, 1918

Bad News, Bad Investment, Bad Health

June 29, 1912 Cecil Smith, E.D.'s brother, died. It was an untimely death and a sorry one. A young man, just reaching the pinnacle of a proud career as an engineer, he had been engaged in a big irrigation scheme in Idaho, U.S.A. called the Gem Irrigation District. With a couple of multi-millionaires as investment partners and a strong engineering firm as partners, Cecil probably felt his personal backing was well covered.

When his "inopportune" death came, just before W.W.I., the whole scheme was falling apart with a great deal of money at stake. Cecil's partners (who had been persuaded to embark on the deal by Cecil) asked E.D. to put up some money which he did and for good reasons.

The Fourth Generation

First, my brother had been very successful, had earned and obtained a very high reputation. His name was at stake and I did not like to see this venture fail. He had been unable to sell the bonds, (his partner) also could not sell them but I thought surely in time they would be good. Another motive was of course to save my brother's fortune or part of it for his boys, Arthur and Harold. Thirdly, one partner had acted so honorably by putting in $100,000 after my brother's death, I was persuaded to risk $50,000.

From a small beginning, E.D. got in deep. By 1919 his loss was up to $65,304.18. In return for this investment, Cecil's estate got $70,000 worth of stock in Boundary Investment. Not only did this stock crash but it brought down with it several other interests that had been tied in with it, leaving E.D. feeling betrayed. Contracts had been broken, takeovers had gone through without proper board approval and worse.

I have spent for ten years now about as much thought and had as much or more worry over the affairs of my brother's estate as over our own rather large business with its many worries.

E.D. Smith 1922

Armand wouldn't have been surprised if, including the interest, E.D. had lost as much as $250,000 on this debacle. "It put the family company in a bad way for the Big Depression soon to follow and set E.D. Smith and Sons Ltd. back many years."

Cecil Brunswick Smith 1865–1912

E.D.'s only brother, Cecil was born in 1865 the year the American Civil War ended. He graduated in engineering from McGill and the College examinations in the Faculty of Applied Science ranked him either first or second in all courses and he won the Governor-General's Award.

His resumé was impressive. As Chief Engineer of the Hydro Electric Power Co. which investigated all possibilities on behalf of the government for power for

Jack Harper was farm superintendent for over 45 years. He used to go out by the old drive shed early in the morning and shout at the top of his voice, "seven o'clock and nothing done!"

Cecil Brunswick Smith

Ontario, he was in great demand because of the interest and potential of Niagara Falls. In 1906 he was with the Honorable Adam Beck and Colonel the Honorable J.S. Hendrie on the Hydro-Electric Commission.

Later he designed and constructed great power plants in many Canadian cities and the firm he had organized, Smith, Kerry and Chase of Toronto undertook even bigger projects.

In Idaho, when beginning the plans for the irrigation of that state, he became ill and his doctor ordered him to return home for he had scarcely three weeks to live. During his final few days, E.D. apparently was with him constantly.

Most Smiths enjoy quite a long life, but he died from cancer at 47 just as his career was taking off. It ended on an unhappy note because of the huge Idaho project that went sour. Had he lived a long life, he may well have turned this investment around and made a success of it because he was good at his job.

He left his wife, Mary Jemima Dempsey. They had three children: Cecil Culloden, who died when very young; Arthur Latrobe, who drowned in 1913 one day before graduating from the Royal Military College in Kingston; and Harold Sylvester.

Going Strong at 75 Years of Age

> E.D. Smith is a man of vision who dipped into the future far as the eye could see. His sterling qualities, his fair dealing, his honesty are such that his many customers have had unbounded confidence in his integrity.
>
> M.W. Matchett, Accountant
> on the occasion of E.D.'s 75th birthday

Whatever success I may have attained is due to being aided by my good wife, who is a thorough business woman and comes from a thorough business family. From my youth I have worked as hard as I could and as well as I could. My mother sacrificed many things to give me a good education. My policy has been: 'Play fair, be just.' Later on I decided to go into the nursery business and found it very hard work. I was successful in getting around me a good class of workmen of sterling qualities, honest and dutiful.

E.D. Smith on his 75th birthday

The Fourth Generation

Meanwhile, back at the plant, fruit growing, fruit distribution and jam making were thriving. Canadians had developed a taste for this wonderful pure jam and they proceeded well into the 20s in this manner. But by mid-20s, the raw fruit business started slipping away with the advent of more competition.

Time For a New Strategy

This precipitated the beginning of the greenhouse business because they figured it would complement the nursery business and they could use the same engineering staff for heating the greenhouses as heated the plant.

> About 1929 we discussed whether we would go into the greenhouse business or the wine business. I guess if we had gone into the wine business we would have been millionaires but mother was opposed to making anything alcoholic so that settled the matter.
>
> Armand Smith

So we started into the greenhouse business just before the Depression and "in conjunction with every other business lost our shirts."

The Great Depression

Business climate in general was poor and E.D. made several very bad investments, ending up losing just about as much as he made. "Honest E.D.," worldly as he was, still believed in the integrity of others and was several times "taken" by those with fewer scruples.

In business, his word was as good as his bond everywhere. Over a period of 30 years the bank loaned him money without him ever signing for it. He made hundreds of verbal contracts with farmers who trusted his word alone. (An example of "business with a handshake" which we will see more of later.)

Every North American company that existed during the Depression has a story to tell. Our story is probably similar to many. We proved the old cliche, "when the going gets tough, the tough get going," to be true.

The Great Depression

Let me explain first, what some of the specific problems were.

By 1930 E.D. Smith was in trouble because trucking took over from the rail shipping. Farmers found they could deliver their own fruit themselves. E.D. Smith had some control over the local rail situation, but not the trucking business.

They lost a lot of their customers out west because there was a drought on the prairies.

Cut-throat competition in the east caused some sales to be down as much as 50%. In an attempt to keep customers, selling prices were lower but costs remained the same thus reducing profits.

For several consecutive years the Smith farms lost money.

The greenhouses had been carrying the business but in hard times flowers became a luxury and sales were way off. Also, the retail flower shop, Winona Flowers, in Toronto on Bloor Street near Sherbourne, returned less and less of a profit and in fact became a drain on the company.

The time had come for Armand to face the problem and the employees head-on.

The prosperous times that other industries enjoyed for the five years previous to October, 1929, were not enjoyed by us. Certain of our Departments made money, but others always lost heavily, so balancing up, we had no easy money to lay aside. Any member of the Board of Directors would be more than pleased if you would make it a point to say what steps you have taken and what new ideas you have

thought of to cut down expenses, without decreasing efficiency.

I have to stop here to notice that this sounds like modern day downsizing and house cleaning.

To you who sell, now is the time of all times to exert yourselves and scheme and think of every conceivable way to get our products on the market at the best prices possible. During these hard times we cannot afford to have serious mistakes made, either of commission or omission.

We have been pretty lenient in the past; we have always taken sentiment into account in our family organization. We have considered that by the excellent co-operation and friendliness we have had, it has worked out economically all right and much more agreeably than a hard-boiled corporation where figures only counted. We want to carry the same principle along, but when we are in for a fight (and we do not look for this Depression to be over very quickly) we have got to have staunch fighters with us too.

We very much regret that, owing to present business conditions, we are unable to give our usual Christmas contribution to our employees. It goes against the grain to do this.

The Smiths took a 10–20% cut in wages and issued no dividends. January of 1931 they re-negotiated contracts of every employee and almost without exception offered lower hourly wages, about 2 1/2 cents per hour lower, and lower weekly wages, about $1.00 or $2.00. Some who were due for an increase were not lowered but remained the same.

My success has been aided by the faithful men and women who have helped me all these years and I feel that success will come to any concern that builds up a faithful and honest band of workmen around them.

E.D. Smith 1928

The Great Depression

The names on record who received these lower offers were such people as William McLean, Henry Weigand, I.I. Butner, Mrs. Anderson, Mrs. E. Getrick, H. Librock, W.J. Nicholson, Milo Wilbur, Miss H. Grant, Miss J. Carpenter, Miss A. Barr, Miss C. Gordon, Miss O. Hawe, Miss E. Dennison, Miss E. Dunkin, O.M. Pettit, Miss E. Denny, Miss V. Smith, Miss I. Johnson, Miss Y. Mackay, Miss N. Langdon, Miss S. Speirs, Miss M. Vine (owing to your father's ill-health and your becoming more experienced, we are not making any change), Miss E. Campbell, Miss D. Keown, Fred Rogers, Levi MacDougall, Miss E. Howell, Nelson Jacobs, Russell Hamm, Norman Hamm, A. Jacobs, Charles Shaw, J. Davies, George Honey, L. Langdon, W. Butler, Sid Jones, Miss Isabel Wills, Albert Swick, J. Watson, W.C. Dawe, J.C. Hodgson, W.N. Langdon, C. Baillie, R.H. Savery, M.W. Matchett, E.J. Wills, Fred Richardson, Anley MacKay.

Of course there was some opposition to such drastic measures but in such a business climate, who could do much about it? Many comments by employees were like the one Mr. Anley MacKay made when he agreed to take a cut in pay and said, "It was the best and only proper thing to do."

> Every man knows that the problem of business right now is not to make profits, but to carry on. Expenses must be cut to the bone. Every employee worth his salt and with any feeling of interest in and loyalty to the business will cheerfully agree to that.
>
> John Watson 1930

What a feather-in-the-cap to E.D. and Armand that they had managed to instill in their workers this sense of loyalty. It was also indicative of the attitude of people at that time. They liked the security of working at Smiths; they liked the area; they had a good sense of the work ethic and quite frankly, they did not have much choice. Most businesses were laying people off and cutting back. People realized a co-operative attitude might help save their job.

The Smiths were no fools and they hired no fools.
Art Van Dyke 1994

The Fourth Generation

By 1932 a few termination notices were given because of less work and less cash. The lucky ones were asked "to stick with the ship and help to get it through the present storm."

In 1931, well into the Depression, Armand said jam was being sold for a ridiculous price. I remember him and my father telling the story that at one time, he brought a case of jam to his house, plunked it down on the table and announced that they might as well enjoy it because it was probably the last one they would ever make. It must have been a very depressing time for him to have hit such a low point. On top of all this, the actual E.D. Smith farms were not doing well and Armand even had them on the market for sale. "With a loss of over $29,000 they are our biggest bugbear."

Year of the Great Depression. Bank would not allow us to pack in the jam factory. Mother died May 15, 1932 at 3:00 p.m.

Armand Smith, diary entry 1932

To try to stabilize the business, he started a campaign of letter writing to the bank and to Parliament, to try to get money, stave off minimum wage, reduce or impose various tariffs, anything he could think of that could help. All the while E.D. up in Ottawa was trying to do the same thing at a higher level. They were a team, both working for the same goals of keeping the business going.

When the bank suggested sending in an Investigator to help the Smiths get on a better footing, E.D. was a bit upset.

Our business is all an open book to you. We have nothing to conceal. We do not need or want anyone to tell us how to run this business, but from our banker we have no secrets.

We thank you for your offer of assistance from your Industrial Department, but we have won our present position by our own efforts and will continue to do the same and feel very sure we know how to run it much better than anyone can tell us, though we are always learning something new. If we lose, we have no one else to blame but ourselves, but we are not going to lose.

1935

After four years of being in the red, E.D. was able to announce to the family Directors at the Annual Meeting that "The jam factory is our fairy godfather and has helped the other departments over the stile." The profits that year were $968.73 which was used to purchase a truck and trailer and a farm tractor. Good thing we did not stop making jam!

The grip of the Depression was lessening.

****

During his tenure in office, E.D. helped draw up many laws, regulations and improvements pertaining to the fruit business. He fought for and won better transportation facilities for fruit in railways and steamships, ventilated blower-express cars, cold storage on boats, improvement of docks to have them equipped with modern machinery to load and unload vessels. He sought protection for Canadian industry in the form of higher tariffs for imported farm and garden products in competition with the domestic equivalent. He was not a Free Trader, unlike myself.

At 92 he was the oldest member of

Mackenzie King's letter

Personal   CANADA   Ottawa,
                           January 20, 1946

OFFICE OF THE PRIME MINISTER

The Honourable E. D. Smith,
   Winona,
      Ontario.

Dear Senator Smith:

      His Excellency the Governor General duly received your letter asking His Excellency, for the reasons given therein, to accept your resignation as a member of the Senate of Canada.

      It has fallen to my lot to advise His Excellency to accept your resignation, and it has, accordingly, been accepted.

      I should not like this severance of your relations with the Parliament of Canada to pass without expressing to you, as I know Members of Parliament would wish me to do, appreciation of your years of public service to our country. The fact that your resignation has been tendered because of your advanced years speaks for itself of the length of your service. Those who know what part you have played will be the first to recognize how worthy it has been.

      May I express the hope that your retirement will afford more in the way of freedom from anxiety, and that the knowledge of the contribution you have made to the public life of Canada may lend its note of satisfaction and reward through the remainder of your days.

          With kind personal regards,

               Yours sincerely,

                 Mackenzie King

The Fourth Generation

the Senate both in age and in years of service and was still serving in the chamber and taking an active interest in his fruit growing, shipping and preserving business.

There is no secret to reaching the age of 92 and retaining full possession of all one's faculties. It's just hard work and good habits. Don't ever be afraid of work and be tolerant and temperate in your habits. However, the work must be properly directed to be of any benefit, for there is no point in working hard without proper direction.

E.D. Smith 1946

The Senator's Predictions

In 1946, on his 93rd birthday he resigned when he was Dean of the Senate. He continued to have tremendous vision and insight and cared deeply about the future.

He believed that World Wars would not occur again as long as the United Nations held the secret of the atomic bomb.

Even though the Federal Government had gone greatly into debt and the family allowance alone cost one-half as much as the entire outlay of the government at one time, he predicted that:

Canada will pull through and will probably enjoy a great wave of prosperity.

I visualize a hard concrete road across Canada from the Atlantic to the Pacific in the not very distant future, and hard surfaced roads increasing in mileage from year to year until the whole country is so covered with

Ernest D'Israeli Smith 1853–1948

them that people can drive on them to within a very short distance of every home in the land.

I visualize a great desire of millions of people of Europe to come and settle in this favoured land, and I hope conditions may prevail that will enable us to take advantage of this, but with discretion. There are plenty of desirable Europeans to fill up our vacant lands or to operate our vastly increased factories without letting in undesirable elements.

We need to increase our population with an influx of desirable people so that we will be able to carry the heavy load of taxes with which we will be burdened for a very long time.

I visualize the lessening of manual labour. The tremendous inventions that have been brought about, although depriving the working man of some of the elementary callings of the past, have opened up to him a much wider field, where more brain power and less hand power are employed.

I have no use for the theory that all wealth should be divided equally. It won't work now and it won't work in years to come. I challenge anyone who thinks 'the world owes them a living.' (A politician today could never say anything as blunt as this. They would have to tiptoe around it all without actually saying anything.)

In my lifetime I have seen the formation of this Dominion of Canada from scattered provinces. The increase in population is mostly in towns and cities which is all to the advantage of us country folks. City folks are our customers and we wish them to prosper, but not at our expense.

Some people are talking about the 'New World' that will arise from the war like a phoenix. This war has been so engulfing and technical and terrifying that we take for granted that things will get better because they can't get any worse. Some even have dreams of a world where lazy men and dolts will inherit wealth and comforts and even luxuries without much exertion; they hope that all the wealth in the country will be equally distributed. What incentive then would there be to work hard with hand and

The Fourth Generation

brain, which is how most wealth is acquired? Without this incentive to work, there would be much less done, and so less to divide.

The Senator Retires

I now retire and leave my two sons in charge. Armand, who has served our country well—four years in the Great War 1914-18 and two and a half years in this one: and Leon who has for many years been the head of the Nursery branch of our business and who has consistently carried out the original policy of straightforward, fair dealing. I bespeak for them that high measure of confidence that you have accorded to me in the past.

I may not ever have a better time or opportunity to say to my neighbours and friends in the Niagara District, how much I appreciate the more than friendly relations that have always existed between us. We have bought and sold together in a rather big way for sixty years or more and almost wholly without disagreement. Each of us is entitled to his own personal opinions. I have followed a course that seemed to me honest and straight, throughout all these years and I have found few indeed that did not seem to be actuated by similar motives and so we have lived happily together. I hope that the relations between you and my heirs may continue as pleasant as they have been to me in all the long past that we have been neighbours and friends.

Senator Ernest D'Israeli Smith died "a quiet death," October 15, 1948.

Excerpts from Letters of Tribute Written to Armand on the Death of E.D.

...The district as a whole today mourn with you the loss of one who has played an important part in the development not only of this area but of Canada as a whole.

The Senator Retires

...He was the embodiment of all that was good in the pioneer past of the Winona District and he kept alive in our hearts the love of these noble traditions.

...He was a member of the old school and his passing has made the world much poorer.

...He gave us our first start in Canada. We will always remember him as our benefactor.

...Mr. Smith strongly believed that the incentive to work is the greatest assurance of plenty for all, and through his life he lived up to this belief in deed and word.

Christina Ann Armstrong—Mrs. E.D. Smith 1861–1932

Once upon a time, in a belt of country in the south of Scotland dwelt some of the most renowned of the Scottish Lowland clans. Among them was the powerful clan Armstrong. Our archives provide the lines from a poem "Lay of the Last Minstrel":

Ye need not go to Liddesdale
For when they see the blazing vale
Elliots and Armstrongs never fail.

Legend has it that a Scottish king had his horse killed out from under him and, when lifted from the ground onto his swordbearer's horse and saved, he rewarded the fair fellow with border lands, gave him the name of Armstrong and awarded him a crest bearing an armed hand and arm. Some members of the family display the crest even today. My great-grandmother, Christina Ann Armstrong brought the spirit of that crest with her when she moved to Winona on March 24, 1886 to marry Ernest D'Israeli Smith.

Was he attracted to her raven black hair, dark brown eyes, tall dignified posture, regal and intelligent visage? Or her keen business sense and strict focused education? Or her father's thousand acre farm?

I think the answer is 'yes' to all of the above.

Suffice it to say, he married a young lady with a strong family history along with a strong sense of self, such as his own.

The Fourth Generation

Christina Ann Armstrong Smith
1861–1932

I find myself thinking the words "a woman ahead of her time" fit very nicely once again. You will see why when you find out her story.

It is actually not surprising that E.D. married her, for don't people say most men tend to marry someone like their mother? Brought up on a farm, she had a strong work ethic, she loved animals and was very knowledgeable about plants and flowers, could ride a horse and was a good cook. Like Damaris, she was vitally interested in the role women could and eventually would play in world affairs and in this way set her sights high. However, her accomplishments had to do more with the issues she saw around her, right at home.

Her only daughter Verna, wrote that Christina was most anxious to help women make the hard work in their lives easier. It followed that she bought the first manual washing machine, and then the electric model as soon as it was available, and the first electric stove. Imagine how she would have praised disposable diapers!

She wanted women to be worldly but remained adamant in her idea that first of all a girl should learn to be a good housekeeper—know how to buy and cook and bring up children—before going further afield.

She loved being in her home, with her family and the door was always open to her children and their friends. Being the wife of a Member of Parliament and then of a prestigious Senator, meant she had to spend a lot of time in Ottawa attending social functions such as the Opening of Parliament, and related political niceties. The story goes, that after she presented Verna to society, around 1906, she was relieved to find she could spend more time at home because Verna became a "polit-

Christina Ann Armstrong

ical social butterfly" and helped her father as a secretary and hostess. I get the impression she raised more than a few eyebrows from time to time as she too probably acted in a more modern way than was accepted at the time.

We might not have been too pleased today with some of Christina's rules. Strict Sunday observance was understood, with only hymns and classical music allowed and NO WHISTLING!! Not any card playing and no dancing either. She believed in children having lessons in piano, voice (in order to learn better speaking through proper breathing) and anything else that could improve their capabilities.

Without looking for the limelight, Christina was a great helpmate to E.D., a model wife and mother and self-sacrificing to an amazing degree. She was always interested in the welfare of others, a mainstay in the local church along with her husband who was a warden for 37 years.

The employees almost worshipped my mother. I don't think there was a sick child or a baby born that mother didn't help the parents in some discreet way. Being the daughter of a farmer and the wife of a man that had originally been a farmer, she took a tremendous interest in farming which was still her great love until she died.

Armand Smith

The Women's Institute

A tragic event, the death of a small, young child started in motion one of the most powerful women's movements of all time and set Christina's place in history, quite separate from her husband's.

The young eighteen-month-old son of Adelaide Hoodless, a friend of Christina, died from drinking tainted milk. Adelaide's grief and guilt were unimaginable. She realized he had died because she was not aware of the properties of milk, or of other foods for that matter. It became her mission to help educate women in the management of their homes and families.

Believe it or Not! The Women's Institute gave a fruit canning lesson in a Turkish village!

The Fourth Generation

To do this, she needed an organized attack. She began by trying to convince the education system to teach girls domestic studies in school. Believe it or not, years ago only girls could study this but now boys too can learn how to cook and sew. I think they call it "Home Economics" or "Household Studies." You can thank this lady. She was so forceful in her arguments that Mr. Erland Lee invited her to speak at The Farmers' Institute, comprised only of men, on a night when women were invited.

At this meeting she stressed the importance of a similar organization for women. She realized what a lonely, restricted life farm women led and their horrible lack of education. The outcome was a society which had its humble beginning in Squire's Hall, Stoney Creek, in 1897, and called itself simply The Women's Institute.

During W.W.I a Women's Institute chapter started in England and the Queen herself was president of one of the branches.

The real purpose or object of this first Institute was to raise the standard of homemaking. This is shown conclusively in the following statement recorded in the early minutes; "A nation cannot rise above the level of its homes, therefore, we women must work and study together to raise our homes to the highest possible level."

Fifty Years of Achievement

Today, as the world's largest women's organization, with seven million members worldwide, I must say it is quite humbling to know it all started just a couple of miles from where we live. The old Erland Lee homestead on top of the escarpment is now the Women's Institute Museum and displays beautifully just how it was, the night the Constitution was drawn up and signed. We have the added pleasure of knowing that E.D., Erland Lee and Major Carpenter were the ones who put the original Constitution together and the crowning achievement—Christina was asked to be the first President.

Hours of operation of Erland Lee Museum:
10 am to 4 pm Monday to Friday, Saturday closed,
1 pm to 5pm on Sunday.
Location: 552 Ridge Road East, Stoney Creek, (905) 662-2691

The Women's Institute

What a perfect person for the job. In her attitude she was an activist but in her actions, a homebody.

So what actually did the Institute do? It found resources and people to teach about home sanitation, home building, cooking and sewing. Through its magazine it taught how to wash, drain and dry dishes. To us this may seem primitive and easy but that's because we already know about the importance of washing dishes—heck, we just throw them in the dishwasher. Back then they had to learn to build the fire to heat the water without filling the house with smoke; make the soap using lye and ashes without chemically removing all the skin from their hands; and even sew the dish towels from old flour bags.

As the size of the organization increased, the scope of work widened to include child welfare, school health inspection, education, laws pertaining to immigration, women and children.

Even today, there are millions of women worldwide who are part of an organization that Ernest and Christina helped to establish.

Verna Rowena Smith Conant 1888–1992 (104 years!)
E.D.'s only daughter

As far as I know, my great-aunt Verna never had a real nine-to-five job. As a young lady, E.D. put her in charge of the fruit pickers during the busy summer season and the label room at other times; she worked like a slave for him in Ottawa; she wrote letters to newspapers and gave speeches to organizations; her husband was the Attorney General of Ontario and for a short time in 1942 was Premier of Ontario!

She was a professional volunteer!

She was the first chairman of the Voice of Women.

She was also an outspoken representative of the Women's Institute.

We must defeat Germany at any cost. We must keep up our morale in Canada in order to help Britain. We have been given the privilege to vote, a privilege to guide our country, and that vote carries duties and responsibilities. Have we lived up to that obligation? Records show that less than 50 percent of women use their franchise.

> Verna Conant, June 12, 1941 in her address
> to the Fort William Branch of the W.I.

The Fourth Generation

On one occasion her basement full of old cases of food products came in very handy. Two years after the atomic bomb was dropped on Hiroshima, the American Can Company in Hamilton was very concerned about how far the radiation had spread and to what extent it had affected food. When the E.D. Smith company was asked if they could answer this question, they knew just where to go. Verna's basement! Sure enough, she still had plenty of everything that had been processed since the bombing and a case of each was taken to a sophisticated lab to examine the contents. No radiation was found.

Armand (her brother) wrote to her in 1964 and was impressed with how busy she was.

> How you can stay up till two or three o'clock in the morning after giving a dinner party, then the next day carry on in the usual way at meetings, etc, entertaining again at night and carrying on continually is really something. Of course you have quite a bit of your grandmother Smith in you—made of iron—and of course father was a tremendous worker.

Verna was a bit of a hoarder and never threw anything out. She bought and stored cases and cases of E.D. Smith products in her basement and boasted that her larder was so well stocked she could feed 50 people at any time on a moment's notice.

Probably one of the first to "reduce, reuse, recycle," she would drive from Oshawa to Winona, arrive at the plant with her car full of empty jam jars, tin cans and bottles—50 years ago!! Another Smith ahead of her time.

Like Damaris, her father E.D. and her brother Armand, Verna was a diarist and a lover of history. She kept scrapbooks of newspaper articles, letters, photographs and memorabilia which would have been lost in the shuffle of time without her. This is a good lesson to us all, to treasure and preserve little bits of our daily life so future generations can try to understand us, just as we are trying to understand them.

THE PAST IS THE ONLY THING YOU CAN COUNT ON.
Judge Robert Meagher 1995

Elizabeth Smith

Elizabeth Smith 1859–1949

E.D.'s second sister Elizabeth was born two years after the Depression of 1857, the year after Sylvester built his big house, the year before the Civil War started in the United States and eight years before Sir John A. MacDonald became Prime Minister of Canada. She lived to see the atomic bomb in action, television, telephone, jet planes and antibiotics. She probably lived in what historians would call the most fascinating period of history to date.

At a time when women were not admitted to medical school because of the horror of gore and the insensitivity to it that men thought they had, here is a girl who had probably dissected more bloody carcasses by the time she was 10 than most third year medical students.

> Farming furnishes many subjects and much material for scientific enlightenment. One very interesting study to me was the study of physiology, which the removing of the fat off the insides and intestines of the animals killed for the table afforded. This was an opportunity par excellence and I availed myself of it.
>
> Damaris McGee Smith

She too was influenced by her mother.

Virtuous Energy

When she took the Medical School Entrance Exam in 1878 and failed, she was devastated. Had she been a man, she would surely have passed the exam but the laws and institutions basically barred women either through legislated means or by simply not accepting them. Rather than deter her, these attitudes charged up her indignation and gave her the courage and determination to overcome these barriers.

To earn money to continue, she was obliged to teach school for a couple of years.

> Have received a couple of letters from Elizabeth lately in the last of which she has received a cheque for $18.50—her first earnings & they come in very opportunely. She is getting on well with her school which is a small one; & has two music pupils at $7.00 per quarter, gives $1.75 per week

for board & likes her boarding place in fact everything runs smoothly only that the place is lonely for so social a spirit as Elizabeth's & her only source of enjoyment is writing long letters to her friends.

E.D. Smith

She and her contemporaries formed Canada's first great feminist wave. Dr. Emily Stowe (who earned her medical degree in the U.S.) was practicing medicine illegally in Canada in 1876 but practice she did. These ladies helped set up the Toronto Women's Literary Club which was really a sham, a screen for their suffrage activity. A clandestine, undercover, subversive, conspiring group (or so they were called at the time) who had to meet under the guise of a literary club in order to hold meetings. Seven years later, they could openly call themselves the Toronto Women's Suffrage Association without fear.

In 1883, Dr. Jennie Trout, the first licensed woman doctor in Canada helped found the Women's Medical College at Queen's. The next year, women were admitted to McGill University and the momentum of the Woman's Suffrage Movement picked up speed.

Elizabeth struggled with the world and herself most of her life. She revelled in the fact that things were improving for women and that she had something to contribute to this end but she despaired that she could probably not reap the benefits of it all.

Having earned some money she went back to Kingston in 1881 where she could continue "the real business of my life, the study of medicine." With the help of Adam Shortt a new friend who guided her through these critical months, she persevered. They married in 1886 and he went on to great achievements. She did not.

Elizabeth did become a doctor but discontinued her practice after her three children were born, Muriel Gwendoline, George Ernest and Mary Lorraine.

Now I claim that a woman should have a voice in making laws that so nearly affect herself provided she is qualified in other respects as men are required to be.

E.D. Smith

E.D.'s Three Other Sisters

She tried to be involved in many causes and hoped to maintain an intellectual interest. She actually ended up not well, bitter, trodden down by disappointment.

The world was truly a more complicated place than she had imagined.

E.D.'s Three Other Sisters

Mauritana 1856–1946   The closest in age to E.D., she was quiet, studious and taught school on top of the escarpment. In 1887 she married Hervey Coon, a widower with a daughter Helena, and lived on a farm in Norwich. They had two daughters Alice Alexia (Mrs. Charles Hurlburt) and Edna Gladys (Mrs. Wm. Deacon and Mrs. Alfred Bourne). Mauritana was a home-loving woman, close to her family and church.

In 1936, after her husband died she moved to live with E.D., then a widower and they both profited by companionship until she died in 1946.

Gertrude 1861–1962 (101 years old!!)   This third daughter of Sylvester and Damaris was a well educated lady who loved debating, planning programs for groups and her garden. Damaris lived with her for the entire 27 years Gertrude worked at the Hamilton Post Office—widowed mother and old maid daughter. In 1913, when Damaris died, Gertrude took over the role of family historian. She also drew up her own plans for her own house which she had built to her specifications.

She was an upright woman, if ever there was one and her sense of duty to family went beyond the usual.

Violet Bernice 1872–1954   The youngest child in the family, she graduated from Queen's University in 1897. Even though shy, she taught English, French and vocal and spent some time teaching in Saskatchewan. She lived several summers in Paris and the students she ended up teaching at Oshawa Collegiate Institute were lucky indeed to have such a fine lady to teach them the joys of the French language. She went to live with Gertrude on retiring.

Many thanks again to Verna Smith Conant for becoming the family historian after Gertrude and keeping notes on all her aunts and uncles.

I pass it on to those who would pause and have a glimpse into a past generation that still imparts solid remnants of its influence on those who stop to care for family, home and country.

Verna Rowena Smith Conant

(Verna has been included in E.D. Smith's chapter primarily because of her great involvement with the Women's Institute, although being E.D.'s daughter, she really is a member of the next generation. In the same way, Leon, her brother is included in this chapter because he was the prime person associated with the nurseries.)

Leon Launcelot Smith 1900–1946

The younger son of E.D., Leon contributed to the success of the company during the two World Wars and Depression, raised a family and left his mark in the agricultural history of Canada.

The first half of his life he enjoyed his tremendous athletic ability and played on the University of Toronto first string football, basketball and badminton teams. Tall, dark and handsome, living in the Delta Gamma Fraternity, life was good.

The black cloud at the time was a bout of typhoid but although it left him weak for a while, it did not stop him from going dancing at the King Edward supper dance in January 1925. That night, a friend of his, Archer Davis introduced him to the lovely

Leon Smith 1900–1946

Leon Launcelot Smith

Roberta Thurston and the next year after graduating with his Bachelor of Arts, he was out in Port Moody B.C. meeting her parents.

They married in 1927 and had three children, Thurston, Sheila Ann and Geoffrey.

> At that time we did a leading nursery business with all the farmers. There were no nursery sheds to work in, in case it rained—the trees were heeled outside with one shed in the centre that had a cover but the sides were open. Under this shed the boxing was done. All trees were delivered, of course, by teams of horses except what the farmers came after themselves. The drivers would be pretty tired after delivering nursery stock into the late hours and there was one team in particular that all the driver had to do was tie the reins around the whip stock and the team would come home. We had to stop this because although the team would come home alright sometimes it wouldn't turn out wide enough for passing other vehicles on a mud road and we had to enforce a rule that the teamsters had to stay awake!!
>
> Leon Smith 1932

Leon Joins the Business

As early as 1922 he had an official position in the nurseries and was soon responsible for the entire development of the agricultural program. He loved his work! Leon actually picked up the slack in the nursery department where E.D. had left off when he became a Senator. Like E.D. he preferred to be outside, working the land and running the various farms. Armand did not. He was happier inside, in the plant overseeing the factory, and expanding the manufacturing facilities to develop markets for the produce of the farms. The two of them complemented one another perfectly. The one company E.D. had started now had more than enough room for two Smiths.

When finally completely in charge of the Smith farm and nursery—true to tradition—he kept good relations with the employees and gave them the privilege to purchase left-over nursery stock in the fall for a fraction of its value. He encouraged pride and neatness by offering prizes to the best kept garden amongst the company houses.

The Rose King

Leon's knowledge of roses was unequalled by any grower in Canada. He went to Europe in 1938 where he made contact with McCready's in Ireland, Pawlson's in Denmark and other leading rose growers, to import their best varieties of roses to Canada. Thereafter Leon became a rose specialist of international reputation. He established a rose test garden at Helderleigh where over 600 varieties were planted and where he could study roses and decide which varieties were best suited to Canadian soil and climate. This garden which bordered #8 Highway was open during the summer months to the public and attracted thousands of people.

Roses are like my children. I know them all.

Leon Smith

AWARDED A SILVER MEDAL AT THE PAN-AMERICAN EXPOSITION, BUFFALO, 1901
Fragrant, Hardy, Vigorous.

Dorothy Perkins, A New Pedigreed Climbing Rose.

E. D. SMITH
HELDERLEIGH NURSERIES
WINONA, ONTARIO

Helderleigh Nurseries

The great expansion of the E.D. Smith company between the two wars, in spite of the Depression, was thanks in large part to Leon and the nurseries and greenhouses. Nursery stock, planted on over 1,000 acres of Smith farms, was shipped to all parts of Canada: shade trees, shrubs, roses, perennials, ornamental plants and fruit trees. They even got into the landscaping business and had jobs as far away as Port Hope.

Many of the big apple orchards in Trenton, Ontario, the Annapolis Valley of Nova Scotia and the Niagara Peninsula were planted with

Helderleigh Nurseries

trees from the Helderleigh Nurseries. Some of the seeds for these trees came specifically from trees in the mountains of Tennessee. In 1911 600,000 apple trees were planted.

Leon's right hand man, was a lady, Julia Carpenter. She knew just about everything he did and was a great help at the Winona Flower Shop in Toronto that they used as a retail outlet. Evelyn, Armand's wife, would travel to Europe and buy china to sell in this shop.

Since apple trees need to be planted very early in the spring, Leon got the jump on the competition by having trees ready to dig up and ship before the ground thawed. How did he do this? By putting one full acre of trees under glass with their roots dug in, he could protect the trees all winter, from freezing. In this way, they could be ready for shipping much earlier than if he had to wait until the ground thawed. They would then arrive at their destination several days before the ground did thaw, ready to plant the minute it softened up. Some people might have said it was an impossible idea, but he made it work. Innovative.

York Nurseries

E.D.'s wife, Christina Armstrong Smith's family owned a beautiful piece of property in what is now North York, part of Toronto, at Bathurst and Wilson. Leon made it into a working farm and nursery supply enterprise managed by E.D. Smith staff.

During the 30s, the Smith farms in general had trouble making money but Leon did well with the nurseries.

> I feel you deserve a lot of credit for the way you have taken hold and re-organized the set-up of the York Nurseries, to at least bring it out of the red. If you can even make it break even while retaining it as a profitable outlet for the parent company, you will at least have considerable satisfaction.
>
> Mr. Ingram—Canadian Bank of Commerce 1940

Alastair, his nephew, can remember working there planting or digging up trees and his most favourite job, driving the truck to make deliveries. He would ride his bicycle to work from Oriole Gardens and took great delight in receiving his Senior Matriculation early (high school grade 13 equivalent) because working on a farm was considered a war effort.

The Fourth Generation

Leon had his hands full at an extremely turbulent time. The war had taken Armand away and he found himself running the whole show by himself. On top of it all, Leon was not well and he became dragged down by his illness and the enormity of his responsibilities.

I am not as optimistic for the last half of the year. We cut our grower contracts by 25% in view of the export business being wiped out. Two years ago we had approximately 80,000 bushels of tomatoes packed at this date, while now we have barely 3,000 packed as tomatoes are ten days to two weeks late.

Retail sales at the nursery are only about 50% but the greenhouse crop looks promising. I feel the sale of jam will improve as the demand gets higher again, even with a war on.

Leon Smith, August 1940

It's the innovator who gets ahead.

E. Llewellyn G. Smith

Treetops

Our present home in Winona, was built by Leon in 1929 and he probably had hoped to live there forever. But as early as 1926, he knew he had a health problem. It started with occasional weakness; he would go to write his name and not be able to hold the pen. On a business trip to England he and Roberta went to see a Dr. Riddick, a neurologist who told him the bad news: Post Encephalitic Parkinsons.

Roberta remembers.

I was sure he would get better. The doctor looked at the ceiling. Then he looked at the floor and then he looked me in the eye and said, "You are too intelligent for me not to tell you the truth. He will never get better."

Treetops

Becoming anxious about his condition, Leon sold Treetops, and moved to Toronto so his family could get settled there. Geoff, Leon's youngest son was nine when his father died. He really just remembers him as a sick man. He feels his Dad got the family all in order and well cared for, before he bravely took his life with a gun, on November 10, 1946.

After his death, his treasured books on roses were given away to people who would appreciate them. There were 35 acres of roses to sell off and the void of his death was keenly felt because no one knew better what to do with them than Leon. This demonstrated to the family that there was no Smith knowledgeable enough to carry on, so the nursery business was closed down, the 600 acres at Jordan sold, the York Nurseries sold and the Winona Flowers shop closed.

By 1948 they could report the most profitable year in the history of the company to that date, thanks mostly to the sale of the nurseries and land. But Armand could see "a fight ahead now for all lines and no nursery to help overhead."

The Senator enjoying the Helderleigh Nursery rose garden

The Fourth Generation

Most of the money that had been invested in these enterprises was put back into the company for the continued manufacturing of fruit products including our jams, jellies, marmalades, pie fillings, all kinds of tomato products, maraschino and glacé cherries. I mention jam first because it has always been there to pull us through.

Money and Power Cause Problems

Geoff believes his mother Roberta probably has some bitter feelings towards the Senator. When Leon predeceased him, apparently the Senator changed his will so that Leon's children didn't get the same share of opportunity and ownership of the company that Armand's children did (Llewellyn and Alastair).

In fact, Roberta ended up getting more for her shares than she could ever have imagined and gave her money to her children. Then her daughter's husband, John Shortly, with several others, caused quite a furor in the family when they attempted to sell these shares. (See: The Great Share Scare)

Roberta is on her own again now, well into her nineties, living in Florida. She is still a big, strong, healthy, good-looking woman and when she visited Toronto in the summer of 1994, she thought nothing of jumping on the subway to go and visit friends.

****

Life is full of circles. Roberta married Chris Morrison, a fellow she had known before Leon. My dad bought Treetops back and now it is the home of my family.

My brother Llewellyn has enough vision from E.D. and the past to last the next thirty years.

Sharon Seibel 1995

Ernest D'Israeli Smith

His first core purpose was to try to find a more remunerative way of farming. He came to appreciate the capacity of the soil and if properly utilized what it could produce. He went on to add value to the produce of the earth by preserving the fruit to keep it from spoiling, grafting trees to make them healthier, being able to ship fruit further because it was kept cooler. Building on the superb foundation of land, attitude and education that the previous three generations had given him, he soared.

His tremendous self-confidence based on solid research and faith, allowed him to take his well planned ideas to the limit. Each time a door closed, he opened another.

Because he worked so hard himself, he almost intimidated others into doing the same. He was a leader, taking people to places and ideas they would never have experienced otherwise.

He aspired to lofty goals and possessed a vision of the future. He was a convincing figure of authority.

Hard boiled common sense, belief in a reward for a job well done, disdain for those who did not strive to improve the world, a genuine concern for the plight of mankind and belief in the greater good, made him the ideal Senator. His children were instilled with a value system that although strict was not static. The Smiths had never been afraid of change, of speaking their own minds, of taking perhaps the road less travelled.

THE FIFTH GENERATION

NOT JUST JAMS AND JELLIES ANY MORE

Armand Armstrong Smith 1891–1972

RAVENSCRAIG

The Fifth Generation

The Smith Family	World Events
1916 **Armand** marries Evelyn Hannah Gibson	1918 end of W.W.I; worldwide flu kills 20 million
1918 **E. Llewellyn G.** born	1919 CNR organized
	1920 RCMP established
1921 Leon joins the company, now called E.D. Smith & Sons	1921 Agnes MacPhail first woman elected to parliament
	1922 insulin discovered; Billes open first Canadian Tire store
1923 Alastair A.G. born	
	1926 first demo of T.V.
1927 Leon marries Roberta Thurston	1927 first air mail in Canada; Fidel Castro born
	1928 penicillin discovered; women get the vote in England
1929 Leon builds Treetops and greenhouses; **Armand** V.P.	1929 stock market crash
	1930 beginning of the Depression
1932 Christina dies	1931 Saltfleet incorporated
1933 raw fruit shipping discontinued	1934 Long March in China; Dionne quintuplets born
	1935 William Lyon Mackenzie King prime minister
1936 fire at the plant	1936 King George V dies; King Edward VIII abdicates; King George VI ascends; CBC created
	1939 W.W.II; Canadian troops land in England
1940 the Brigadier's accident	
1942 Judge Gordon Daniel Conant Premier of Ontario	1940 women in Quebec granted franchise; Battle of Britain
1942 start of HP in Canada	1941 Pearl Harbour attacked; Bismarck sunk
1943 **E.L.G.** overseas	
1945 **E.L.G.** marries Elizabeth Ann Jane Sifton	1944 Normandy Invasion; Stephen Leacock dies
1946 Leon dies; **E.D.** resigns as Senator	1945 end of W.W.II;
	1948 Mohatma Gandhi dies
1947 nursery business closed; Sharon born	1949 Newfoundland becomes 10th province; Louis St. Laurent becomes P.M.
1948 **E.D. Smith** dies	
1949 first Lea & Perrins produced here; Daphne born	1950 Korean War
1950 start producing diet spreads	1951 population of Canada 14 million
1952 Alastair marries Jessie Maben	1952 King George VI dies
1953 Gordon Conant dies **Llewellyn S.** born	1953 Queen Elizabeth ascends throne; Stalin dies; 8,734 cases of polio in Canada
	1954 Toronto subway opens; Hurricane Hazel hits

THE FIFTH GENERATION

NOT JUST JAMS AND JELLIES ANY MORE

The shareholders recognize and pay tribute to the fact that through good times, bad times and war periods, the Company has been able to carry on and grow which in large measure can be attributed to the many skills of Armand Smith. After all, there are not many concerns of our kind in Canada which can claim such continuity of business operations under one name and remain independent.

E. Llewellyn G. Smith at shareholders' meeting
when Armand retired from Chairman of the Board 1965

Armand Armstrong Smith 1891–1972

Grandfathers have an impact on one's life and mine was no exception. I remember him as a smiling, kindly gentleman, a bit stooped because of a bad hip, with a cane in his hand, welcoming us at the door of Ravenscraig, his home. He lived just across the road from our farm property, so my sisters and I often saw him and my grandmother, Evelyn; we called her Gaga. To us he was Granddaddy but to the rest of the world Armand Smith was the Brigadier.

I looked up to him and felt he took care of us. My earliest recollection of this was on the farm. The weather had changed, sunshine replaced with overcast skies, soon followed by thunder and lightning. My cousins Derek and Maben and I were out in the fields; not a safe place to be in an electric storm. There he came, driving his Cadillac through muddy, bumpy orchards to find his grandchildren. Being only partially mobile with a cane, rain falling and high winds blowing, he rescued us; put my bike in the trunk and safely transported us home.

Since I was 19 when he died and had been away at school for a few years, I remember him best through stories I have heard about him. Behind his tender face lay a courageous man of rock solid values.

The Fifth Generation

I saw this really tough side of him for myself when I was 13 years old. My parents were away on a holiday and left me in the care of a babysitter. A horrible, frightening thing happened. Our house was broken into, we were robbed, tied up, threatened with a gun and told we would have our heads blown off. They wanted money. I didn't know where any was so I gave them $4.00 I had earned cleaning out the swimming pool. They left us tied up in the basement.

When Granddaddy heard what had happened, he was enraged. He took his gun from the cabinet, loaded it, then marched up the hill to our house and spent the night with us. With the gun tied to his leg in a sling, especially made for the purpose, he slept on the bed fully clothed. He protected us with every ounce of his 75 years.

A local man, Brian Chadwick, reported the get-away car to the police and the thieves were caught. It's probably a good thing the Brigadier didn't get them.

After hearing that story, you will believe the hair-raising adventures to follow and appreciate the military side of the Smiths.

The Military

In all of history, there are few generations that have escaped the scourges of war. Silas came to Canada because of a war. Ananias fought for his country's right to be a country. Sylvester lived through local uprisings and was very aware of war in other parts of the world. E.D. did not go to war because of his eyes, but he encouraged the local militia to train at our plant, stored their supplies and ammunition and supported them in every way and waved his son Armand good-bye twice, in two wars. Leon his other son had his own war effort. Armand's older son, Llewellyn, became a Major and served in W.W.II and Alastair served as a Lieutenant but did not go overseas.

Armand Meets W.W.I.

Prior to the war, Armand had been pulled out of university by E.D. because he was needed in the business. One of his first tasks involved setting up the jam factory in England. With the declaration of war in 1914, Armand returned home and it was not long before he was back on a ship, returning to England,

Armand Meets W.W.I.

this time in uniform. His letters home, although fascinating, must have made unsettling reading for his family.

I was nearly killed in a Belgian cottage, two nights before the armistice, when the Germans let off all their surplus bombs on us. I had just told our cook that he was late in getting supper ready and I was leaning against a sideboard having a glass of beer with my other hand resting on the shoulder of another officer, when a bomb went off outside the window. It killed the mess waiter and the cook had over 40 wounds in him and the officer on whose shoulder my hand rested was shot through the stomach. You could hardly find a single place on the sideboard that was not marked by shrapnel except for where I was standing. It's almost impossible to believe that with everyone around me shot, that I did not get a wound.

I was made acting Second in Command under Lieutenant-Colonel Bert Hooper. We were the farthest advanced on the right flank of the Canadian Corps, to the right of Mons. I accepted the last German prisoner taken by the Canadians—I had to keep him at headquarters until a guard could be found to take him to the cages because the Belgians were screaming to kill him.

About this time, both Hooper and I were pretty sick from being gassed.

****

Armand returned to England with Hooper only to find Hooper's wife dead and his own wife Evelyn very sick, and Llewellyn his baby son, in need of an operation that would give him only a 50-50 chance of living. He had contracted the influenza that was devastating the country and the continent. Armand got the head surgeon at Guy's Hospital in London (Armand always went to the top person—even when buying grass seed as we'll see later). These must have been very difficult times for him: the war, his sick wife, his baby's operation, the business, the dying, the global upheaval. To a young man still just starting his life, the world must have seemed like a pretty scary place.

ARMAND WAS AWARDED THE MILITARY CROSS.

The Fifth Generation

Somewhere in France, April 12, 1918

We marched our feet off for several nights and then after living in the open another night, we went in to relieve certain Imperial battalions which the Germans had pushed back and cut up frightfully. The one we relieved came out with only 96 sound men. Well, when I took over from the Imperials, they had a sorry tale to tell. They had beat it so quickly that they left some of the wounded behind, and we had to have them carried out, and bury a number of others.

Our ration party was put out of business, and so we had to go without grub for a night and a day. The next night I was ordered to tape out a new trench ahead of our old one. I got to work on it under machine gun fire, but I got it done.

In the meantime, Heine's (the German's) machines came over thick as bees, as many as fifty being in the air at once. Well last night I had to get to work on the new trench again and had two companies on it and liable to lose heavily. Well we expected something to happen, as the day had been quiet, when suddenly a golden flare, was dropped from Heine's lines, and then—bango! His whole artillery opened on us, and the air became blue with smoke. Up went the flares from our front line and S.O.S. and back came our artillery. My, it was beautiful! There we were in a shallow trench *we had just dug*. Shells were falling on our old trench we had left and we found ourselves in a sort of no-man's land in comparative safety.

I got all my men ready, bayonets fixed, Lewis guns ready, and waited, lying low in the shallow trench we had dug. Heine did not come over on us, but on the next battalion to us, but our artillery was so good it cut them all up. While all this racket was on, and we expected to fight it out on a sort of forlorn hope, I honestly never felt cooler or better. I went along the line, talked to the men and had a smoke. It was a wondrous sight that night, not come to many, a real grandstand seat.

For the last six days I have not had more than two hours of sleep at odd intervals, always sleeping in my whole equipment without a blanket and out in the open with a

Somewhere in France, April 12, 1918

rubber sheet if possible under me. However I feel fine, but dirty as the devil, as we have not had a wash for five days, as it was enough to have our drinking water carried in. In battle you feel you are doing something real, and it is a queer thing when you get roused. I was wishing Heine would come last night, and generally the men were cocky too.

Can't you just see him, chomping at the bit, daring the enemy to come so he could have a go at him? (Just like he did when we were robbed.) It seems he relished, even welcomed a challenge and then attacked it. Tariffs, union organizers, competitors, wartime enemies, a debilitating hip injury and company balance sheets, he took them all on. In later years he would tackle Walt Disney, croquet mallets and crabgrass, but that's another story.

Major A.E. Kimmins

The E.D. Smith company had great respect and pride in all the gallant young men from the Winona area who went to fight, with special considerations for those who worked for the company.

Kimmins became General Manager of E.D. Smith in 1910 and no decision was ever made until he had been consulted. He was to Leon and Armand what Clare Proctor, Ron Lake, Brent Carroll and Bob Cunliffe were to me. A mentor. Enlisting at the beginning of the Great War, Kimmins gave his life in the Battle of St. Julien, April 23rd, 1915. E.D. acknowledged the importance of this in his tribute to Kimmins.

E.D. Smith Speaks in Touching Terms of Brave Man Who Died A Hero's Death While Leading His Men

Major Kimmins was my right hand support for 21 years. He possessed an unusual degree of all those manly virtues and qualities that have made the name of Englishmen respected and admired throughout the world.

The Fifth Generation

> His example was worth an ines-
> timable amount in the neighbourhood
> elevating the moral tone of the com-
> munity in which he lived. I was most
> fortunate in having such an influence
> exerted over my sons, growing up as
> they have been where his influence
> counted for much. I feel the loss only
> less than I would one of my own
> immediate family.
>
> E.D. Smith, Hamilton Spectator, 1915

Military training continued between the two wars and Bill Reekie remembers that during the 30s, "C" Company trained at the E.D. Smith plant and even stored all their ammunition there. During the fire of 1936 it all went off!! No casualties apparently but more than enough excitement.

Troops would train and march from Galt, to Long Branch, to Winona, stay over at the plant, and then on to Niagara-on-the-Lake. The Dragoons was another regiment supported by E.D. Smith. Bill and his friends have memories of making some pocket money by supplying the thirsty soldiers with drinks.

Brigadier Armand Smith Goes Back to War

Armand's diaries of W.W.II begin in 1940 with the flavour of the Old Boys' Club coming together once again to take on the enemy. Entries talk of luncheon here and there at various prestigious clubs, of discussions concerning high ranking officials from W.W.I. and what their strong points were, of cocktails and the Lieutenant-Governor's tea party, and of the 48th Highlanders' Ball.

General McNaughton himself worked at returning officers to their own units. The troops were definitely rallying.

In spite of the complexities of planning for war, Armand kept family life and the business well in mind. By this time, he was the chief person running the plant, with Leon managing the nurseries and greenhouses and E.D. directing his senatorial duties.

October 30, 1939 Called to District Headquarters Toronto to be told I would take over the Hamilton units until the 1st

Canadian Infantry Brigade staff was formed. I had been given the command of the 1st Brigade three weeks previous.

On Monday, December 4, 1939, Armand was promoted to Brigadier. I wish I could have been at Helderleigh to see him. The neighbours, co-workers and family assembled to give him a hero's sendoff. When they presented him with a bedroll to take with him, the Senator was "considerably affected" by such a moving sentiment. We will hear about this bedroll later on. If only it could talk!

The family would speak of this day for years to come. Here, a local fellow who had already distinguished himself in business and in war, was about to leave again, along with several other members of the community. Pride swelled high in their minds and sadness deep in their hearts for this party emphasized the enormity of the commitment.

December 5, 1939 Entrained from the Toronto Exhibition grounds for overseas. Evelyn and all the family saw me off. Sad parting. Llewellyn, soldierly, and Alastair, 16 years of age—5 years younger, rather broken up. Both boys would have liked to have gone with me. Llewellyn was already in the Royal Hamilton Light Infantry as a Lieutenant, having enlisted on the outbreak of the war. Evelyn a brick as I know what she is going through. Am Commanding Officer of the train.

Brigadier Armand Armstrong Smith C.B.E., M.C., E.D., 1891–1972

Crossing the Atlantic

December, 1939
Fog....Smooth sea....No escort....Fog....Still no escort....Ship alone....Still no escort....Partly clear.

The Fifth Generation

Up before dawn and went to the bridge where I met the Captain. Now in very dangerous waters off Ireland. Enemy submarines and possibly raiders. As it became lighter we could make out a tip of a mast on the horizon but we didn't know whether it was a German ship or one of our convoy. If it was the German battleship, and we knew there were 2 German raiders out on the loose, we were dead ducks. There were anxious moments as it came closer and closer. Fortunately for us it turned out to be a British war ship, one of our convoy. Before long we again rejoined the convoy and were protected by the 2 battleships—Resolution and Repulse, 1 aeroplane carrier and 10 destroyers.

Landed in Scotland

Cold as the devil, no batman, no pyjamas, no heat.

Miserable night. Water pipes in men's barracks frozen. No heat. Wired home Christmas wishes. Coughing and feeling rather low.

In France

January 9, 1940 Listened to a lecture given on the conditions and the Maginot Line. Although billeted in a chateau and given an excellent guardsman as a batman, the room was very, very cold. Must remember to wire Evelyn for her birthday on the 13th.

January 14, 1940 Really very sick for most of the week, with coughing and feeling very poorly. Forgot to send Evelyn birthday wire after all.

Visits King on Return to England

January 24, 1940 King's visit. Presented to him. My Brigade lined the streets and were very good. Lunched with the King and senior officers at the Officers' Club. His Majesty looked very well.

The Brigadier's Sword

Visits King on Return to England

****

Over the years, quite strong ties had developed between the Smith family and England, including the fact that it was where Silas' parents were born and the family always considered they were of English "stock"; my father was born there near the end of the First World War; we had extensive business dealings with the importing, exporting and making of jam; our largest customer for tomato purée was in England; and when Armand found himself there once again in W.W.II, he seriously contemplated moving the family over.

They never did commit to such a drastic move but the most important British "relationship" ever, as far as the company was concerned, would happen within the year.

A Great Honour

February 22, 1940 Went to Westminster Abbey, London, to be present at Lord Tweedsmuir's (former Governor General of Canada) burial service. I felt what a tremendous honour it was for me to sit with and be one of the representatives of Canada in the seats of the mighty. I couldn't help but think

At a luncheon in March 1940, Armand sat beside Vincent Massey, who was at the time the High Commissioner for Canada in the United Kingdom. (The same Massey whose name is associated with the famous farm equipment company.) Wouldn't it have been fun if he could have known that in the future, his granddaughter Daphne, my sister, would buy and live in the Massey home near Port Hope in Ontario!?

how I, a comparatively humble resident of a little village in Canada, should be given such distinction.

April 8, 1940 Went to Wellesley House and met the King— shook hands—talked with him and lit his cigarette. Later spent some time alone with him and had a nice talk. He looked fit as a fiddle, laughed, seemed to have a mind of his own and only hesitated once in his speech. Received secret documents re an invasion.

Evelyn in England

On April 25, Evelyn, my grandmother, arrived to be with Armand. The North Atlantic had become one of the most dangerous places in the world and she crossed it by ship, to be with her husband. A brave lady.

May 4, 1940 Big day—inspection at 1020 hours of the 48th by Athlone and Princess Alice. I accompanied them on their inspection. Evelyn and Mrs. McNaughton were ladies-in-waiting to Princess Alice. Thence 48th Highlander's cocktail party. Thence dinner—then home. Athlone and Alice aught to be satisfied.

May 10, 1940 Germany invades Holland.

May 24, 1940 Entrained for Dover. Owing to General McNaughton having gone to Calais, Dunkirk and back to London by destroyer and motor, it was decided to return us to Aldershot as too late to get to Calais and do any good. We would only be sacrifice troops. We disembarked. (Later we found out that General McNaughton had seen Churchill. It seems to me that for political reasons we Canadians were not sent in as it was either sure death or capture and it would have been bad politically for the 1st Canadian Infantry Brigade, also the first Canadian troops to be in action, to be wiped out). Churchill and Eden, however, did send in, as a possible forlorn hope and maybe to encourage France, the Rifle Brigade and the Welsh Guards. These troops fought nobly to defend the perimeter around Dunkirk but they were eventually all killed, wounded or captured. German armour was altogether too much for troops without proper defensive weapons. Neil Perrins, who came out to see me later in Canada, was in the Welsh guards as an officer, was taken prisoner and spent the balance of his war years in a German prison camp.

May 25, 1940 Back to Aldershot. Went out to see Evelyn. I have arranged for her to go back home as owing to the food situation in England, it is not right to have any person here that is not necessary for war purposes and she could do

BY APRIL 17, 1940 THE BRIGADIER HAD SHAKEN HANDS WITH THE KING SIX TIMES.

more good at home. Further strain with Evelyn because of having to say good-bye twice when she fully expected to never see me again because we realized by this time that we were sacrifice troops.

May 31, 1940 Evacuation of Dunkirk commences.

Here's a romantic touch. Evelyn's departure had been temporarily cancelled.

June 6, 1940 Saw Evelyn. King and Queen visited us and said "au revoir." Evelyn looked fine and was temporary lady-in-waiting to the Queen. The 48ths had their Majesties to tea. All my units were inspected. My nose has a boil inside it and is red as a beet. I took the King in for a chat and was with the Queen for half and hour. Both very easy to talk to and charming. Evelyn had quite an experience with the Queen which she may tell her family.

She certainly did! Her fairy tale stories of being with royalty were enchanting!

A Grave Decision

June 12, 1940 Left for France. Arrived at our destination Sable at dawn. One lone R.T.O. met us with an interpreter and told us we must withdraw immediately to Brest as the Germans were breaking through—Paris had fallen and all the forces left in France were pulling out immediately. There was not another staff officer to be seen. We wondered if the R.T.O. was a Fifth Columnist (a civilian within defense lines who secretly assists the enemy). When we asked the R.T.O. if anyone in his family had distinguished themselves in the Empire, he said he had only one, a fellow named Captain Oates who had gone to the Antarctic and died.

I was now faced with a grave decision. I tried to check with the engine driver to see if this fellow was bona fide. If this R.T.O. chap was a German or Fifth Columnist and he was in league with a turncoat master, even answering the questions he did satisfactorily, there was still room for possible fake as the Germans were very smart on this sort of thing and it would be disastrous if I pulled out with my advance column and then found that I had been tricked. If I did this and it was wrong, no doubt I would be court-martialed and would face ignominy for the balance of my life. On the other hand, if we didn't pull out and detrained and the bona fida order was to retreat, we would be left 275 miles in the interior of France without food, with only rifles and a few bren guns. We would have all been killed, wounded or taken prisoner. *So I decided not to detrain the men* and I gave orders for the French train crew to take us back to Brest.

The men on the train were very thirsty because of the hot trip, very little water because they consumed too much of it and some of them thirsty because of drinking wine given to them by French people, through the windows, against orders, when the train was held up at various points because of refugees. The French engineer now refused to take our train back. He said "la guerre fini"—the war is finished. I gave orders he must take us back. He refused again so Haldenby put in the cab a Highlander Sergeant Major who was acquainted with engine driving and another man to help drive and stoke the engine. They told the French engineer that he had a choice of being shot if he didn't take us back or we would give him bread and wine and treat him well when he landed us at our destination. Then on the cowcatcher and in the cab, Haldenby placed Bill Hendrie, Bill Darling and a few other ranks, including an interpreter, with revolvers and rifles.

Whilst this was going on, I had detached a party to go and get water in large cooking kettles. Haldenby was anxious to move on but I decided to wait until I got sufficient water. It took us half an hour to get this done. I took this chance because if the troops had no water they would not be in fit condition to fight or march.

June 16, 1940 Arrived back in Southampton by ship. Nobody knew about us until about ten minutes before our arrival. Up to that time General McNaughton had believed we were stranded and wiped out in France. We had gotten

A Grave Decision

the farthest into France, 275 miles but we were the first back to Britain by reason of being lucky.

My transport with radio equipment was all ordered to be destroyed in Brest by the British Commandant—not burnt but hacked to pieces with axes. There had been no space to load it onto the ship. This as a preventative to the Germans seeing fires and smoke which would give them a guide for their bombing planes. Rogers, our transport officer, salvaged my bed roll out of one of the trucks and threw it on board ship. (He probably went against orders to do this, but this famous bedroll had developed quite a history and Rogers was not about to let it be destroyed.)

August 13, 1940 Two air raids. When necessary, we are all in slit trenches. Mine looks like a grave. I sleep in the bottom of it and have a telephone in a recess in the earth. I have a tent under the trees camouflaged which I use in the daytime and also for sleeping at night unless there is an air raid warning.

> The main thing in my life at that time was to get my Brigade over to France to have some fighting and to show that I knew how to command in battle.

The Air Force

At the end of August, two planes collided—one an English Hurricane and the other a German bomber. Had set up headquarters in a stable and the German was brought to me. A young fellow, S.S., not hurt—fanatic Nazi. Our pilot had bailed out and was brought to me then too. I took him in to meet the German who had collided with him and he immediately offered the German his hand. The Hun refused to shake hands and spat at him. I sent the Hun up to Division H.Q.s. It was a good thing for him that our men outside didn't know how he had behaved or they would have made short shift of him.

****

No praise is big enough for the magnificent job that the British air men, including the Mother Country and all the Dominions, did in defense of Britain. The successful defence of Britain at this time, sparked and maintained by the most wonderful words and actions of Churchill, saved Britain, and therefore might be said, saved the greater part of the world.

September 9, 1940 Big raid against London last night. Heavy damage but spirit of people still fine.

Mail from home. Annual statement and remarks by Leon—very good. Waiting for the Hun to come over.

The Duke of Gloucester inspected the 48th. At the tommy gun range I asked the Duke if he would care to shoot. He whispered to me that he didn't wish to shoot as he would made a d... fool of himself. Ordinarily he is a good shot but Royalty, when they do anything in front of the public always have to do it a bit better than average.

Went to see Shirley Temple in a movie. Bombs dropped outside shaking the theatre.

The Accident

When we wake up each day, there is no way to know what will happen in the next 24 hours. Most days are uneventful, but every once in a while, along comes one that can change your life. Friday, October 18, 1940 was just such a day for the Brigadier.

Enroute to do an inspection, sitting in the back seat of a staff car, a large Army Service Corps truck came out from a minor sunken road, didn't make the turn properly and came forward on the wrong side of the road.

We crashed head on.

At first it seemed that Chand, our driver, got a cut and concussion and was taken over to a house. Colonel Graham had a slight concussion but was able to get out of our wrecked car.

I was the one that got it.

I was thrown into the front of the car, my knees ahead, puncturing the leather and smashing against the iron framework, driving my left leg back into the hip joint

The Accident

socket and bursting, or rather breaking through the side of the same. I couldn't move my left leg.

They got me out of the car and laid me on a seat of the car in the ditch and a kind English householder, I remember when I came to, was trying to get some tea into me. From that time on I didn't lose consciousness but was suffering considerably. Someone got an ambulance from the Dorking County Hospital where they put me on a slab and x-rayed me and said they found nothing. There was no doctor in the hospital at the time and the nurse seemed to be a poor one. She x-rayed my leg and knee but not my hip.

Dr. Wansborough at the hospital, put me under anesthetic and pulled my leg out. I then laid on my back with my leg in a sling and they said it would take three or four months to recover.

It turned out that no leg bones were broken but I have a compound hip fracture. Lying in one position is going to be a test of endurance.

Back at home, Evelyn heard about the accident over the radio!
Every day the Brigadier entertained an incredible number of visitors. General McNaughton gave him the best compliment possible when he assured him that his Brigade would be held for him until his return. No one knew how serious and debilitating the injury was and that he would in fact never really return to active duty.

Little did I know what my future held.

December 12, 1940 Sat up in a wheelchair for the first time. Played quite a bit of chess. I plan a reception in my hospital room on Christmas Day from 5:30 to 6:30.

Christmas Day My room was filled with guests all day. I had the room decorated; I gave each nurse a nice handkerchief as a present. Colonel Lawson put my crutches on the side of the wall and said anybody that would offer him 5 cents for them could have them. (We could not have known that I would never be able to walk again normally and that within a year he would be killed in Hong Kong where he was in command of the Canadian troops.)

January 11, 1941 I was moved to Garnons, a convalescent hospital with 36 officers, all Canadian. Leg muscles hurt and I have spasms.

E.D. Smith Company Visits HP Sauce

Not only was the Brigadier's military life changed by this accident, so was the future of the E.D. Smith company. In a strange way, without the accident, the company would probably be very, very different from what it is today.

January 24, 1941 Motored to HP Sauce, Birmingham. Met Mr. Bayliss and Mr. Wright who took me around to the local factory Home Guard and to the city Home Guard where I looked them over and said a few words. Arrived Mr. Bayliss' home—late, for dinner. Mrs. Bayliss and two daughters all very hospitable. Good dinner—up late talking. Mr. Bayliss helped me into the bath and looked after me like a brother.

January 25, 1941 Although Mr. Bayliss wished me to stay longer, I left HP at 11:30. Returned via Evasham and had a look at my old 1914 factory. The cook kitchens and part of the storage rooms were there and I saw two copper pans which were likely there in 1914.

A Dismal Sight

February 1, 1941 In London, went down into the subways to see the refugees and sleepers—very, very dismal sight. These people have all been bombed out although some are just ordinarily scared. They sleep on the subway platforms and on the steps going down to the platforms. The cold draft surges over them; old people, little children and babies. How these people can stand it one never knows. They lie on the train platform within three feet of the trains that come and go. In places the only way you can get to a train is to step over their bodies. There are three classes of people down in the tubes: rich or poor that are bombed out and are staying down there temporarily; the very poor who stay there all the time because they get free shelter and can't afford to go out into the country or have no friends there to stay with; and simply scared people that are still carrying on their business in London.

The Hip is Very Bad

February 3, 1941 Doctors told me I was worse than at Christmas, that the new cartilage on the left hip bone had dried up and because of lack of circulation there was a portion of my hip bone that had decayed. Further, that I had arthritis in the hip bone, further, that I would never command an Infantry Brigade again, further that I couldn't do anything for two months and after that, if I got somewhat better, I could only take an administrative job. Further they recommended that I be sent back to Canada.

After all my ambition to command the First Brigade into battle this is what happens—life.

If I have to take an administrative job I prefer to return home.

The Brigadier Sails Home

February 27, 1941 Sailed for home on a ship with a valuable cargo of 1900 soldiers and navy men, all ranks. There are only two passenger ships in our convoy—ourselves and the Empress of Canada but we have three destroyers and an armed merchant ship as escort. Cold, rough sea.

March 9, 1941 Landed at Halifax. Who should get on the ship, to my great and pleasant surprise, but

Evelyn Hannah Gibson Smith
1895–1981

The Fifth Generation

Evelyn. I have an idea that Evelyn didn't know I was in such bad shape.

March 12, 1941 Arrived Toronto. Verna, Leon, Gordon, Roger, Llewellyn and Alastair met us. Then for the day it was a scramble. They met me with a wheelchair. Leon got a large reception room in the Royal York where I had to meet representatives and photographers from the Spectator, Globe, Telegram and Star.

June 23, 1941 Reports about my leg and hip from doctors at Christie Street Hospital in Toronto were not good.

Thus endeth this chapter. I am out of the army.

****

The army however was not taken out of him. The diary entries he made while lying in a full body cast after his hip fusion are touching, because they show his frustration and disappointment.

December 7, 1941 Dr. Gallie called and cut the cast from my knee to the toe in a hinge so as to gradually get the use of my knee. Japan bombed Pearl Harbour. Peculiarly, when the nurse came in she said nothing, although she knew, about the bombing of Pearl Harbour. She didn't realize the tremendous significance of it and she only casually mentioned it after half an hour. I immediately of course told her that meant the United States was in the war.

December 8, 1941 Yesterday Japan treacherously attacked the United States and British Pacific bases. Britain, United States and Canada declare war on Japan. My knee bends about three inches.

December 9, 1941 United States has evidently lost heavily at Pearl Harbour. My leg cast from knee to toe will be broke off.

December 19, 1941 Germany and Italy declare war on the United States and in turn the United States declares war on them. My cast which was hurting my heel, now fixed up by cutting the heel out.

The Brigadier Sails Home

Although honourably discharged from the military with an eventual 80% disability, the disappointments of losing his command and of being physically disabled were hard to take. However he did return to take over active control of the company at a very pertinent time. Leon's health was failing quickly and a Smith was needed at the helm. It also fell into place at this time that the connections he had made in England with the H.P. people after his injury, made for some exciting business news on both sides of the Atlantic and led to bigger and even better years for E.D. Smith & Sons.

Leon Fights His Own War

Leon, Armand's brother, who had not been well for a long time carved out his own war effort and proudly left his mark.

In 1922, a militia company was formed at E.D. Smith & Sons, made up of employees and men of Saltfleet Township. When the commanding officer Major Morris D.S.O. died, Captain Leon Smith assumed command. It was a very efficient company and because of it many of the men fought in W.W.II. Leon was very much a part of the military world.

He was also one of the founding members of the Winona Patriotic Citizens Committee, formed August 14, 1940, with him as president. The meetings were held at the E.D. Smith plant.

The object of the Association shall be to raise funds by various means, to supply comforts to the members of the Canadian Active Force who enlist from the Winona area, and to assist other patriotic associations, including the Canadian Red Cross and do all such things as shall contribute to the successful conclusion of the war.

Mandate of the W.P.C.C.

From 1940–1946 the W.P.C.C. raised $45,170 by organizing carnivals and concerts and encouraging donations. My heart really goes out to Leon who in his younger days was so physically active, strong and athletic. It must have hurt him deeply that his brother and nephew were able to fight for their country, but because of deteriorating health, he could not. The fact that he took on this added duty shows his determination to help "the cause" when we know he more than had his hands full just finding enough strength to run the business.

The Major—Ernest Llewellyn Gibson Smith

My father, E.L.G., had two commissions in the war. Discharged after six months because of deafness in one ear, he reapplied when the rules changed and he was accepted although he had to start at the bottom. This man was determined to fight for his country at a time when many were looking for any kind of excuse not to.

He met my mother in Brockville at R.O.T.C. training. She later joined the Canadian Red Cross Transport Corps and learned to drive an ambulance. It's a safe bet to say most sons would probably have difficulty imagining their mother driving an ambulance. Not me. My mother has such a stoic streak of loyalty, commitment and inner strength that if I were a wounded soldier and she the one I was depending on to get me to safety, I would have no worries.

At any rate, my dad ended up in France a Lieutenant. Like his father before him, he had several humbling experiences that left him wondering how he managed to stay alive. One such time occurred when a stove blew up, burning his face and hands terribly. He was stretchered out to England and the fellow who took over his position was killed the next day.

He was promoted to Major and completed his duties with great distinction but strangely enough doesn't like to talk about the war. So it is with the fathers of friends of mine, some of whom were in very similar positions. Unlike the gallant, swashbuckling tales of World War I that the Brigadier would write and talk about at length, World War II soldiers that I know just wanted to get the job done, go home and forget the whole thing ever happened.

They are very proud of their participation but seemingly find no glory in it. Is this perhaps where my generation developed the nerve to endorse anti-war demonstrations, to dare to say "take the toys from the boys"? Maybe.

As it turned out, by the time my mother qualified for the ambulance position, all the jobs for Canadians in Europe were gone. That meant she would have had to sign up with the British for a minimum of six months with no compassionate leave given. She chose not to accept this position because she

The Major—Ernest Llewellyn Gibson Smith

probably would have lost contact with the handsome Llewellyn, whom she married June 16, 1945.

After the war my father did not continue his association with the armories, much to his father's regret and much to my mother's relief.

War Memorial

Brigadier Armand Smith , C.B.E., M.C., E.D., (Commander of the Order of the British Empire; Military Cross; Efficiency Decoration) was Chairman of the Saltfleet War Memorial with the unveiling of the smaller block monument on Sunday, June 12, 1949. He had to deal with a surprising number of problems associated with its construction, from the cost, who would pay, who should pay, what it would be made of, who would build it, where it would be located and even some wondering why it should be done in the first place.

Even though Canada was spared any fighting on our soil, as a people we were very involved and the Brigadier knew the memory of this just had to be preserved.

When he received the following letter from a friend, Mr. Burton, he must have felt proud to know he had been largely responsible for the existence of the addition to the Saltfleet War Memorial that commemorates W.W.II.

My son who lives near the monument told me of an incident which occurred there on Sunday, June 19, 1949. A car drove up with two men, apparently father and son. The young man had the bagpipes and the older man appeared to be a veteran. They first arranged the wreaths on the monument and after tuning his pipes played by the young man, the two of them marched completely around the grounds playing the Lament, after which they stood before the monument and played the Last Post, then saluted and left.

The Fifth Generation

Saltfleet War Memorial. The large monument erected in 1922 commemorates the lives lost in W.W.I. The smaller block monument was unveiled in 1949 in memory of lives lost in W.W.II and later in the Korean War. Seventeen of the men listed, worked at one time for E.D. Smith & Sons.

Armand Carries On

Armand Carries On

Whether it was good sense or good management or good luck, E.D., Leon and Armand seemed to cover very well for one another over the years. War, politics, sickness took their toll but there was always a family member running the company.

By 1930, Armand was in the plant, Leon was in the fields and E.D. was in Ottawa.

They had just had two years of great expansion and expenses of $93,000 for greenhouses, the florist shop, a new manager's house, modern equipment and the purchase of some land beside the property.

Armand supported the greenhouses wholeheartedly because he was looking for other businesses which might be more profitable just in case the buying and selling of raw fruit went down the tubes.

Minimum Wage Threat 1938

Armand wrote to the Industry and Labour Board to discuss the looming possibility of a minimum wage. In his letter he noted that the E.D. Smith company operated under different conditions and shouldered additional costs that many others did not and would be more severely hurt by a minimum wage.

His main argument was that the company was in a poor location and he could not afford to move the plant. It was not a port city; rail was no longer available; everything coming in or going out of the plant (including raw fruit) had to hauled by expensive trucks; the work force lived in the city, not in the country and he had trouble getting labour.

Half their tomato export went to England and was being threatened by the hearty tomato from Hungary. He pointed out that now they were competing in a Worldwide (Global) Market and a minimum wage would raise his costs and make him uncompetitive.

Since the company at its own expense had an independent water supply, they were not a drain on the municipal coffers.

The consequence of being a seasonal business meant that at peak times it became expensive to transport workers from Hamilton.

On the other hand, E.D. Smith workers had so many additional benefits that more than made up for any advantages of minimum wage.

The Fifth Generation

Ketchup Wars 1930

The major ketchup producers today are trying to sell us ketchup that is thicker than the competition's. Things have not changed much since Armand's day!

I needed a thicker ketchup, one that would stand the blotter test (one that did not show a liquid ring when dropped on a blotter). Got a tip-top chemist with a laboratory specializing in food industry problems. We selected the best—not the cheapest—Dr. Gephart Ph.D. of Harvard. If he solved the problem, we would give him a large sum of money and a different amount if he did not.

He made tests and said he had finally solved it. They didn't work out. He was absolutely baffled. We paid him on the basis of not having got it. Mr. Boehm and myself continued experimenting. I made numerous experiments myself on the kitchen stove to no avail.

In an issue of the "Glass Packer" was an article on this and they put it to Heinz that he was using pectin. Naturally we tested pectin in a hundred different ways. We advanced so far that we could get this ketchup thick, but the pectin added would cost as much as all the tomatoes put together in the boil.

Dr. Gephart had so much money at stake, he would have got it if he could have. Illusive!

A British chemist was approached by our Mr. Hodgson who said to him, "If you get this, we will give you $500.00." The man said, "You may as well hand over the $500.00 now, as I can solve this problem—I am sure of it." Later we received word from this man that it was not pectin at all but another procedure entirely. We took up this procedure and it didn't work. The chemist did not come after the $500.00.

The steps we took in this ketchup problem are confidential, even as regards the use of pectin. If we get this, we think it is going to be worth a lot of money to us and if any other manufacturer goes after it, we want them to go through all the expense that we have.

Minimum Wage Threat 1938

These extras included the availability of continuous, steady work and an entire family could be employed at peak times; free, clean, running water (when even some of the finest homes in Hamilton did not have it); fruit at a discount. They could grow their own food on E.D. Smith land around their homes and supply themselves with free wood from the mountain for heat. They had no transportation costs for getting to work because they walked. There had never been a strike and everyone was very loyal.

Added benefits such as the company sports teams, fire department and picnics made the environment more enjoyable and safer. Human nature tells us we should "belong to a community of our peers" from which we gain security, friendship and a sense of belonging. Nestled comfortably at the foot of the escarpment, the inhabitants of Winona "dug in" between Hamilton and Grimsby and proceeded to experience life to the full without need of the big city.

The adult male was making between 19 and 27 1/2 cents an hour for a 60-hour work week and salaried people from $19 to $30 a week.

Even at that time, these wages might have seemed low but Armand's argument boils down to the fact that he figured the company could not afford to pay more in wages AND provide all these extras.

The biggest incentive of all was extremely cheap accommodation supplied by the company.

Company Houses

Those who worked for E.D. originally were farmers who were already living in the area. He shipped their fruit, paid them to pick his and eventually employed them to manufacture fruit products and build the business. Apart from seasonal workers, those who had a job with E.D. Smith were never out of work. It was a time of expansion, of innovation, of new directions.

After W.W. II, post-war expansion heralded the need for more manpower. E.D. Smith started recruiting from England, Scotland and Holland so successfully that many of these people arrived not looking for work, because they already had at job at E.D. Smith, but rather looking for a place to live.

The Fifth Generation

E.D. and the Brigadier realized this housing need and first built dormitories and then actual company houses. What a coup for a young couple just off the boat from a country that probably had very little housing prospects and even fewer job opportunities—to arrive in a geographically beautiful area, have a place to live, pay next to nothing in rent, and it all came with a job attached; a job which earned a living wage at the time. To top it all off, they soon discovered they were working for honest, decent, hard-working people.

This whole set-up laid the seeds for a mutually loyal relationship which in turn spawned an attitude that encouraged generation after generation to work for the E.D. Smith company.

We do feel a moral obligation to men who have come to the country and taken one of our houses, to give the heads of the houses practically steady work. They have here no opportunity to get jobs any place else.

We give work during the winter time whereas if we did not have a community spirit and feeling for our own people we would lay them off and let them look elsewhere for a job.

Armand Smith 1950

The freedom to choose work did not exist for those who wished to stay in the Winona area. This was not Smith's fault but it was basically a "given" that most young men in the area would work there or would have to move away to find a job. Art Parker tried it and it didn't work. He couldn't live closer to work, have more security, have more beautiful surroundings, have fairer, more honest people to work for than Smith. This lack of choice and freedom must have been hard to swallow.

This is a great example of a symbiotic relationship that today would be called a win/win situation.

People are attracted to family companies and food companies for many similar reasons. One is for job security. There is an accepted feeling that family companies are more paternalistic than faceless multi-nationals. Family companies have local ownership and community spirit and commitment. Food companies may not be as dynamic as some others, but they are stable and after all people have to eat. When you combine a family company with a food company to create a family food com-

Armand Has His Hands Full

Art Van Dyke had $100 in his pocket when he arrived in Canada with his family in 1951. As a teenager during the war, in Holland he participated in the Underground movement and with hoses tied onto his bicycle rims as a tire, would ride past enemy lines, note on a piece of paper where anti-aircraft guns were, put the paper in his mouth and ride back past the German checkpoints and tell his contact person.

After the war he worked as an airline mechanic in Indonesia for a year and a half. Then the E.D. Smith company offered him a job.

For $10 a month the company provided him with a little, insulbrick house across from the plant and he worked on the pumps and then in the machine shop. They had never had it so good. Mrs. Van Dyke remembers her garden, the huge playground for her four children (the fields behind the house), and the running water. Considering the times, she could not imagine a better place to live. Art says, "I had a real good deal at Smiths." He hooked up his own hot water heater; the company paid when the toilet broke and both he and the company thought they had the better bargain. His children picked fruit with "young Lew and his sisters." He worked for three generations of Smiths who "cared."

When people heard the approaching "tap, tap, tap" of the Brigadier's cane, they made sure they looked busy. One time, the Brigadier saw Art sitting on a fence and said, "I see you are doing nothing." Art could reply, "That's right. When I am doing nothing the line is working. When I am busy that means the line is down." With a wave of the cane and a bit of a "harumph" the Brigadier was on his way.

When the plastic chain on the apple line fell off, he stayed up all night to fix it and his wife made sandwiches for him.

By 1967 he was draftsman and project engineer and his job was eventually replaced by a computer. He "got out just in time." Some "empire building" had been going on and he was not surprised when people were let go because of overstaffing. It "caused a lot of hurt but they did the right thing."

pany, the values of stability, loyalty, security and community become very entrenched, certainly at E.D. Smith.

Armand Has His Hands Full

When he returned from a holiday in Florida in 1941, Armand told Leon he would take over the jam department but would do it without going into the office! By September he was back in hospital for his hip fusion operation. This must have been a difficult way to run a jam business while at the same time negotiating an important contract with the HP Sauce people—all from a hospital bed without fancy telephones and fax machines.

His friends tried to cheer him up by telling him he could have the leg cast cut off in two months and the body cast in three months. But Armand noted, "It didn't work out that way, it was much longer."

Other Concerns

As well as running the business, Armand had many other items on his agenda.

> War clouds hang heavy. The U.S. and U.N. troops in Korea are being driven out. The U.S. is spending billions on rearmament. Canada has sent the 1st Brigade of Princess Pat's to Korea, holding balance of Brigade back. We expect war taxes in 1951.
>
> Armand Smith 1950

When Chris and Arie Bergschoeff's father, Arie, was sick, the Brigadier let it be known that his car was in the yard, available for them, twenty-four hours a day if they needed it.

Their housemaid was knocked down by a motor car and ended up with a broken leg in a cast; they found out that R. Mitchell, the comptroller, had stolen from them over a four-year period and Armand says, "I stuck to my guns and had him in court." Helderleigh, the home E.D. had lived in until he died, was boarded up and put on the market for sale. It did not sell easily.

The good news was the jam department made more money than expected and business was "generally booming." The time was right to upgrade the jam manufacturing process.

Other Concerns

Jam had always been cooked in big open kettles, not unlike the way you make jam in your own kitchen, but on a larger scale of course. With the purchase of the new vacuum pans to cook the jam, they knew they were on to something innovative and special. It meant the jam could be cooked at a lower temperature and this helped maintain the flavour of the fruit. Some workers were at first a bit suspicious of these strange looking contraptions and worried about them blowing up or causing trouble. It just didn't look like jam cooking. Well, it was and it gave us a jump on the competition for a while. Our pure, high-quality jam was now even better.

> At the christening of Llewellyn Sifton Smith, born May 15, 1953, Armand gave him his $5.00 lucky gold piece that Verna had given to him when he went off to W.W.I.

As seems to happen so often in the history of the company, when one door closes, another one opens. When E.D. lost money growing corn and grains he started selling fruit trees. When this became so successful, he starting shipping the fruit. Again, success caused a glut of fruit so he started making it into jam. The two wars and Depression gave the company a roller-coaster ride but introduced them to HP Sauce. When Leon died and the nurseries were sold, the money was used for expansion at the end of the 40s which helped them stay on the leading edge of the industry at that time. The sale of Helderleigh came right when money was needed for the purchase of the vacuum pans. And then, when the raw fruit business no longer seemed viable or profitable, the fruit-processing business did.

Expansion in Food Processing

In the early 50s all the efforts and available money turned in the direction of manufacturing jam and processing fruit products in an even bigger way. This in turn lead to great expansion in the food-processing business. Consumers were poised and ready to accept prepared foods.

Armand was not alone. By 1953 Llewellyn added advertising responsibilities to his job as Vice-President in charge of production and Alastair took over the purchasing and management of HP Sauce and Lea & Perrins. They were a good team.

IN 1951 SALES WERE $1,917,924.
96.5% FROM JAM AND FRUIT PROCESSING, AND
3.5% FROM FARMS AND GREENHOUSES.

The Fifth Generation

The Brigadier Retires

In a family business, it is a blessing to have children who are interested in joining the firm. It is a tough decision though to know when to let control pass from one generation to the next. Armand allowed himself to be president only nine years, until 1957 and then Chairman of the Board eight years, until 1965. His father, E.D. held on officially until the very last minute and although he had not been very active in the day-to-day routine, he still had control. Armand may have felt a bit disappointed he was not handed the reigns earlier but he certainly gave them over to his children as soon as he could but he did not make the share ownership clear for some time and this caused considerable trepidation for his sons.

So in 1965 Llewellyn became President and Chairman of the Board and Alastair Executive Vice-President. The Brigadier continued to be involved but to a lesser and lesser degree.

Walter! Disney

This is a good time to tell you a story about how upset Armand was at Walter! Disney and his portrayal of the United Empire Loyalists, his pioneer ancestors. Young people today don't remember "The Swamp Fox" but their parents do.

It was a production that portrayed the Revolutionaries as being extraordinarily smart and courageous and the British as stupid or drunk or both. He wrote to Walt Disney Productions, the CBC (which aired the show in the late 50s) and even the sponsor Red Rose Tea and said, "I don't know how many people would appreciate you being a sponsor."

He must have had some impact because the Disney people wrote the sponsor on November 27, 1959 and said, "We have had a great deal of consternation about this type of programme and consequently the CBC Programming Department has requested that we discontinue "Swamp Fox" series.

Another victory for the Brigadier.

During the late 60s the desks of E.L.G. and Alastair were constantly full of little blue inter-office memos that Armand, although "retired," kept sending. They included everything from reminding them how well he did at public school, to discussing land prices and insurance. He certainly did keep his hand on things.

Walter! Disney

His bad hip prevented any rough and tumble sports in his life but croquet became an important, favourite pastime. Attention turned from business concerns to the details of ordering an imported croquet set from England. Delivery, length of handle, and roundness of mallet required considerable correspondence.

He personally took an interest in Llewellyn and Alastair's lawns and wanted to be informed immediately if they were experiencing any difficulty with them. When he wanted information on lawns and seeding he contacted radio personality John Bradshaw a well-known expert in his field. Whenever corresponding with companies he would always introduce himself as the Chairman of the Board and the letters would be addressed to the head of the particular firm. Armand was a top-drawer person who liked to deal with top-drawer people.

The Sauces and Their Secrets

As a youngster I can remember every once in a while an unusual atmosphere blanketed the plant. People would whisper, partitions would spring up around the cooking deck, a strange but intriguing odor would linger. A door with a special lock was about to be opened.

HP Sauce brewing days.

During two weeks of every eight, my uncle Alastair, who always walked to work, would stride across the road, dressed in a white lab coat and disappear into a secret room.

Eric Durber, the most trusted foreman in the world, had called him to come to complete the H.P. recipe because even he could not. Tamarinds, shallots, raisins, dates, malt vinegar, tomato paste, sugar, molasses, garlic and onions all rested in huge kettles up on the cook deck waiting to become HP Sauce.

Colman's mustard from Montreal was one of these ingredients and from the midst of this intrigue springs romance, for Alastair married Jessie, the daughter of the president of Colman's.

Alastair and my dad were the only ones in their generation who knew what spices to add to the brew and in what quantity. Single-handedly, he would physically weigh them out very officially into a big, stainless steel pan, stir them around and then pronounce the concoction ready to be added to the simmering kettles.

He would then hang up his white chemist's coat, resume his duties as Purchasing Agent for the rest of the day, but return the next morning to mix enough spices for that day's brew.

The History of Spices

Perhaps this is a good time to back track and fill in some of the fascinating details about the origin of this complicated sauce.

I could tell you about the Roman invasion of England and what spices they brought with them, or even tell of the Norman Conquest of 1066 and the cinnamon, ginger, mace, cloves, grains of paradise, saffron, cardamom, nutmegs and galingale! they introduced. But suffice it to say, valuable spices have played a long-standing role in the English diet. Spices were definitely big business. Landlords would even sometimes accept them in lieu of rent money.

Business has wings.

Armand Smith

In the 1400s a sea-route to the Orient opened up the spice trade even more. The British East India Company was founded for trading purposes and spices were at the top of the list. So precious were the spices that they were paid for in gold and seamen employed to unload the cargo were provided with suits without pockets!

Discovery of HP Sauce

Already by the 1800s "store-bought" sauces were starting to come on the market but it took a fellow named Samson Moore, owner of the Midland Vinegar Company in Aston Cross, England to bring a commercially produced sauce to the world, at a price the masses could afford. The rich were eating plain, wholesome food and the poor were eating monotonous, tasteless food. Certainly both would enjoy the added zest of a good sauce. Even today the English may have a reputation for plain food, but they excel in their chutneys, relishes and sauces.

Discovery of HP Sauce

Mr. Moore knew the timing was right to introduce just such a product. He basically had the sauce but now he needed a name for it.

When visiting the shop of a Mr. Garton who owed him money, Samson smelled something good cooking and saw a little cart with bottles of "Garton's HP Sauce" in it. Apparently Mr. Garton's wife's homemade sauce had been spotted on a dining table in the Houses of Parliament, hence the name. Samson forgave the debt and bought the name right away.

Not only did he have a sensitive nose for sauce, he had a keen mind for marketing. Anxious though he was to launch his product, he waited until it was fully endorsed by a reputable Dr. A. Bostock Hill, Birmingham's first Medical Officer of Health; it had a prestigious drawing of the Houses of Parliament on the label; and he had decided on the now famous shaped bottle.

So in 1903, just two years before E.D. Smith launched his first pure jam in Canada, Samson's HP Sauce was for sale in England. The parallels between these two men are many: their consumer product was introduced at just the right time; each product a natural progression from an already established business: from fruit trees to jam, from vinegar to sauce; both from a family business with very high moral standards; each with a vision of the future. Both men balanced their love of life with their energy, ambition and acute business sense. (The more I see of life and business the more I realize the importance of this word, balance.)

The prize goes to Samson though for originality in advertising. To get everyone talking about this wonderful sauce, he filled up small, covered wagons with miniature bottles of it and then when he couldn't arrange to have them pulled

The Fifth Generation

by ZEBRAS! he settled for donkeys. Even this created quite a stir. He had made his point.

Now the colonies were after the sauce and New Zealand and then Canada started to import it.

Because of the nature of the sauce itself and good advertising techniques, the Great Depression did not harm the sales of HP but rather enhanced them. With slogans such as:

It's the taste that saves the waste—HP sauce.

Today England expects every man and woman to be economical, use HP sauce and make the most of every scrap of fish or meat or cheese.

The sauce that's right for meat that's left.

Lea and Perrins

The ads were quite obviously directed at lower-income families so to hit the higher-end market they bought Lea and Perrins Ltd. which had a much snobbier appeal. It too was a sauce but in a daintier bottle and only a very polite few drops were used at a time. Although very well received, only a small segment of the market bought it.

Let me just take a minute to tell you the fascinating history of the discovery of this sauce. In 1823 a Mr. Lea and a Mr.

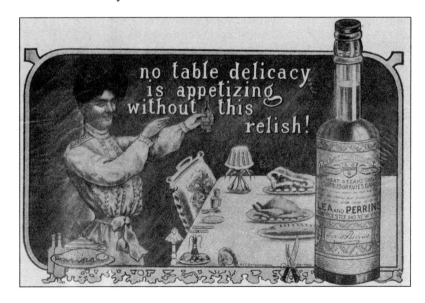

Lea and Perrins

Perrins, chemists and druggists, started a business in Worcester that included groceries. Lord Marcus Sandys, ex-Governor of Bengal, came into their shop one day and handed them a recipe for a sauce he had greatly enjoyed while in India and requested the two men make it up for him, which they did. Great scientific procedure was followed but when it was tasted and found to be abrasively powerful, they thought they had invented "liquid gunpowder." They loaded it all into their basement, planning to dispose of it at a later date.

Some months after, they dared one another to taste it again before throwing it all out and to their utter astonishment, it had mellowed into a spirited, toothsome sauce of rare piquancy. They bought the recipe at once and by 1838 produced it commercially.

E.D. Smith and HP Sauce

Now skip about 100 years and know that HP Sauce of Birmingham was Smith's largest English customer for tomato puree. Remember, there had been several British connections between the two companies over the years. Armand had lived there before the First World War where he started a jam manufacturing plant; during the war he spent a lot of time in England; Evelyn his wife came out and his first son, Llewellyn my father, was born there; at the beginning of the Second World War, he was posted once again to England. He became friends with one of HP's directors, Mr. Ralph Bayliss, as we saw in Armand's war journals. Mr. Bayliss actually suggested that some time they might want to have their product made in Canada and he promised that if that ever came to be the case, he would give Smiths the first opportunity. In August of 1941, export to Canada of HP Sauce was stopped during the war and he gave us the opportunity to make it here, for at least the war years.

> On one very special occasion, Mr. Bayliss had his Home Guard inspected by Brigadier Armand Smith in a most interesting scenario because it meant Armand the supplier (of tomato purée), was inspecting HP, the customer.

The ships crossing the Atlantic had no space for such luxury items as sauces. They were filled with soldiers, supplies, ammunition and weapons, refugees and wounded.

The Fifth Generation

At the time, the Brigadier was in and out of hospital with terrible pain and difficulties with his injured hip. Alastair remembers that before Armand agreed to take on the responsibilities of manufacturing the sauce, he put the question to Alastair, Llewellyn and several key production people, "Boys, can we do it?" The answer, a resounding, "Yes! We can do it!"

We gladly accepted the job of making the sauce.

This was a perfect match. Just as the E.D. Smith company had always supported any war effort by sending jam to troops and billeting soldiers, the HP Sauce Company did the same by sending HP Sauce to troops (the movement of British troops could be traced by the exports of HP Sauce), becoming firefighters and by forming their own Home Guard.

So, Armand announced:

I feel that this is certainly a very worthwhile acquisition to our business as this sauce will be put up during the winter months which will enable us to have a profitable enterprise running during that period of the year when ordinarily profits run out of the bung-hole because of inactivity. There are a few points to iron out but they have now given me personally their very valuable formula.

Ah, the secret formula. You can imagine that the success of HP Sauce world-wide had prompted other sauce manufacturers to try to produce a similar one. They could not. It had evolved to such a state that it was THE ONLY SAUCE LIKE IT IN THE WORLD and HP was determined no one else would ever know how to produce it without their authorization. It meant a very special relationship had to exist between them and Smith for this all to happen.

Many letters crossed the ocean.

CONFIDENTIAL

Dear Mr. Bayliss:

E.D. Smith & Sons Limited and myself are quite willing to safeguard the secrecy of your recipes and methods. No doubt you would want a deed made out between yourselves and E.D. Smith & Sons Limited. You may wish to communicate this secret process and give me instructions to enable E.D. Smith & Sons to manufacture the sauce in a

E.D. Smith and HP Sauce

satisfactory manner. I would need to disclose the general process to Mr. Honey who is our factory superintendent. He has been with us since he was a boy, (with the exception of four years that he spent in the last Great War) and is thoroughly honest. As I am General Manager of our firm, and as Mr. Honey is a busy Superintendent, the actual cooking of the sauce could not be done by either of us, but the process could be so divided up that a cook would not know the whole process or ingredients. The firm, myself and Mr. Honey would be glad to give sworn affidavits, bonds, and the necessary penalty clauses could be included in the agreement. You could send out a cook to us when we are making this sauce. We would pay him, but if there were idle periods, we would expect him to help in our factory at other work.

We have no hesitation in saying that subject to getting the proper ingredients, we can certainly make this sauce to your satisfaction and our firm is, as always, out to give you an absolutely square deal. Our firm is a family concern, the shareholders being Father (Senator Smith), my brother, sister, wife and myself and we prize too much, our good name and the family's business record of integrity, to do anything that would lower us in the eyes of such a famous, world-wide British concern as your own.

Yours truly,
Armand Smith 1941

What a cloak and dagger operation it turned into. In September 1941, a trustworthy man carrying a plain brown package, left England by ship with instructions to find his way to Winona, Ontario. Words such as "secret mission" are not too strong. Presumably this fellow was not told what he was carrying, only that it was "for the eyes of Armand Smith, only." In fact, he had one-half of the list of ingredients that go into HP Sauce and they were written using code letters. The code was explained in a second secret delivery made in December of the same year, along with the other half of the recipe. Under separate cover still came the actual description of the method of preparation and necessary plant design.

MORE HP SAUCE IS SOLD THAN ANY OTHER THICK SAUCE IN THE WORLD.

The Fifth Generation

A great deal of trust came into play here. Never before had the guarded secret been entrusted to anyone else. Armand took the responsibility of this secret very seriously.

Dear George:

HP Sauce are tying the firm and myself up very, very tightly and we have got to tie up our employees tightly as well.

Now the main thing, George, is that you and I are the only ones who know the complete formula and you must not give that formula to anyone, including those who have signed affidavits. You and I certainly do not want to give anyone any information except that which pertains to what they do. For example, Mr. Lamont will see an invoice but then he should not be allowed to go into where they are cooking; Wilbur will see certain cooking but he should not know everything. Mr. Leon has the right to go into your building and see what is going on but you have no right to give him any information as to the general formula and how it is made.

Armand Smith, Christie Street Hospital

It seems from this letter that Armand's brother Leon probably never knew the whole story, mainly because his focus stayed with the greenhouses and roses, but obviously Alastair knew the secret some years later. At any rate, it makes a good story that people working at the plant at the time loved to tell, that even the brother, one of THE Smiths, did not know the secret. It lent magic and gravity to the issue and added to the intrigue and importance of the product.

HP Sauce must be one of the most interesting foods in the world when you consider the origin of some of the ingredients.

We use African S from Nigeria or Sierra Leone in the form of the plain washed root, usually described as "unbleached whole S." Calicut S is very similar, but if you have to resort to Jamaica S, which is much weaker in flavour and usually supplied bleached, it may be usually from Trinidad or Grenada, described as pale to reddish, and Zanzibar or Madagascar Q. West Indian cane molasses vary somewhat in flavour and if there is any choice in supplies, one with a rather burnt liquorice type of flavour is preferred.

Armand Smith 1942

One of the biggest problems was getting permission to export and import all the necessary spices. If some tended to be on the exotic side, governments could take some time deciding whether or not to allow them into the country.

We have just heard from the Export Licensing Department of the Board of Trade that our application to export to you 6 tons of tamarinds and 1 ton of N spice mixture has been refused.

Just as secret as the ingredients was the combination of them. This was so confidential that England cautioned, "If you have to buy these spices already ground in Canada, they should be bought separately in disproportionate quantities to conceal the composition of the mixture."

The agreement stipulated that for the time being, E.D. Smith & Sons Ltd. would make the sauce, not sell it. W.G. Patrick & Co. of Toronto had been the sole distributors for many years and they would continue to sell it.

Of course I do not know whether we will continue to do so after the war but it is good to have such a close connection with such important people in England. They are the same concern as Midland Vinegar and also Lea & Perrins and one never can tell where this initial combination may lead to.

E.D. Smith put in a lot of new machinery, bottle cappers, fillers, labellers, all capital expenditures and in July, 1942 had sold 35,000 dozen and could not keep up with the demand. "This contract is quite profitable and is going to stand us in good stead." A wire from Birmingham congratulated Smiths on the excellence of the sauce and stated that it was as good as their own in every way. Thus one of the biggest problems was solved. The complexity of the recipe, the difficulty in obtaining all the ingredients and the hours necessary to learn the technique of putting it all together had finally paid off.

The Fifth Generation

I find it fascinating to see how business and personal correspondence were discussed in the same paragraph in letters between Armand and Bayliss.

> I am glad to hear that you are getting about, but it is very disappointing to know that you will still have to use a crutch for so long. I thoroughly understand the position as far as the agreement you have made with HP Company and my only hope is that you will be able to thereby recoup some of the expenditure which you put in so generously for the sauce.
>
> letter from Ralph Bayliss, 1942

> We have made our first sample and I think it is very good. Incidentally, you handle your garlic the same way as we do. Thanks very much for sending me Christmas greetings.
>
> letter from Armand Smith, 1942

I would be interested to know how many legal documents were issued in the whole Smith/HP Sauce agreement. Probably none at first. This was business done with a handshake. Armand's military reputation, the E.D. Smith reputation and that of Ralph Bayliss and the HP people were impeccable. These gentlemen, from long-standing fine families enjoyed the trust of one another. These are the type of people to be in business with!!

I like to refer to it as "the personal factor" that helps maintain integrity in business. It cuts through red tape, facilitates meetings and gets the job done. Today, often all the legal hoopla takes precedence over the actual business dealings and somehow that seems a waste. In my zealousness to treat business this same way I have made a few mistakes. But that's a later story.

Not to say there was never a formal agreement. Indeed there was for it would have been silly and naive not to; however both sides agreed that:

> in submitting formal agreements of this kind, we venture to think that the spirit of mutual co-operation implied in them counts quite as much as the formal agreements.

E.D. Smith and HP Sauce

By 1946, Armand was pleased to report, "The latest run of sauce just completed looks fine. I think we have got it now." The enormous complexities of formula and number of ingredients explain why it could take five years to get it right. Sometimes substitutions had to made if some ingredient were unavailable; the mineral content of the water could change the formula; spices gain or lose flavour depending on their age; vats used in England differed a bit from those used here so the gallonage per brew could change and that would throw off the correct proportions; temperature coils in the vats operated at different speeds and sometimes the margin of error had to be less than one degree or the sauce would gel or be too thin. The list of problems is endless.

Because E.D. Smith adapted so well to making the sauce, HP Sauce, which owned Lea & Perrins as well, saw it as a very small step to have both sauces made in Winona. At first the Lea & Perrins came over in concentrate form but was soon made from scratch right alongside the HP.

E.L.G. Visits HP

The cooking/brewing problems are the same today as they ever were but something else has changed dramatically—business relationships. Back then, business dealings took place on a very personal level. When my father arrived in Birmingham in 1945 to visit the HP plant, Mr. Wright the plant manager wrote to the Brigadier:

> After the first flood of war talk, we thought it might be useful if he could see the simmering and F addition here. We did it in exactly the same way that we recommended to you i.e. we did not allow the temperature after addition of F to exceed 95 degrees C. He will probably be able to tell you, after seeing the operation at your end, whether your simmering is obviously very different from ours or not.

Back then, a Smith was able to handle all the details, one-on-one with the head of HP, but today both sides have replaced this personal element with professional chemists, plant designers and economists. This became the new style of business and required quite an adjustment. I'll explain later the huge transition my dad made along with the vision he had, to see just how and why changes were necessary.

My mother and father remember a good example of this personal relationship. They drove to New York to pick up Colonel and Mrs. Perrins for their beautiful September visit to Winona. They stayed at Ravenscraig with Armand and Evelyn where a black tie dinner party was given for them.

They followed a well-planned, typed itinerary that included a trip to Niagara Falls, a visit to Sherwood Inn in Muskoka, luncheons and cocktail parties. All very lovely and proper.

This was business in the gracious old style. The men enjoyed their after-dinner port and the ladies chatted in the living room. You get the picture.

My mother possessed a particular charm and entertained beautifully. She had a knack for making her guests feel at home. My sisters, Daphne and Sharon and I give her a lot of credit for the success of the HP and E.D. Smith relationship.

This too has been one of the secrets.

Alastair Visits HP

When Alastair went to England in 1947, he was in for a shock. With the war over, people thought things would return to normal and the cruel hardships would be a thing of the past. Not so. Food continued to be rationed, unemployment was high, unrest in the workplace meant things were generally not good. He says some English people were so disillusioned he would hear such comments as, "Who won the war, anyway?"

He stayed with the Bayliss family for a few months, went to work with Mr. Bayliss and learned the sauce making business from the raw ingredients to the sealed bottle.

Back at home, Mr. Howard Lee took over from George Honey and continued Alastair's sauce-making education for some time.

The original secret formulas for both sauces were kept in a vault in Hamilton. Armand used to say that if for some reason he died quickly, his successors would be told what vault the secrets were in.

"LORD MAKE US NOT LIKE PORRIDGE,
THICK AND SLOW TO STIR,
BUT LIKE HP SAUCE, QUICK AND READY TO SERVE."

Lord Bishop of Birmingham 1975

The Secret Ingredient

By 1950, E.D. Smith was making both HP and Lea & Perrins from scratch *and* fully in charge of all selling and distribution.

When Smith started manufacturing the famous Lea & Perrins sauce, they were saddled with yet another secret. This time not only was there a secret formula, but a secret INGREDIENT. Again, it was Alastair who was in charge of adding it to the batch each time. The brewing and cooking of Lea & Perrins took place only about three times a year but each time a specific ritual was strictly observed. Alastair, in his white coat again but this time over a pair of well-worn overalls, would go deep into the cellar at Ravenscraig to the cabinet where the Brigadier kept his shotgun and retrieve some of the INGREDIENT to add through the bung holes of the barrels of Lea & Perrins sauce. He would walk down the carefully-partitioned corridors, through the locked door to the room of barrels, each holding 65 imperial gallons, all alone; close the door, carefully measure the right amount of secret INGREDIENT into each barrel, cork the bung holes and leave.

Before he could return to work, Alastair had to walk home, hang the incredibly smelly overalls outside and take a shower.

Honestly and truly no one knew what INGREDIENT Alastair put in the sauce. Today though, legislation states that ingredients must be on the label; product information must be made available to consumers at any time and the food industry as a whole is very regulated in this way.

So, what is the secret INGREDIENT? Am I going to tell you what it is?

No.

The secret ingredient being added through the bungholes

AS OF 1985, LEA AND PERRINS WAS SOLD IN 142 COUNTRIES AND NEXT TO COCA-COLA WAS THE MOST WIDELY DISTRIBUTED BRAND NAME PRODUCT IN THE WORLD.

The Fifth Generation

The Sauces and Their Impact

When E.D. Smith's main products were jams, jellies and pie fillings there wasn't enough volume to justify a full sales force and most selling was done through brokers.

The reputation of the sauces was so powerful that when we started manufacturing and selling both sauces, there was a huge demand for them. Every store and restaurant was obliged to carry HP Sauce and Lea & Perrins Sauce. Every home and institution became a customer. The time was ripe for a national sales force of our own that could be kept extremely busy now selling a full line of products.

In the long run, HP Sauce saved E.D. Smith & Sons' bacon. The fortuitous timing at each stage of development shows Armand's good business sense. I guess the thing to learn here is that in business "status quo" is not the ideal goal. It's comfortable, but not for long.

Armand retired to Chairman of the Board in 1965 a happy man, knowing he had set the company up with yet another "flagship product."

The Sauces and Me

My own involvement started when I was 12 and my parents arranged a family rendezvous in Ireland and England. As part of the trip we had a fascinating visit to Worcester—home of Lea & Perrins, and Aston Cross, a suburb of Birmingham where the HP Sauce company is located. At Worcester we stayed in Mrs. Perrins' house. My it was cold. I certainly wasn't accustomed to the dampness.

I sat in at a meeting where my father was presenting a Canadian advertising campaign for Lea & Perrins Sauce for their approval. The English are to this day quite particular about all elements. They are proud of their "original and genuine" sauce and although they had great respect for our marketplace and country, they were not about to let "Colonists" direct change.

Visiting the factory, I was struck by the amount of regimentation. Very little could be done with-

If it wasn't for the profits of Lea & Perrins Sauce, the Royal Worcester China would likely not be with us today. After touring this handcrafted operation, I was told that the Perrins family for years underwrote the operating losses of the China works.

out the approval of another. At the time I thought it was because of the special secret. Only later did I realize that it had more to do with the British classes of society within a plant environment.

Here, over 1,100 people were employed in a sprawling factory, in a decaying neighbourhood. The building was 11 stories high, crossed streets and roadways and smelled of vinegar and sauce production. I stuck close to my father!

Sir John Lewis, the Chairman of the Board, arranged for a car and driver for my mother, sisters and me. We were taken to Coventry and shown the new cathedral which replaced the one which was totally bombed by the Germans in W.W. II. The only thing which remained untouched was the alter and cross. Coventry was the heart of England's industrial and wartime enterprises. It was badly bombed. Here, we were fortunate to stay in Sir John's own home with central heat, and Corn Flakes for breakfast!

****

My next 30 years of sauce involvement included a three-month work period in England, salesman on the road, marketing manager, new-product developer, executive-in-charge and finally being an owner ushering in a new and difficult period of transition in E.D. Smith's history.

Production and Marketing

In England many substitutes of ingredients and changes in processes were made through the years, but in Canada our formula and recipe remained largely unchanged. So much so, that when Hanson Trust acquired the brands, one of the first things they did was to send people out to Canada to learn what we were doing right. How is that for a change?!

Over the years the production of the sauces has been just as important to the success of our business as the selling of them. When we began the business after the war, we put together a production team of Armand, my dad, Alastair, Albert Swick (bottling expert), Eric Durber and George Hardyman (head shipper). Our second generation team lead by Chris Bergshoeff, Bobby Chaisson, Abe Knegt and others stayed the course and built the business. Congratulations to all for helping to maintain the quality of these successful products!

**WHEN ARMAND RETIRED IN 1965
E.D. SMITH SALES EXCEEDED $8 MILLION.**

The Fifth Generation

HP in the U.K. was positioned as a thick brown sauce to cover and improve the taste of cheaper grades of meat. In Canada we marketed it as the best steak sauce in the world. We always took a premium pricing position. Our challenge through the years was how to expand on HP's fine name with other products. Regrettably our attempts failed: from a great tasting Hamburger Sauce (a combination of ketchup, HP and horseradish), to a line of simmering sauces called Sauce 'n' Savour. Although we beat General Mills in market-share position, we both lost the war with items ahead of their time. Today, Uncle Ben and Ragu dominate the category.

Lea & Perrins is a fabulous product but has low overall consumer awareness and is only used selectively in salads or stews, or as liquid spice in bloody Marys or Caesars. Our challenge through the years has been to educate the consumer to use it on more occasions. We found that consistent advertising and on-pack recipe ideas worked.

One big success story was the launch of coating and dipping sauces for the foodservice trade (i.e. restaurants and institutions). With the rise in popularity of roadhouses and casual fast foods, we created a full range of complementary sauce products and continue to lead the category today. Another benefit of being in the sauce business is we used our HP reputation and expertise to make Winona "the sauce capital of the world."

We have been extremely proud to sell HP and Lea & Perrins. In an era when it was tough to gain attention, our customer's buyers and merchandisers always had time for us. I think it largely was because they liked to use the products themselves in their own home or on backyard bar-b-ques.

Regionally we have always dominated in Western Canada. Many people have suggested it is because of the strong British origin, especially in B.C. Quebec has been our weakness, especially with Lea & Perrins. As a rule the Quebeçois are not big brown sauce users and virtually all thin sauce is Soya with Chinese food. In Atlantic Canada, our premium-priced position has hurt us. My trips through the region continue to highlight the fact that Maritimers are very value conscious. I might add that the H.J. Heinz Company has done a remarkable job in both Quebec and the east and to their credit hold sizeable pieces of the market.

The People

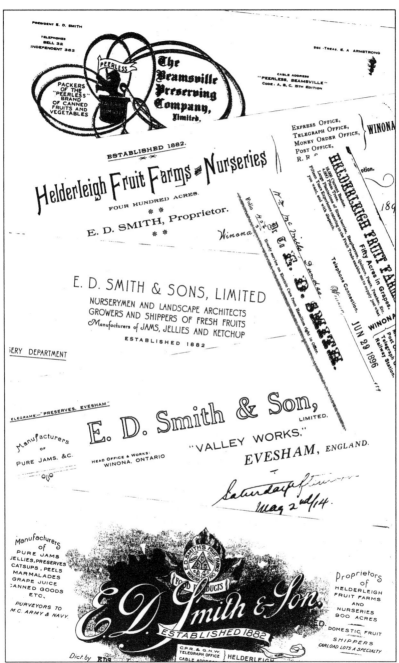

Letterhead through the years

The Fifth Generation

The People

At age 22, I spent three months in the U.K. working and touring not only within HP and Lea & Perrins but visiting other Imperial Tobacco owned food companies. In each case I was welcomed and made to feel part of the family. Each of the people I met took great pride in their work. It was almost as if their particular contribution was so important and required such skill the whole place would shut down if they were absent. The British workers know how to play hard as well. They love their football (our soccer) and their pints of lager or ale. I couldn't get over how much beer the average bloke (guy) could consume. In fact, in the HP plant at Aston Cross there was a social room where at noon the fellows would down a few pints before returning to afternoon work.

Most of this came to an end when market forces and keener competition entered the picture. A unionized shop floor rebelled and within three years 750 people at HP lost their jobs as state-of-the-art bottling lines and computerized process controls were installed. An era had ended.

On our side of the water, the production and sale of HP and Lea & Perrins was treated with utmost respect. Our people gave it priority over time spent on E.D. Smith products. Each person who knew anything about the product was bonded, meaning that we signed a legal document stating we would not divulge our knowledge to anyone outside those who needed to know. With each production run, samples were sent off to England to let our colleagues know that we adhered to the specifications.

Friendships developed. Along the way Imperial acquired Smedley Foods, an innovative vegetable canner who developed the U.K. frozen food industry. Michael Smedley, second generation, engineered a subsequent merger with HP Sauce, the impact being our importation of up to two million dollars worth of Smedley goods from the U.K. for resale into the Canadian market. Agents and distributors from around the world came together in bi-annual purchasing and sales conferences. People such as Gordon Trueman, Irvine Reid, Richard Burdon and in later years Pamela Street, all made the job more challenging and interesting. At E.D. Smith we had many people through the years handling the sauce account. Each had the complex job of balancing the needs and aspirations of both companies while making a mark for themselves. The countless hours of briefings, ad agency submission reviews, budget tabulations etc, I am sure gave each one of us sufficient skills to enter the political arena if we were ever to choose that course in life!

My thanks to Ron Lake, many years Vice-President Marketing and Sales; Jack Brokenshire, Bruce Maddox, Chris Wilkinson, Dave Running, Chris Powell, Brian Jones, Doug Ladoucer and others who have charted this course.

The Commercial Side

Up until Imperial Tobacco of the United Kingdom bought HP and Lea & Perrins in the early 60s, dealings with E.D. Smith were done on this now "famous handshake" basis. With Imperial's acquisition a formal contract was put in place, the terms of which were similar to what had taken place before. Remarkably, the contract was renewed every five years with essentially the same terms and conditions. Remarkable because it survived an ownership change and over 15 different U.K. Managing Directors.

These contracts provided an equal sharing of the pre-tax profits after a provision for factory, administration, sales and marketing overheads were applied. The conventions used provided incentives for each partner to help the other's business move forward. For example, the bigger E.D. Smith became, the less overhead charged to HP and the higher royalties generated for U.K.'s benefit.

E.D. Smith financed the Canadian business and charged the partnership a bank rate fee of interest. U.K. received a quarterly cheque without having to invest any capital whatsoever. For our part, the sauce business was crucial to our growth and survival. *If there was a lesson learned, we made it into too big of a success at the expense of our own business and in many ways lost our own independence.* In some of the lean years, income derived from the sauces accounted for over 70% of our pre-tax profits yet less than 15% of our overall sales. This all changed in 1994.

Enter the French

After paying some 32 times earnings to acquire the worldwide rights for HP/Lea & Perrins sauces in a market where 10 to 15 times is more the norm, B.S.N. (now Danone International

Brands) of Paris, France needed to pay for the acquisition. Consistent with the strategy of consolidating decision making, reducing costs through factory closures and re-investment in building strong brands, they bought us out of our old agreement and fundamentally changed our long-standing relationship. As stated in our new agreement, it was done in a "spirit of partnership." As part of the deal we had to give up manufacturing of Lea & Perrins which returned to Worcester England. We also lost the marketing responsibility in Canada for both HP and Lea & Perrins' retail sizes, while retaining food services. We remained as sales and distribution agents for both sauces and continue to produce HP as a contract packer. With this new arrangement, Danone is pouring millions of dollars into introducing new HP/Lea & Perrins products reaping a much higher profit per case, with aspirations of doubling the business by the year 2000. For E.D. Smith, we received cash towards our own business and a longer contract term with performance and bonus clauses. All in all it is a major shift for E.D. Smith that at first seemed like a backward step but so far has helped bring better focus and commitment to our own E.D. Smith brands.

We want to put our name on the table.

E. Llewellyn G. Smith 1995

Armand Armstrong Smith

The Brigadier was first and foremost a military man and it gave him an identity quite separate from E.D.'s. Being exposed to the army and war and having a quite high rank at a young age, set him up in life as a man of authority to be respected and even feared.

He dealt with people in a very fair way but there was never any doubt that King and country and business came first.

A typical second-generation owner, he ran the company for his father but then independent of E.D. brought home H.P. Sauce. He made this connection that would last more than 50 years. It was his contribution to the business. The fact it provided winter employment meant the company could operate fully all year and this provided the 'glue' between the seasons and there were no layoffs.

A gentleman to the extreme. Another leader. To be the son of a Senator, a commanding officer in the army, and the president of the largest company in the area gave his life a gravity of purpose. He had little use for anyone who did not do things properly. This forced everyone in his circle to rise to the highest level they could.

Through two wars and a depression he held the company together. There was no time to be a visionary. Opportunities presented themselves and he made them work by dint of strong character and integrity—both inherited from his father and grandfather.

After the death of Leon and E.D., he tied up a lot of loose ends, sold off some of the business and that allowed him to finance and focus on food processing, paving the way for today.

THE SIXTH GENERATION

HARVEST OF VALUES

Ernest Llewellyn Gibson Smith

D. Larson '95

TREETOPS

174

The Sixth Generation

The Smith Family	World Events

The Smith Family

1953 **Llewellyn S.** born

1957 75th Anniversary of E.D. Smith & Sons; **Armand** retires as active head; **E.L.G.** President; Alastair First Vice-President

1960 **E.L.G.** President of Ontario Fruit Growers Assn.

1964 big plant expansion

1965 **Armand** retires as Chairman of the Board

1968 big fire burns administration building

1969 bought Ware Foods; national sales force created

1971 start to make filling for donuts; Daphne Smith marries Ian Angus

1972 **Brigadier Armand Smith** dies; Alastair resigns

1973 Caro Angus born

1974 Sharon Smith marries Robert Seibel

1975 **L.S.S.** marries; Daphne Seibel born

1976 bought McLaren's

1977 "Partners in Progress" sales meeting

1979 Douglas Conant retires; **Gerard Llewellyn** born

1981 Evelyn dies

1982 100th Anniversary of E.D. Smith & Sons

World Events

1957 John Diefenbaker elected Prime Minister of Canada; Lester Pearson awarded Nobel Peace Prize; first broadcast of Front Page Challenge

1959 St. Lawrence Seaway opens

1961 Bay of Pigs confrontation in Cuba

1963 John F. Kennedy assassinated

1964 Canada gets a new flag

1967 Expo '67 in Montreal; Montreal Stock Exchange admits female members

1969 man lands on the moon; Dwight D. Eisenhower dies; first flight of the Concorde

1970 F.L.Q. forces War Measures Act

1971 Nikita Krushchev dies

1973 oil crisis in Europe and U.S.

1974 famine and civil war in Ethiopia

1975 CN Tower completed; end of Vietnam war

1976 Howard Hughes and Mao Tse-Tung die

1977 first flight of space shuttle; Elvis dies

1980 Terry Fox forced to stop Marathon of Hope

THE SIXTH GENERATION

HARVEST OF VALUES

Strive for good quality. Be it in people, machinery, bricks or mortar.

E. Llewellyn G. Smith 1979

E. Llewellyn G. Smith—The Major

E.L.G. made quality work for him. Under his leadership the company grew ten-fold in sales and profits!

Born in Godalming England in 1918; educated at Winona Public School, Lake Lodge School, Trinity College School and Bishop's University; my dad returned from W.W.II in 1945 with the rank of Major in the Royal Hamilton Light Infantry. He went to his father to tell him he was about to be married. "That's all very well and good, but what do you want to do in your life?" the Brigadier wanted to know.

He remembers answering, "I've been thinking about it and if you've got room I think I'd like to come into the family business."

He had no concerns in this matter. There was always room for another Smith.

I happened to be the eldest son of the eldest son and in the old European or British tradition it became the natural and logical step. My family is inclined that way.

E. Llewellyn G. Smith 1985

The Sixth Generation

As in my case, E.L.G. did not begin his career at the top. As youngsters and students we all picked cherries and worked on the shipping platform and farm during many summers. But when my father started full-time my grandfather told him that he should start at the bottom and he became assistant to the purchasing agent. Not assistant purchasing agent, but assistant to the agent.

A few months spent cooking jam is good therapy for anybody with an exaggerated idea of his own importance.

E. Llewellyn G. Smith

Like his father before him, my father married a lady of independent means. In Armand's case, he married the daughter of the Honourable William Gibson, a Liberal Senator. When he died, a friend said of her father, "He was a genial, loyal, kindly hearted Scot, and a businessman of exceptional quality." He had owned a stone quarry at Beamsville he inherited from his father and then went into the contracting business big time. Imagine Armand, the son of a Conservative Senator, marrying Evelyn with her background. Family business is definitely in our blood.

My mother, Elizabeth Ann Jane Sifton, came from a strict, forthright family with a strong belief in the work ethic and sense of responsibility. They too were another remarkable, highly successful Canadian family in business.

> Father was at the banquet and the people were very kind to him. What pleased me too was that I was able to have Llewellyn and Alastair present. I hope it helps to bring along the worthwhile traditions of the family.
>
> Armand, writing to Verna, 1935

Most discussions around the dinner table at home concerning business, largely centered around two topics—the impact of weather on various crops and incoming visitors from H.P. Sauce. In later years it would expand to include the relationship of the Canada Permanent Trust (now Canada Trust) Company, and its role of administrator of E.D. Smith shares

E. Llewellyn G. Smith—The Major

and other share ownership issues. Whether by design or omission, Dad kept his business thoughts to himself during family hours. There was no question that he had a lot on his mind. My mother and father led a very active social life. Between this and the business worries, it was a full plate.

During the 50s, under Armand's direction, E.L.G. worked in all departments and showed himself to be a leader, ready to take over the reigns when the time came.

75th Anniversary of E.D. Smith & Sons Limited

The year was 1957 and E.L.G. was President, Alastair was first Vice-President and the Brigadier was Chairman of the Board.

At a "family party" the company held to celebrate this event, many prizes were given out and the Brigadier was presented with a gold watch. In his thank-you speech he reminisced.

He remembered Albert Kimmins who had built the house next to his; Jack Hewitson, who had come to E.D. when he opened his first office in the old stone house which later became the boarding house, and was office manager for many of the early years; Jack Harper, farm superintendent for over 45

E. Llewellyn G. Smith

Elizabeth Ann Smith

The Sixth Generation

years; Charlie Everett, a young German who came down from the mountain in 1880 and worked for over 50 years, laid all the original tile drains on the company property by hand and packed thousands of nursery boxes; A.M. Cocks the first jam superintendent; Billy Dawe, the outstanding fruit buyer for over 45 years; factory superintendents such as George Jacobs, Gifford, Bill Boehm, George Honey; sales people like Joe Hodgson, Stuart Watson, Andrew Truesdale, Walter Belyea, Art Bundy, Harvey Lambert, Hank Weigand, Charlie Cummins, Bill McLean, the Hamms, Mrs. McConnell, Ed Ruddle, Andrew Durfey, Steve McCoombs, Levi McDougall.

He went on to include Arthur Parker, father of Arthur Parker Sr. and grandfather of Arthur Parker Jr., "one of the best foremen we ever had"; Tom Davey, father of Mrs. Durber, Mrs. Hardyman and Mrs. Bell; Amos Swick, father of Albert Swick; James Barr, father of Annie Davies; his uncle Elijah Armstrong,

At 75th Anniversary, family members include (L-R) E. Llewellyn G. and Elizabeth Ann Jane, Margaret Armstrong, Verna Smith Conant, Armand (the Brigadier) and Evelyn, Alastair and Jessie, Douglas Conant and the two girls Sharon and Daphne.

75th Anniversary of E.D. Smith & Sons Limited

e grand prize was an all-
pense paid trip for two to
orida for fourteen days, won
Miss Florence Farraway.

shareholder and manager of the Beamsville Preserving Co. and father of Miss Margaret Armstrong; Marlow Wilbur, father of John and grandfather of Gerry; George Winchester, father of Joe; Fred Hardyman, father of George and grandfather of Douglas; Archie Nichol, relative of Alice Lymer.

He remembered his brother Leon who died in 1946 and was head of the nursery department; he was followed by Arthur Gilbey, Nursery Sales Manager, father of Clarke and grandfather of Maynard; Mr. Langdon, cashier father of Miss Norah Langdon.

The notable feature here is the amount of multi-generational "home grown" talent we have had working for us. I have come to appreciate the strength of this in our work force.

You can rightly be proud of the achievement of these First 75 Years. It is in itself a testimony to your good administration, to the high quality of your products, as it proves also to what extent your Company has won and kept the confidence of people.

Alphonse Raymond 1957
Alphonse Raymond Limited

Fire and Water

Even when I was young, some of the worst stories in the neighbourhood were of fires. Barns, buildings, crops, animals and people were burned and destroyed. In the country, when a fire gets going there is very little one can do. Even today. The E.D. Smith company started its own fire department for that reason years ago—it was sorely needed.

Dreaded fires came from no one knew where. They united and swept like a devouring demon before the wind, and licked up with their tongues of flame a large portion of the dead timber and let sunlight upon soil that had long been a stranger to it.

Damaris McGee Smith

The Sixth Generation

For Mr. Smith's factory a considerable quantity of water is required and fresh, pure, clear water is essential. This is drawn from a spring found in the rock on the top of the mountain by drilling. This water is carried from an underground spring in pipes to a cemented and covered reservoir on the side of the mountain. From here it is drawn by as good a system of water pipes as is found in any of the towns.

The Globe November 2, 1907

In 1910 Major Kimmins organized the fire department at E.D. Smith. This was a service vital to the area and the company. They may not have had the finest of equipment but they put out a lot of fires.

Kenny Foster tells the story of a brush fire once up near Treetops, the Major's place. They took "the old fire truck that Albert Swick and Jack Beard had made out of an old Packard car with the gravity-fed fuel pump and we got that fire out, we did." When they were just about finished, the Major invited them all in for some refreshment. They never forgot it.

Kenny and the boys had a lot of laughs about the old days but on a serious note he would say that the very reason he wanted to work at E.D. Smith was because it was a total community that took care of its people and itself. The fire department was just one example.

Just as important to him was the fact that the company maintained this totally independent water supply from Lake Ontario. It was company workers that dug the ditch to the lake; that hauled the pipe; that ran the pipe hundreds of feet out into the lake. A reservoir was built up on the escarpment that the water was pumped to. Then

Then
Below each second story window in the Homestead is an iron ring. A rope long enough to reach the ground, was attached and used to climb down the outside wall in case of fire.
Now
Dial 911

Fire and Water

under pressure, every company home that E.D. Smith built had running water.

The pumphouse at the lake was manned and supervised by company personnel and right there on the beautiful shoreline they maintained a beach for all employees to use for picnics and parties and swimming.

As far as Kenny was concerned, the Smiths did not ask the outside world for anything. They carved their business and life right out of the land.

Let me tell you why I find this so impressive. They didn't sit around waiting for the local municipality to lay pipe to supply the water service. E.D. Smith needed an incredible amount of water RIGHT AWAY.

We have a four inch main pipe to Lake Ontario and our own pump. Water used for cooling purposes; vacuum pans require a lot of water; small young nursery stock needs a lot of water; employees in company houses had running water installed for them at no extra charge; we use 16 million gallons a year; cost of running pumphouse $5,500 per year; when the wells go dry it saves the cost of hauling water.

Armand Smith 1938

Albert Swick was the first E.D. Smith Fire Chief and the Stoney Creek Fire Department would help them with drills and practice sessions of fire-fighting procedures. In 1942 Eric Durber became the Fire Chief until 1966 when Chris Bergshoeff took over.

Eric felt that the "finest hour" of the fire truck and the volunteers was at the end of W.W.II when the boiler room caught fire during tomato season. The fire broke out on the day shift and the fire department was able to contain it and extinguish it in less than two hours. By working on repairs all night, production was able to resume the following morning.

The older company fire truck sometimes didn't start right and during one emergency they had to use the flower truck to pull the company fire truck all the way to the top of the escarpment. That's the truck that nearly tipped over one time because there were too many firemen on it. Ah the joys of a volunteer fire department! At least they were keen and always turned up.

The Sixth Generation

Abe Knegt went to the bank one day and on his way home heard the company fire siren go off. Being a volunteer fire fighter, he followed the fire truck down the road to his own house!!! Apparently it was a grease fire that was quickly put under control and the company paid all his damages. The old E.D. Smith fire truck was finally retired in 1973 to a restaurant in Toronto called the Fire Hall (now home of the Second City Revue).

E.L.G. at the Helm

The 60s marked an unprecedented economic growth in Canada and the demand for consumer goods increased dramatically, precipitating the need for expansion and increased manufacturing efficiency. E.L.G. was in his element here because he loved machines; he was a plant man. Nothing pleased him more than to buy a new label machine or filler. In 1964 plant expansion and equipment quickly ate up $1,000,000. He put in a $250,000 waste management plant which had become necessary. Increased productivity, better working conditions and streamlined manufacturing all indicated money well spent.

Dad believed in having only one manufacturing facility. This way Smith eyes and ears were always on site.

A strong diversification program is changing E.D. Smith and Sons Limited's image as a jam maker.

Jam making still figures prominently but a broad range of tomato products—many produced under private labels for chain stores—and a booming business in fruit pie fillings are helping to change the emphasis.

Part of the answer lies in marketing. The company has been able to distribute its pie fillings and tomato products on a national scale while regional competition has kept its jam sales largely in Ontario, Montreal and Winnipeg.

Hamilton Spectator, July 24, 1967

"A" for Achievement

The provincial government presented the company with the "A" for Achievement Award on February 7, 1968. E.D. Smith & Sons had proven itself to be a company making outstanding contributions to the economy through increased plant size, employment, export sales and research and development.

Our food industry ranks among those that employ more people, pay more wages, use a higher value of raw materials, and produce a higher value of products than most large industries.

In Ontario the food industry is a paramount contributor to the Province's vigorous economic development.

Today, the Canadian consumer is earning more and spending more. He's also eating more—and eating better. And the manufacturers and merchants who seek profit and expansion have to keep up with the customers' demands for low-cost products that are new, different and exciting.

With all this in mind, I sincerely congratulate the Management and Staff of E.D. Smith and Sons Limited for winning the Provincial Government's "A" for Achievement Award."

Honourable Robert S. Welch, Q.C.,
Provincial Secretary and Minister
of Citizenship at awards ceremony

Maple Leaf Mills

The metamorphosis of the sales force continued. Ever since H.P. Sauce had become such a large part of the line, E.D. Smith had been able to justify its own sales force to complement the brokers.

Then, an interesting change came about. One of the side lines at the time for E.D. Smith was the packing of glacé cherries for Maple Leaf Mills. Alastair was the contact person with them and at the end of the 50s Maple

In 1969 when the Federal Government banned cyclamates, E.D. Smith was forced to discard a large part of its inventory, leading to the first year-end loss in over 30 years.

Leaf came to him with an interesting proposal. They suggested the amalgamation of the sales forces of both companies. Presumably this would be more efficient and Alastair found the idea pleasing because he was sure it would give E.D. Smith an even higher profile. So, they proceeded with the idea and that gave them a sales force of 125 people. Alastair would visit Maple Leaf in Toronto every week and kept on top of the whole situation.

Back at the plant, E.L.G. saw the whole story in a different light. He and his brother did not agree on this arrangement at all. Whereas Alastair saw it as a big plus to the company, E.L.G. saw it only as an attempt by Maple Leaf to slowly take over his company. In spite of the disagreement, the arrangement was put in place until 1967 and sales soared.

Our policy is to remain totally independent.

E.L.G. Smith April 28, 1960

This story shows the lack of communication between my dad and my uncle. Some quite hard feelings resulted from this issue and maybe if they had talked about it more together, they would have each better understood the other. Family businesses suffer from this dilemma perhaps more than other enterprises.

A Tiger by the Tail

But it was time for a change in the corporate and sales structure anyway. E.L.G. knew that "the times, they were a'changing." Experts in sales and marketing, manufacturing, finance and data processing were added to the staff for the first time ever. New packaging and design were tested and introduced. This way, the company was able to keep pace with the multinational food corporations whose operations were growing quickly too.

A New Product Development Committee began its work. The Consumer Service Division assessed the needs of the customers. They came up with new diet products as the consumer became more health conscious. The Special Food Services Sales Force started selling to more institutional and industrial accounts.

A Tiger by the Tail

We virtually have a tiger by the tail. One thing I will say,
contrary to anything you have heard, E.D. Smith & Sons
Limited still belongs to the Smith family. It has not been
sold out to anyone and gentlemen, we don't put turnips in
our jam!

Bill Reekie, speech 1965

The evolution of the development of the new corporate
structure included several very interesting additions to the
staff. Alastair was Vice President of Sales and had been
approached by Dick Loftus who thought he had some marketing ideas for E.D. Smith. The bottom line is they came up with
a very strong Marketing Sales Force under the direction of
Richard Ferguson, the famous Olympic runner, who had
worked for General Foods and Beecham.

Rich, a very much take-charge type of person, in just three
months hired 35 salesmen across Canada to replace the Maple
Leaf sales force.

On January 1, 1968 he launched the first national E.D. Smith
sales force. (They did keep Pratt Representatives as agents in
Newfoundland.) He inspired and motivated the salesmen by
telling them they were the best in Canada; gave them cars with
radios and air conditioning; he aimed for $10 million in sales
and when he achieved the goal everyone got a pen and pencil
set engraved with "ten million—thanks." In 1968 he held a
sales meeting at the Park Plaza and wives were flown in from
all parts of the country and given a dozen red roses.

As part of the split with Maple Leaf, E.D. Smith put themselves in the position to assume the brokerage for the St.
Lawrence Starch Co. Ltd. of Port Credit in April 1968. St.
Lawrence Starch closely paralleled E.D. Smith as a very long-
established, family-owned business. Their Corn Oil, Corn
Starch, Corn Syrup and laundry starch were well known products in Canada. Later we even took over and handled all their
exporting.

The E.D. Smith company was left reeling with Rich's excess-
es and enthusiasm. They had never seen anything like it. He
really put them on the map.

He worked hard, played hard, could be at the poker table
until four o'clock in the morning and still be on the job by
7:00 a.m.

E.L.G. HIT A HOLE-IN-ONE, JULY 4, 1966
AT THE HAMILTON GOLF & COUNTRY CLUB.

The Sixth Generation

> If you ever come out to the airport to meet Mr. Smith and me again with a dirty car, you won't be working here any more.
> Richard Ferguson to salesman 1968

E.D. Smith & Sons Limited had the reputation of being a "sleepy little company in Winona." That was about to change. People like Ron Lake who was working at J. Lyons Canada at the time, was told, "If you meet Rich Ferguson, you will want to join the E.D. Smith team." He did.

A year and a half later Rich left and Ron took over his job and became Director of Sales and Marketing.

Next they decided they needed more professional help in the factory and found a graduate engineer from the University of Western Ontario, Bill Jeffries.

On the financial side Douglas Conant became Treasurer and Vice President Finance and Administration and Clare Proctor, a chartered accountant, came on board.

The Administrative set-up looked like this in 1969:

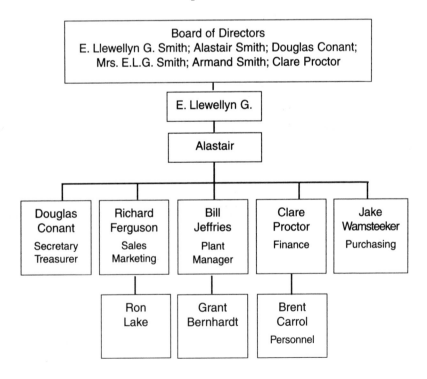

A Tiger by the Tail

My father's philosophy was: "It is better to acquire than be acquired" and with this strong executive committee in place he was ready to expand. Acquisitions included the Ware Foods operation which served the institutional food industry; McLaren's, the pickle people; Dessert Wagon brand of frozen pies and desserts; and the Stafford brand of products including ice cream toppings. The company had really turned into quite a tiger.

Tomato Season

Not a person who ever worked for Smith could ever forget tomato season. It meant 24 hour days for six to eight weeks pro-

cessing the fresh tomato crop into ketchup, tomato juice and chili sauce. An endless line of truckloads of tomatoes from over 82 Ontario growers came into the yard.

In earlier days the tomatoes were manhandled into the plant in baskets but by 1970 they were inspected, and cleaned by floating down a flume at the back of the plant, each flume with three inches of

*IEN - Local produce was
ed "fresh pack" so in tomato
ason the yard was full.*

*- Ingredients come in from
ver the world in partially
essed form. Picture shows
to paste shipped in "aseptic
pack."
L. Larry Eggleton
R. Tony Morabito*

water going through it at the rate of 900 gallons a minute. No wonder we needed our own water supply! Bill Reekie, the factory manager said the company could produce 325 bottles of ketchup a minute on one line and the plant had five lines. One line could produce 400,000 bottles of ketchup a day.

Today, no tomatoes come from local growers, but rather from California or Chile in paste form. Smith still sources very high-quality products and produces a superior ketchup and the recipes are still secret.

Helen Janicki

For 30 years Helen Janicki worked on the tomato line watching ketchup bottles go by and never once complained. She felt well looked after and secure in her job. Born in Poland, she came to Canada, found this job and stuck with it. "Nothing ever bothers me at Smith." Some of her friends found it difficult to believe she was never laid off and never collected unemployment insurance. She was proud to work extra hard in tomato season because she knew it was important and she was extremely proud of the company and its products.

She has photograph albums filled with pictures of E.L.G., company Christmas parties, friends she worked with on the line and even every letter the company sent her. The people she worked with were special and she remembers George Hardyman's kindness to her when her husband was sick.

She is typical of the people who have been the backbone of our company and our country over the years.

Today she lives in a very nice, modest apartment near Hamilton and hopes to live long enough to read this book.

Garden Cocktail

Most people in the food business could only dream of having a product as successful as Garden Cocktail.

In the early 70s, Bill Reekie came across a product called Veg Crest, in the United States. He brought home a sample of it

Garden Cocktail

and thought a similar product could be made at E.D. Smith, especially because of the tomato business.

Within the year, Alastair realized the potential of this product so they made up a few thousand jars, test marketed it in London and Peterborough and found it was quite well received. The decision was made to go with this new product. They prepared a well-planned spectacular launch! All salesmen travelled with a refrigerator, serviettes, glasses and lots of Garden Cocktail. In every store, to every manager, buyer and customer they could find, they introduced them to a sample. Clean, cold and fresh, it was like "sipping a salad."

As Ron Lake says, "We romanced the product." He and everybody else loved it. They put up displays of 1,000 bottles; it was mass marketed; they couldn't make enough to supply the demand.

For the first couple of years tanker trucks from Chicago brought in the fresh mix of ingredients and Smith added only the tomato, but then they realized they had the knowledge and the machinery and people to press the juices from all these fresh vegetables themselves. And they did just that. Fresh. Right in Winona.

Every drop of Garden Cocktail was made from 100% fresh ingredients. The logistics of making this juice added to the hectic tomato season because that was when it was made.

The residue after pressing the juice from the celery, peppers, parsley, carrots, onions and dill was at first sold to pig farmers for feed but in a short time, the efficiency of the pressing was so superb that the residue was too dry to even call hay. The process for extracting juice from tomatoes and apples became so effective as well, that the residue had no nutritional value left at all and was hauled away for compost.

IF YOU THINK GETTING BLOOD FROM A STONE IS HARD, YOU SHOULD TRY PRESSING THE JUICE OUT OF DILL.
Bill Reekie 1994

The Sixth Generation

The juice extracts were pasteurized and then pumped into huge 8,000 gallon storage tanks, ready to be used in the production of Garden Cocktail.

Imagine pressing, mixing, bottling, warehousing, financing, selling and distributing such a product. It was all made in a six-week period and sold in a fifty-two week period. It tied up a lot of space and money but became another flagship product. Unlike HP Sauce, this product had our name on it and was called E.D. Smith Garden Cocktail.

No other such product on the market tasted so fresh.

This product carried us right to the end of the 80s and it was sold in 1989, much to the surprise of many who thought it was a big mistake. In hindsight, it was a good move. Just as Leon's nurseries and E.D.'s house were sold to get money to plow back into the company, so was Garden Cocktail. Not only did it provide money for new product development and updating, it eliminated the cost of storing and financing inventory. One door closes and another one opens.

Lady luck has played an important role. But, when she came we were usually ready for her.

E. Llewellyn G. Smith

The Great Share Scare

The day before the Labour Day weekend in September 1981, my son and I were told that all minority shareholders, all of them relatives representing 46 per cent of the common stock, had banded together to sell approximately one half of their total interest to a large U.S. company, right away, with the balance to be sold over a seven year period. My wife, son and I (all Directors) held a meeting that afternoon and decided to fight the takeover. We had until Thursday night to come up with a counter-strategy, as the Board Meeting of the foreign company was on the Friday morning. Their Management Committee had approved the purchase and the majority of their Board were Management members.

BY 1981 SALES WERE OVER $65 MILLION.

The Great Share Scare

We had little sleep that week. Money talked. Many legal documents had to be signed, a new numbered company had to be set up. My immediate family now control over 99 per cent of the business and the bank was quickly paid off. The moral of the story:

— if possible, have binding shareholder agreements

— maintain a good working relationship with your principal banker

first issue CAFE Newsletter March 1984
in speech by E.L.G. at the founding
meeting of CAFE, January 25, 1984

To fully understand what happened here, it is necessary to go back a few years. The business inheritance of the late E.D. had passed down through Armand, Leon and Verna to 27 descendants!

You have to know too, that only family members owned shares, so we are talking about some pretty close connections here. In 1965, a number of significant circumstances came together. Armand resigned and E.L.G. became Chairman of the Board, Verna Conant resigned as a Director and Douglas Conant joined my father and Alastair as the third main person running the business.

At this time, succession duties and death taxes were in place and several of the more major shareholders became nervous. They were concerned that they would be taxed on what they were potentially worth, not on what they had in the bank. The gravity of the situation was so severe that they were prepared to see the company fold.

What to do?

Clifford Sifton

Salvation came in the name of Clifford Sifton, my grandfather, my mother's father. Through a trust he had set up for my mother, she had enough money available for her to be able to buy shares, with her father's approval, from all these worried relatives, to the point that she controlled just over 50% of the company.

My mother in effect gave my father his own company. She then also had enough faith and trust to have him run it.

The Sixth Generation

If her father had not held such a high opinion of the Smith family and if he had not had the money to make this happen, so be it. But, in both cases he did. My mother came to the table when the chips were down and saved the whole show. She did not have to do this. But she wanted to.

As in every case where a great deal of money is at stake, people can become jealous and resentful when they should in fact be grateful. This is just such a case.

But wait. There's more.

****

Members of a family business bring to the business what they inherit or what they receive as successors. In Armand's generation, both he and Leon brought the same "ownership right" to the company but Armand married Evelyn Gibson, a lady from a wealthy family so to see the two families side by side, one would think Armand's to be more prestigious.

History repeats itself in a way with E.L.G. and Alastair. Because E.L.G. married a Sifton from a well established Canadian family and because he and his situation were so well received by them, he had a more solid financial backing than did Alastair.

This led to some financial inequalities that troubled Alastair. In the early 70s, Alastair's wife Jessie pointed out to him that he had a problem that his brother did not have. The problem being, if Alastair died, the Death and Inheritance Taxes would tax him based on his ownership of considerable shares in the company. He was making a "reasonable but modest" salary and such a tax would put his family in the poor house. Such a tax would apply to E.L.G. as well but he had the money to cover it.

Alastair approached his brother with three suggestions. One proposition was to go public. Another was to take out life insurance policies on one another. The third one was that E.L.G. could buy enough of his shares to give him the money necessary should a crisis arise. So in the early 70s my father arranged for part of Alastair's shareholdings to be acquired by E.L.G. family interests.

Alastair thinking that the company would benefit by having HP own a significant amount of shares, approached the sauce company about acquiring a strong minority position. If successful, this would have solved the concerns of other minority family shareholders. It's unfortunate that he did not consult with his brother first.

HP's Sir Alex Alexander was very surprised and asked E.L.G., "What is going on here?" As it turned out, my dad made sure the answer was, "Nothing."

Alastair worried about what his brother thought of him. He wondered if E.L.G. thought he had chickened out and put himself and his personal concerns ahead of the well-being of the company. He wondered if it would be perceived he was undermining the company. He was just worried about his future and that of his family. Art Parker, who worked at the company over 40 years, says he thinks it worked out for the best this way. Alastair was a fine person, but E.L.G. was the better boss.

> The Great Share Scare took place exactly 100 years after the company was founded. People have questioned why, after 100 years the company is not bigger than it is. E.L.G. will reply, "You really should ask, 'How did it manage to survive so long?'"

Does Alastair regret his decision? Probably. He'll slap his forehead today and say, "What was I thinking of back then?"

If things had worked out differently maybe I wouldn't be the one writing this book. There is no doubt in his mind though, that he did what he thought he had to do at the time.

Now to get back to the Great Share Scare. In 1981, a block of shareholders, Alastair, Douglas Conant, Roger and Frances Conant, and Roberta Smith Morrison's son-in-law John Shortly, representing 46% of equity, together as ringleaders announced to E.L.G., my father, they were selling out to American-owned General Foods. They did not discuss this with him first. They went behind his back and as far as they were concerned, it was a fait accompli.

But such a buy-in meant the Canadian Foreign Investment

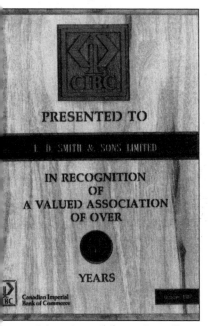

PRESENTED TO

E. D. SMITH & SONS LIMITED

IN RECOGNITION
OF
A VALUED ASSOCIATION
OF OVER

YEARS

Canadian Imperial
Bank of Commerce

...ecognition Award from Canadian ...mperial Bank of Commerce

The Sixth Generation

Review Agency was involved and an extensive review needed. During the wait, dad and I moved fast, raising $3 million for a sunset loan to set up a new numbered company and another $3 million to redeem the shares of these family members to offer them quick cash in place of any future outside deal. The best and cheapest way for a company to get money is through a loan at the bank and over the years E.D. Smith had established a wonderful working relationship and had a sterling record with the C.I.B.C. Clare Proctor, President of E.D. Smith at the time went to the C.I.B.C. to meet with George Lethbridge, who was considered to be one of the top bankers in the region, and said he needed this huge amount of money by Monday morning. George said, "You got it! No problem." A smart move for the bank and a big help to us.

It worked, but as E.L.G. put it, "The heavy borrowing pushed the owners and company from a comfortable to an uncomfortable debt-to-equity ratio." Hardships included slashing capital expenditures, reducing the product line and "pretty punishing measures" such as salary freezes.

Alastair Smith   *Douglas Conant*
Like E.L.G. they are both grandsons of E.D.

The Great Share Scare

Such is the price of success. Maintain good relations with your bank, as E.L.G. had said in his CAFE speech and "attempt to avoid unnecessary surprises."

Could he have avoided this unpleasant surprise? It had never occurred to him that a multinational company like General Foods would have any interest in having a minority share in a private company like his. Perhaps this was naive because if they had managed to gain that much control, you can be sure they would have pushed further to eventually gain a majority.

It probably also never occurred to him that some fringe members of the family, some "outlaws," would try to undermine a company they had inherited shares in, just to get the money. E.L.G. had such profound respect for and belief in the company, it was inconceivable to him that anyone would try to destroy it.

In defense of the "outlaws," they were living with these shares for which they received very low dividends, 3%–6% at a time when bank interest was 15%–16%. They wanted their money invested at a higher rate. They approached E.L.G. with all kinds of options but he always politely insisted that the company could not afford it. He honestly believed this. What he could have done is put in a "redemption over time" policy that could have made them happy.

Now here is the clincher.

Douglas Conant and Alastair were on the board of E.D. Smith and were part of the group behind John Shortly when he approached General Foods. As members of the board, they had access to all the papers of the company and their inappropriate behaviour concerned us. However, General Foods withdrew their offer when they saw it was not going to happen. Rather than make a large issue out of this, as a family we decided to take the high road and not get into the mud.

It was a blessing in disguise that it all happened so quickly, otherwise it would have dragged on and on causing perhaps a deeper rift in the family.

How do we feel when we meet with these family members today? Just fine. In Alastair's case, he probably honestly thought he was acting as a broker in the best interests of himself and those he was representing. As the brother, he was compelled to be the spokesperson and thought it the honourable thing to do. Douglas too, is such a fine gentleman that we choose to believe he was ignorant of the implications and breach of law involved.

Canadian Association of Family Enterprise (CAFE)

The whole incident could have become very nasty and did not. For families and businesses who realize that families in business are unique, there are two lessons here.

The first one deals with the idea of establishing organized family meetings, sometimes called Family Councils where the paramount interest is communication. On a semi-formal, regular basis, talk. Don't talk to just the immediate family members but include all the "tacked-ons" and "outlaws" because in many cases, as we have seen here, they are the ones that stir up the discontent often because they don't know what is going on. If they did, they might understand and sympathize with the business concerns better.

The second lesson is the issue of succession. Plan for it ahead of time. The year after this Share Scare I also took over the business. It was too early. At 30 years of age I was too young but as Maynard Gilbey will say, dad, "threw me the gauntlet" to see what I could do.

The Share Scare prompted E.L.G. to seek out information on family business associations. He found a lack of organized support for families in business, and ended up with Gordon Sharwood among others, founding CAFE, the Canadian Association of Family Enterprise. He saw a great need for it.

Since its start in 1984, CAFE has grown from the original 14 members to a total membership of over 650 family firms, with chapters in seven Canadian cities. CAFE has become the voice of family business in Canada and it provides a powerful resource to keep families in business on the path to success.

Recognition Award from CAFE

Canadian Association of Family Enterprise

CAFE's goals are to educate and inform by providing a stimulating program, allowing members to share information and professional advice. By fostering a greater awareness and understanding of family enterprise, CAFE is building a network of supportive family businesses throughout Canada.

Succession is obviously CAFE's #1 issue. For many family business owners, asking them to discuss succession is like asking them to plan their own funeral. Therefore CAFE has a big job. To help, CAFE's main tool is the Personal Advisory Group. These are teams of 10 to 12 members who meet regularly to share experiences, ideas and information in absolute confidentiality.

When a business is seen and cared for as a child, its family will not let it strangle in its own pettiness. The family will want it to grow up, to become bigger, healthier and more vigorous.

Gail Regan of Cara Holdings
(CAFE newsletter, March 1984)

100th Anniversary

In 1982 the company hosted the "Harvest of Values" promotion to mark its 100th anniversary. Winners of a competition won books on the Group of Seven and letters poured in from across the country.

...I am a firm believer in your products!

...I will tell my friends to be sure to use E.D. Smith products.

...mille remerciements pour ce cadeau formidable "Le Group des sept" aussi pour vos produits délectables.

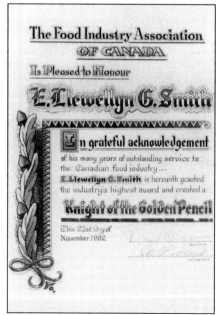

Recognition Award from Food Industry

...this note is to acknowledge the receipt of the beautiful "Group of Seven" book. I sincerely thank you. In the future I shall continue to use E.D. Smith products with even more appreciation.

Also that year, E.L.G. was presented with the prestigious Knight of the Golden Pencil Award, the highest award given by the Food Industry Association of Canada, in recognition of outstanding, long-term accomplishment in, and commitment to the Canadian food industry. A part of this commitment included being President of the Ontario Food Processors Association and then Chairman of the Board of the Canadian Food Processors Association.

The words honesty, integrity, hard work, laughter and sincerity belong to E.L.G. just as they did to his father and grandfather. In his life as well as his business, he would feel he had failed if he had at any time let any of these virtues down. He has not failed.

Business-wise "keeping it all in the family" has been a tough job. The survival rate for family concerns through even one, let alone several generations, is very slim. Call E.D. Smith and Sons Ltd. a Canadian survivor. The family has "its roots in the soil."

E. Llewellyn G. Smith

Ernest Llewellyn Gibson Smith

Again the military influence put the Major in a commanding position but he flavoured it with a more benevolent aura. He could afford to take time to care about the people working for him and they loved and respected him for it. The combination of honesty, success and hard work of both him and Alastair, put them on a pedestal in the eyes of the community.

His core purpose to become a national company was successful. The sales force under professional managers tackled the Canadian market.

Whereas the Brigadier had H.P., E.L.G. found Garden Cocktail and made it into the most profitable product ever. He appreciated the fact that his business was based on the soil and the produce from it. Like E.D. he realized these products from the land could have value added to them to continue to make a more remunerative return.

Economically things were booming and he knew just how to handle the situation. He made daring moves in expansion, people and acquisitions. Most decisions were right. They worked. Things just got better and better under his hands.

The generations before him had given him the tools of leadership, good judgement and integrity. These traits, along with his unstoppable optimism and unshakable opinions and a strong supportive wife, pointed him and his business towards continued success.

Everyone loves a winner.

THE SEVENTH GENERATION

BACK TO BASICS

Llewellyn Sifton Smith

The Seventh Generation

The Smith Family	World Events
1979 **Gerard Llewellyn** born	1980 Iran Iraq war
1981 the Great Share Scare	1981 French only signs a must in Quebec
1982 100th Anniversary of E.D. Smith & Son; **Llewellyn S.** President of company; first Quarter Century Club meeting	1982 Laurie Skreslet first Canadian to reach top of Mt. Everest; war in the Falklands; Canada gains new Charter of Freedom and Rights
	1983 experts warn of Global Warming
1984 bought Farmlane Foods; bought Stafford Pie Fillings; family shareholder agreement signed passing ownership to **Llewellyn S.**	1984 founding meeting of CAFE; Indira Gandhi assassinated; Conservative Brian Mulroney wins Federal election in Canada
1985 **Graham Arthur Clifford** born	1985 Mikhail Gorbachev Soviet party leader
	1986 nuclear disaster at Chernobyl
1987 bought Gourmet Baker and merged it with Farmlane Foods	1987 Black Monday on Stock Market; Free Trade Agreement reached between Canada and U.S.
1988 **Claire Irene** born	1988 thousands of Canadians test positive for HIV; Ben Johnson stripped of Gold Medal award
1989 sale of Garden Cocktail; sold McLarens olives and cherries; company begins downsizing	1989 massacre in Tian'anmen Square; Berlin Wall dismantled; Toronto's Skydome opens
1990 sold Gourmet Baker	1990 Nelson Mandela freed; Gulf War begins
	1991 start of G.S.T.
1992 bought Gem Incorporated in Byhalia, Mississippi	1992 crisis in Atlantic fisheries; Civil War in Yugoslavia
1993 Lea & Perrins/HP Sauce agreement renegotiated with BSN; decision to write a book about the family and company	1993 Jean Chretien Canada's Prime Minister; Bill Clinton U.S. President
1994 **Llewellyn S.** marries Susan J. Fleming	

THE SEVENTH GENERATION

BACK TO BASICS

Each one of the Smiths has been the right person for their time.

Art Parker 1994

Llewellyn Sifton Smith

Four generations of Smiths have employed four generations of people. That says a lot for E.D. and for jam. Jam has been the cornerstone of the E.D. Smith operation since 1904 and even though it has not always had the highest sales, it has always been there. In a novel, it would be called the recurring theme. Other products come and go but the jam is always there, just plodding along. It has a strength, a momentum that seems to transcend time. The twenty-something lady working at the library, here in Canada from Hong Kong for just six years, knows that E.D. Smith is jam. She doesn't know that it is Tim Horton jelly donut filling, that it has been Pizza Pizza pizza sauce, that it is President's Choice sauces, that it is A & P's ketchup, that it was McLaren's olives, that it is Habitant Jams, that it is HP and Lea & Perrins Sauces, but she knows it is jam.

Not everyone could consider themselves a wine connoisseur but Canadians have developed a taste for good, pure jam and could consider themselves jam connoisseurs.

Pure jam cannot contain extra pectin. If some natural pectin is lost in the processing, an amount equal to that which is lost may be added. Pectin helps make the jam thick. E.D. established the rules for "pure" jam and the government has used

The Seventh Generation

Smith's recipe as the benchmark for defining the word "pure" in jam.

They Met in the Jam Factory

I am not the company's first fourth-generation employee. Truck driver, fork lift driver and ingredient picker Brian Hardyman earned that distinction back in the 60s.

His father Doug was the garage foreman and even though Doug's office was somewhat smaller than E.L.G.'s, his training methods were similar and he showed no favouritism.

The Spectator did a feature on this family back in 1972 and the story goes that Doug said, "Brian is madder than hell at me right now. It's 4 p.m and I just sent him off to Toronto with a load."

That meant his truck driver son would miss his normal supper. "I didn't want to take Brian on here," Mr. H said. "I didn't know how the other men would react to it. But they found out Brian wanted in and they told me: 'What's the matter with you? Why won't you let your son come and work here?'"

There was no possible reply because Mr. H's two grandfathers, and both his parents, were Smith employees; as a matter of fact his father and mother met in the jam factory!

Another Generation Picks Cherries

My earliest recollection of entering the family business was when I was first paid, picking cherries on the farm at age six with my older sisters Sharon and Daphne and my cousins Derek and Maben. I am not sure if I ate more than I put in the eleven-quart basket but nevertheless it seemed to take forever to fill. I really didn't know the value of things, but we did receive 50 cents for each basket. Picking one or two in a morning was my starting efficiency.

Llewellyn S. with Clarence Vanderheide at controls on cooking deck

Another Generation Picks Cherries

These were the only times I worked with my sisters in the business. Dad, following English tradition, did not consider that either one of the two girls could actually go into the business. I have now bought their shares of the company and my sisters and I know this was my parent's intention. Whether or not they regret not having the opportunity to go into the E.D. Smith business, they certainly have made interesting lives for themselves.

Sharon, whom I unfortunately only see at weddings and funerals or on my trips to England, is running her own stone quarry and craft business. She likes to say it comes from her Gibson blood and her love of gardens and flowers comes from the Smith side. She is truly gifted artistically and enjoys living in the English countryside with her husband Robert Seibel, an international metals trader and daughter Daphne.

My second sister, Daphne is married to Ian Angus a successful lawyer, who is also Reeve of the Township of Hope and they have a daughter Caro, who rides with the Canadian Olympic team. Daphne is an unpretentious, hard working, "Meals on Wheels" volunteer and animal lover. Like our mother, I am sure she could hold her own with princes and kings and yet lives and works on a horse farm. She has one foot in each camp. Both on solid ground.

In 1964 we purchased a cherry harvesting machine which could seize a tree and shake the cherries off in five minutes. A long arm with a clamp on the end is attached to the front of a tractor. The clamp was attached to the main branches of the tree, one by one. When the operator pulled a lever the arm vibrated, shaking the whole tree. The cherries fell onto sheets of a canvas-like material at the base of the tree and rolled into plastic boxes.

During those summers working on the farm I learned about quality, fairness and integrity.

Quality   In those days, Mr. and Mrs. Parker ran the farm. Mrs. Parker would only punch my paycard (indicating a basket) if the basket was completely full of cherries, with or without stems depending on what was needed. As a check that the basket was full and did not have dirt or leaves on the bottom, Mrs.

The Seventh Generation

Parker always dumped the pickers' baskets into another basket before putting it on the wagon to go to the factory for processing.

Fairness   Because I was the youngest picker, my sisters, Mr. Parker, my cousin Gordon Conant, Brian and Barry Hardyman and the others always gave me a hand with the big ladders. They also allowed me to pick from the limbs closest to the ground. Since we were paid on a piece basis, it would have been easy for them to pick from the prime limbs in order to fill their baskets more quickly. Instead they were sportsmanlike.

Integrity   We also were taught to pick a tree cleanly, not leaving any ripe cherries in a difficult (time consuming) position to move on to the neighbouring bountiful tree. The farm experience helped me understand at an early age to do things properly, deliver a quality product and to not take short cuts.

Knowing that I was destined for the business, (it was taken for granted that I would be), I worked hard and was very proud to be involved. Helen Janicki, a lady who worked on the tomato line once said to me when I was cooking jam, "What are you doing in here? A Smith like you?" I think she was impressed.

Learn the business. This way nobody can fool you. It's darn good training. It's best not to go into an executive office until you've learned more about people. After all, if you're a boss, you're supposed to be a leader, and a leader should understand people.

E. Llewellyn G. Smith

I really enjoyed the work. Not because of the hours or the money, but for the inner pride, the sense of coming home exhausted, having done a job well. I pulled my weight. In fact, as a Smith, I always felt I had to pull more than my weight. It was in the blood.

My summers on sanitation duty (yes—cleaning out the washrooms!), on the cook deck, in shipping, out in the yard and on the road selling, helped me realize the dedication and commitment our people have in their jobs and to the company. Day in, day out, our staff give it their best.

At School

One may make an art of the meanest toil by doing it carefully and imparting a finishing touch.

Damaris Smith at school

At School

Business was the only thing I was ever really interested in and I found school a struggle all the way through until university where I could choose electives. Rather than approach each subject with an open mind, I looked upon it in terms of how it would help me in the business.

My pride in the company has got me in trouble. In grade eight I was beaten up for what I am sure was bragging. Even today I find that whenever I start to get just a bit over-confident, things seem to go the other way and reality sets in. My mother's family speaks of an inner pride in a private way. I have learned to value the strength of modesty.

> In grade seven the biology teacher was stumped for an answer when I asked how dissecting a frog would help me to make jam.

My parents believed in their children having a broad education. Each of us was given the opportunity to be educated in Europe and we thank them for this. For me, it was Switzerland for five years, following two years at boarding school in Ottawa. Although there were times of homesickness and emptiness, the experience generated independence and strength. It is here where I learned about team play and leadership. I invariably had the lead role and except for one terrible football season, we won most games. It is at this point that I learned the advantages of team play. In a way, the game today remains the same but the field is much different.

There is a good reason for a student to have plenty of manly games. It rests the mind and teaches self reliance, decision of character and courage.

E.D. Smith 1904 in a letter to Armand

The Seventh Generation

Our suppliers, customers and competitors are mostly larger than ourselves. We have chosen suppliers who are on a fast growth curve like we are, which in turn helps us because they have fresh, modern ideas.

I have always found it interesting to note the difference between customer groups. Some use their power to bully and threaten and these in time have fallen by the wayside or are not what they used to be, while others treat their suppliers as partners and continue, for the most part, in business today. It's all how you play the game. Those who operate with integrity and fairness, win. In more ways than one.

Dad always said that not everybody can be expected to be a superstar, nor do you want it. He implied that it is the team, with each player contributing to his or her own ability that carries the match.

In Europe, I finished Grade 11 and 12 at Ecole Des Roches then moved onto the American College of Switzerland. Many of my friends and roommates were American. It was at College that I met my first wife, an American, born in San Francisco and raised mostly in Spanish-speaking countries. I lived the Vietnam era through the friendship of people who did not serve, either because they dodged the draft, their number was low on the list or they had older brothers killed in the war and therefore were exempt. It is at this point in my life that I really developed an appreciation for Americans.

Travelling in Europe as a Canadian was a different experience than that of an American. Thanks to Canada's war efforts and our continued good reputation, I felt welcome wherever I went. My American friends on the other hand were treated differently. Not a month would go by without one of their embassies being attacked, or one of their airliners hi-jacked or an executive kidnapped. The price of world leadership was high, anchored in jealousy and envy.

I learned about the values that have made America the most powerful nation in the world. The strong belief in Life, Liberty and the Pursuit of Happiness and the determination to succeed. They have a strong sense of nationalism. We could take a leaf out of their book in this regard. They are American first. I would like to see Canadians develop a similar sense of pride, self-confidence and spirit. We certainly have every reason to feel good about our country.

A Great Teamwork Story

A Great Teamwork Story

One moonlit night in 1972, a local couple driving along a stretch of road that they were very familiar with right here in Winona, were practically paralyzed with fear by what they saw. It looked to them as though a giant, cloud-like flying saucer had landed right behind the E.D. Smith plant.

What they saw was our first warehouse bubble. I must admit it did look quite futuristic and out of place. But it did such a great job for us that we replaced it 13 years later with an even better one. We like to think we have good teamwork here at E.D. Smith; well, the removal of the old one and the installation of the new bubble is one of the best examples of co-operation and teamwork one could ask for.

Arie Bergshoeff and Bill Reekie were assigned to begin the plans. They arranged meetings with contractors; Jerry Winchester and representatives from shipping organized the inventory to best advantage; lift truck operators had to work like crazy. It had to all happen over a weekend so as not to disrupt any pick-up and delivery operations. To make a long story shorter, by 9:20 on a Friday night the old bubble was deflated and with the help of 50 people, the new one was in place by 2:30 Saturday afternoon. The planning, the co-operation, the skills necessary, and the common goal of 'getting the job done' reinforced the Smith mission of working together for the benefit of all.

Old pieces of the bubble were cut out and given to employees who could make use of it personally.

I learned about people from all cultures from more than 100 different countries. My grandfather Sifton always said there are good people in every race, creed and colour. You just had to have an open mind and attitude.

At College I was lucky to have some of my courses include visits to Nestlé's world headquarters at neighbouring Vevey. This allowed me to learn about international marketing and how one of the world's best food companies conducts its affairs. I thought at the time how beneficial it would be for me to work in such a business first. I would have had a chance to learn, to prove myself and develop a greater self-confidence. For me, this was not to happen.

Learning the Ropes

Having spent seven years becoming independent and thinking for myself, I approached my parents about working outside the business. Unfortunately my father disagreed and it was suggested that if I had little interest in the firm, then it ought to be sold.

What a blow! Here I was, an impressionable young man who had inherited a tremendous legacy and was told I must do something about it or it would be kaput. Over. All because of me. This begs the question of course of "why in the world would I even consider not going directly into the family business?" Good question.

E.L.G.'s entry salary was $3,000 per year and $9,000 when he first became President. My entry salary was $9,000. Inflation continues.

For me, the answer would have been simply that I needed to make my own mark and mistakes somewhere else first without the Senator (or the Brigadier or my dad) looming over me. I'm sorry I did not explain my case better to gain their support for this idea. CAFE believes this to be true and they advise family businesses to encourage future generations to work elsewhere before coming into the business. Believe me, this is good advice.

Just ask Jeff Stock, the second-generation in Stochem Inc., a CAFE member. He graduated from university, went to work for Pitney Bowes for one year and then came to us for almost two years. We put him in sales, gave him some major accounts to deal with in the private-label area and a territory from

Vancouver to Halifax. He said that working for us was his "proving ground." He found it to be "an exciting, fast-paced, consumer driven job," and was pleased with the amount of responsibility and accountability we put in the hands of our managers. Jeff knows that the "expectation level of family members is much higher in a family business" and no matter how hard they try, they "can never be prepared enough." It is simply expected that a family member will go the extra mile. His experience working outside his own family business equipped him with a confidence of personal performance. So, this spring, the time was right for him to start working for Stochem and he could go happily, with credentials he earned, not just inherited.

My first full-time job at the company was Export Manager. It was a good entry position. The job was responsible for only 1% of the cases we sold and about 2% of our gross sales. The area was losing money partly because of poor management. When Ron Lake took over as head of Sales and Marketing, he was my boss and we had many heart-to-heart talks. Sometimes he would tell me I had done a good job and sometimes he would say, "Lew, some day you are going to be President of this place and I've got to teach you how to do things right." He was a true mentor.

Then I was posted to the factory as Second Floor Supervisor. I was in tears. Being schooled in professional management I thought it was a demotion, not because it was a move to the factory but because it was a move from Manager to Supervisor. In fact the pay even at this level was higher than Export Manager. This was a shift job and I had the benefit of working beside Glenn Coates and reporting to Bill Wright, two professionals when it came to managing people.

Pat Wilkinson in quality control lab

The Seventh Generation

I remember coming in on the shift prior to start up to insure things would go well, despite the fact that the crew had been managing things quite successfully for years. It was at a backyard party at my home for all the shift staff to celebrate summer shut-down that Mary Agard challenged me on this practice. She made me realize that my action was perceived as a lack of confidence in our staff. It was my introduction to management.

Being a Smith and heir apparent had its special job requirements. Despite my shortcomings (and I have many), people around the company read far too deeply into everything an owner's son said or did—out of respect, fear, politics whatever. It had been that way for many years. It is still that way today. My peers at other family businesses experience the same challenges.

As a young man returning from a global experience, I felt that E.D. Smith, like Canada, had to change if it was going to survive in the marketplace. It was the type of change, the acceptance of change, and the rate of change that presented the biggest challenges.

Coloured Hats

The Executive Committee that my father and Alastair had set up in the late 60s helped the company grow in sales, production and earnings. As a team they ushered in change and did it successfully. It was structured change. Being young, impatient and green, I pushed for faster change. I challenged the status quo at every turn. Not knowingly, I made things confusing for those in middle management. For example, I resisted using coloured hats to show position.

However, I have learned that those of us in family businesses, should be aware that employee recognition is vital. This means not only a pat on their back, but their name on the door. Professional managers are just that, professionals, and when they have demonstrated a certain level of expertise, the world needs to know.

My grandfather was a Brigadier and respected those of higher rank and commanded respect from those with lower rank. My father, on the other hand was a great communicator. People worked for him because they wanted to. He had a genuine interest in the well-being of E.D Smith personnel. To this day,

Coloured Hats

10 years after his retirement, he asks about them and they ask about him. There is nothing anyone wouldn't do for him. Dad saw it as one of his responsibilities to help people grow in their jobs. He was liberal with information about the company. He exposed management to new thoughts and encouraged people to upgrade their skills at all levels.

Education is the key to the cultivation of a good intellect, sound reasoning powers and the ability to make good judgements.

E.D. Smith

Prosperity Plan to Profit Sharing Plan

My father successfully implemented profit sharing at the manager level. His wish was to take it throughout the comp-

The E.D. Smith prosperity committee with a cheque to be distributed among the plant workers. The Count Me In program gives employees a chance to come up with good ideas to save the company money. L-R Brian Jones, Nick Pollice, Jerry Parkes, Mark Trottier, Fred Ecker, Lynn Johnson, Llewellyn Smith, Peter Worozbyt and Brent Carroll.

any but was cautioned that for it to be successful it had to be meaningful and we simply could not afford it. With the help of Brent Carroll, V.P. Employee Relations, Nick Pollice and many others, in 1985 a company-wide pseudo-gain sharing program called "The Prosperity Plan" was introduced. Under this plan, we successfully encouraged over 65% of the staff to form teams to engineer and help implement ways to reduce costs and improve quality and productivity. The plan has been written up in several books and magazines. **The rewards both financially and non-financially were significant. I learned that when people are given authority and trust in those areas they know best and management plays coach and facilitator only, results will come back in spades.** Today, in 1995, we replaced and upgraded this to a company-wide Profit Sharing Plan. I have realized my father's dream!

My Mentors

In addition to my father, I have had the opportunity to learn from a lot of people. I am particularly grateful to my best friend, Walter G.R. Wilson. I believe Ulysses when he said, "I am a part of all that I have met," and I would like to mention everybody. However four have been true coaches: Clare Proctor, Ron Lake, Brent Carroll and Bob Cunliffe. Each served 15 years or longer. All of these gentlemen were dedicated to the company, had pride in their jobs, carried and felt great responsibility in their lives. The thing that impressed me most was their individual ability to understand and motivate people. They liked the interface. They were honest, fair and well respected. Each was not afraid to tell it the way it was and provide me with guidance and counsel. It is no small wonder that the firm's best years financially coincided with my father's molding of this team, which also included Douglas Conant, Grant Bernhardt and Jake Wamsteeker.

Personal Problems

Throughout 18 years of marriage and my management development, my life had been in turmoil. Not only did I take on a lot of business responsibilities at an early age but also made the mistake of agreeing to marry a lady whose culture, values and interests were far different from my own. At one point, under her persuasion, I seriously considered selling the business and moving to California. I found myself torn between my wife's interests and those of my Smith upbringing. Every effort I made to bring these together only made things worse. The impact on my business management skills and decisions affected the company's performance. Leadership and focus were missing on my part but Richard Sexton did what he could to keep things together on the business front.

Our marriage ended when my wife filed for separation in 1989 and we divorced one year later.

I learned a lot from this experience. Don't get married too soon; marry someone who thinks the same way you do; hope that both sides of the family support you in your choice. I spent some time determining just what my values are. I came to understand my career aspirations and their impact on family and social life before committing to marriage again. I also had a chance to play Mr. Mom. This was one of the more enjoyable periods of my life. Shopping, skiing, preparing meals and chatting together before bedtime with Gerard, Graham and Claire gave my family a chance to share our values and work as a team.

CAFE and Me

For those of us who are in family businesses it is easy to understand that a potential spouse is just not marrying you, they are joining a family, a family that is in business. The subtle difference is extremely

To find out more about CAFE call 1-800-760-8882.

important. To help deal with this, CAFE recommends setting up a Family Council to establish philosophies and values. Often it is a forum where family members and soon-to-be family members can discuss in an open and supportive environment, future aspirations, individual fit and growth opportunities. Family Councils are a recent development and my guess is that if such a forum had been in place in our family back in 1975, it is likely I wouldn't have become married at that time because some of our basic differences would have been identified in time for us to realize we were not a good fit.

CAFE does far more than this.

The Canadian Association of Family Enterprise has been a valuable tool for me. It exists to advise family businesses such as E.D. Smith through seminars, recommended professional

The Seventh Generation

advisors, group meetings and above all, Personal Advisory Groups—P.A.G.s.

My involvement started in 1985 when I joined CAFE's first P.A.G. In our monthly meetings, we discuss everything under the sun and have grown as individuals, friends and business associates. From this group, as well as from outside experts whom we invite to our meetings, I have learned about setting up a will, a holding company and a Board of Advisors. I have come to have a better understanding of the role of family members in and out of the business, professional management, tax tips and even where to go for a good holiday. Most of all, I have learned about myself and my friends.

To Tom, Derek, John, Larry, Murray, Tim, Warren, Ralph, Bob and David, thank you for giving me guidance and support. I hope I have helped you too.

Because of my strong belief in CAFE, I am pleased to have served as the National President for the past two years. No time has ever been better spent! In addition to the day-to-day excitement, our Annual Symposiums in Whistler, Quebec City, Calgary (Kananaskis) and in 1995, Ottawa, bring together families in business from across Canada.

Family-owned businesses employ 40% of the Canadian work force. Their success is the success of the entire country.

CAFE members certainly know how to have fun too! We have climbed mountains; test-driven Porsches and Jaguars, line danced; skied; eaten at a maple sugar shack in Quebec and in an Indian teepee in Alberta. We have shared tips on how to deal with our children, especially in a family business environment; how to feel better about ourselves; how to plan for succession; marriage contracts; business plans; and as the first Canadian to reach the top of Mount Everest, Laurie Skreslet told us, "how to climb our own personal mountain."

Through CAFE friends John Pigott and Bruce Morrison, I met Susan Fleming and we were married in 1994.

CAFE is also where I found my Board of Advisors.

Our Board is made up of four successful self-starter businessmen, Murray Walker, Don Fell, Murray Hogarth and Bob Forsythe, plus my father and myself. We have five meetings a year and frequent discussions and reports between meetings. The Board gives me independent and objective advice. It allows our managers a chance to present their business unit plans and receive good advice. As my children grow older, the

CAFE and Me

Board will be a great "sounding board." These advisors know the business, they know me and in the future they will come to know my children.

Gordon Sharwood, my dad and others knew they helped to found a wonderful organization; they just did not know how truly beneficial it would be to our company and the entire Canadian business community.

Acquisition

E.D. Smith has bought and sold many businesses in the 70s, 80s and 90s. Each added to the strength of the company, but over time cost the firm plenty and ultimately has not been part of our future. McLarens is an example of just such a business. Although we sold it, many of their people remain with us today.

Every time we made an acquisition or divestiture, it took my eye and the eyes of key executives off the ball of our main business. The result was a decline in earnings in addition to out-of-pocket costs. I have learned that it is best to build a business the old-fashioned way. We should concentrate on internal growth, have confidence and patience in our own team, be creative and take risks in our own area of expertise.

Institutional size ketchup line, overseen by Donna Lee Allison

The Seventh Generation

I did however enjoy these experiences and learned from them. Over time we have owned: a majority position in a multiple-factory frozen baked goods company—Gourmet Baker in British Columbia; Renaissance Cuisine, a start-up operation producing refrigerated and frozen entrees in plastic pouches and trays; and Canadian Made Snacks, makers of salted specialty nut products. I didn't understand my real purpose for getting involved in these enterprises, but I have come to realize that it was my attempt to create or build something on my own. Many successors in family companies have this burning desire to prove something and this looked like my chance.

Free Trade

After studying international economics abroad, it was easy for me to fully support and campaign for Free Trade with the United States. The U.S.-Canadian Auto Pact was perhaps the best example we have of how beneficial it is for both countries. The alternative of protection and isolation would have left Canada poorer.

At E.D. Smith we moved quickly to make the necessary adjustments and thank goodness we acted when we did. With all the media hype and corporate discussion our customers' buyers were under great pressure to purchase from the U.S. Many of our customers had the misguided belief that they

The end of the jam cooling tunnel, with Jerry Parkes

could buy quality products in America for less money and still get the customized services that they enjoyed from E.D. Smith.

We were told that we had to reduce some of our selling prices by up to 25% or lose the business. We chose to retain the business by reducing selling prices and driving costs out of our system. In a business where a net after tax profit of three percent or less is average, it was not possible for us to maintain our margins. We therefore had to turn our assets over more quickly and grow the business to make up for the lower margin. The result was to discontinue or sell off those products with low margins and all seasonal production was converted to become non-seasonal.

Today we receive fruit year round in frozen or aseptically packed bulk containers from Canada, U.S. and world sources. This means we no longer receive fresh produce directly from local farmers.

The end of an era.

The Sale of Garden Cocktail

To realign our business for the North American market, we needed cash. I made the bold decision to sell our flagship product, Garden Cocktail vegetable juice.

It took a year of planning. With the help of Richard Sexton, President of the company at the time, and Jack Woodcock of J.R. Janus, Toronto, a merchant broker, we carefully packaged the brand for sale and strategically timed the marketing of it. The financial outcome surpassed our expectations. We used the excess proceeds to acquire the Laura Secord and Habitant jam brands and consolidate the production at Winona. In one transaction I was able to reduce corporate debt and shareholder obligations, modernize the factory to enable cost competitiveness in a North American economy and to rebuild our branded business—jam and pie filling categories.

This came at a wonderful time for our jam business. Each year, we would discuss whether or not we really should continue making jam. It wasn't returning us a good profit and maybe it was time to give it up. But the argument was always countered with the sentimental idea that it has been jam all along that has kept us going; it has always been there for us and true to tradition, it was in fact the basis for the company in the first place. With the Back to Basics, Build the Brands type attitude we have turned the jam question right around and E.D. Smith jams continue to be the backbone of the business.

The Casualties

Sounds brilliant doesn't it. But there was a down side to all this. It took such a toll on the people who had to step aside to allow change to come in, that we have not yet recovered. We went through two downsizings, reducing full employment by 50%!—in a company that had a reputation for not even laying anyone off! But our subsequent growth has generated more jobs and a higher payroll than ever. However the nucleus had changed.

Many of the people who helped make the company a success in my father's era were retired or let go. To put back the feeling of self-confidence and security in the company's future is the most challenging task I face. Today's staff has different needs and responds to different stimuli. It is today's generation. Nobody walks to work any more.

What this world needs is a permanency of condition that will enable everyone who is industrious to earn a decent living.

E.D. Smith

David Nichol and Private Label

Along the path in rebuilding the company, I recognized that our retail customers were stepping up their interest in promoting their own "house" or "private labels." One day I met David Nichol, President of Loblaws International Merchants in his office to discuss the prospect of E.D. Smith making products under his President's Choice label.

A funny thing happened.

He asked me what was the secret to making good ketchup and what elements made our Garden Cocktail the best tasting vegetable juice. As I started to tell him, he interrupted and said, "Be clear, anything and everything you tell me, I will use against you."

David Nichol and Private Label

Without a pause I continued to answer his questions. At that point we developed a mutual trust and we went on to create 64 items for Loblaws. This earned us their respect and they chose us supplier of the year. Our reputation spread throughout the trade and today we supply every major Canadian retail/wholesale group.

At Loblaws, it was a relationship far beyond two people. Their buying, product development and merchandising divisions worked hand-in-hand with our counterparts. I was particularly grateful to our V.P. Paul Richardson and his staff at our company who coordinated this effort.

The uncompromising demands of Mr. Nichol and his colleagues forced a higher level of corporate performance on our part. To satisfy this customer we changed the way we operated. It became our competitive edge.

We are all creatures of imitation and the higher we keep our standards, the greater good to others.

Damaris Smith

We learned to concentrate on a few categories, and we brought innovation to the marketplace in each of our distribution channels. Our experience at Renaissance Cuisine and with our customer Pizza Pizza enabled us to become Canada's largest producer of pizza sauce packed in environmentally friendly pouches. We now supply many of the leading quick-service chains across the country including McDonald's restaurants.

We also supply leading food service distributors with our own company brands. We have made such a concerted effort promoting our own brands that we now enjoy a leadership position in this area. This means that you not only see our name on the table, but you know the chef is using it in the kitchen.

Our focus on tomato-based products allowed us to expand our product line to include salsa and pasta sauces in addition to ketchup. We achieved this with the help of Los Gatos, a state-of-the-art tomato supplier in California and our top ranked in-house product development and engineering team. With our dedicated work force and a unique offering of package designs, we have been able to expand our business with growth from Oshawa/I.G.A. group, Sobeys, Overwaitea, Interprovincial Cooperatives, Safeway, Loeb and others.

In the case of Loblaws, their eyes were on the United States, where they have much of their business. After finding only a few U.S. suppliers who could meet their needs in terms of price, quality and service, they persuaded their best Canadian suppliers to set up facilities in the U.S. Loblaws was determined to source on a North American basis with a winner-take-all strategy to lower their costs. We realized that this meant that if we didn't have a U.S. operation we could run the risk of losing the Canadian portion of the business. Although Loblaws represented less than 20% of our overall business, I decided to take the plunge.

One of the other major reasons for Loblaws' interest in having their vendors set up in the U.S. was to supply Wal-Mart. Loblaws had an agreement to develop a line of products for Wal-Mart under the Sam's America's Choice label (Sam Walton started Wal-Mart). Loblaws would receive a royalty for every item sold.

Wal-Mart demanded American-based suppliers. At first we looked at building a factory in Arkansas. We wanted to be at least 700 miles away from our Canadian facility and we thought the choice of Arkansas would put us in good favour with Wal-Mart as it is their home state. We ended up buying a company in Mississippi, called Gem Inc. Yes, history does repeat itself. The Smith's again go back to the U.S.A. and invest in a company named Gem!

Time will tell if this was a smart move.

True to form, the acquisition has had its costs, but we are gaining valuable long-term benefit. The indicated level of business with Wal-Mart has yet to materialize but we have however opened 20 new accounts.

This experience has taught us that there are differences between the Canadian and U.S. markets. Although Americans enjoy a larger selection of products, Canadians have been the innovators in product quality and packaging. We have also learned that whereas Canadians make decisions by committee, consensus and compromise, Americans are focused on having individuals make decisions. Neither is right or wrong; we just change cultures when travelling between the two countries.

E.D. Smith—Gem, Byhalia Mississippi

In any case, we are well on our way to being a successful North American company.

E.D. Smith—Gem, Byhalia Mississippi

This company has quite a history too. It was originally founded in Milwaukee in 1917 and relocated to Byhalia in 1952. Two other companies were acquired and moved here: Aerosol Corporation of the South in 1967 and the New Orleans plant of Anheuser-Busch in 1968. The entire company was bought in 1979 by The Androcan Inc. Group of Toronto owned by Barrie Rose. Up until 1989 the company produced primarily household products, mops, brooms, mouth washes, cleaners and syrups. Then the mops and brooms division was sold and the company became much smaller. We bought it in 1992. We liked the proximity to Memphis, Tennessee, which is the distribution centre of the U.S., the large facility, and the core management team.

This U.S. operation is about the same size as our Canadian plant. There, we have nine production lines, 200 people working multiple shifts. Located in Marshall County in the poorest state in the Union, there are a lot of personal hardships. But like in Winona, these people do not quit. They know what hard knocks in life are all about and are very cooperative and appreciative

Byhalia staff—1995

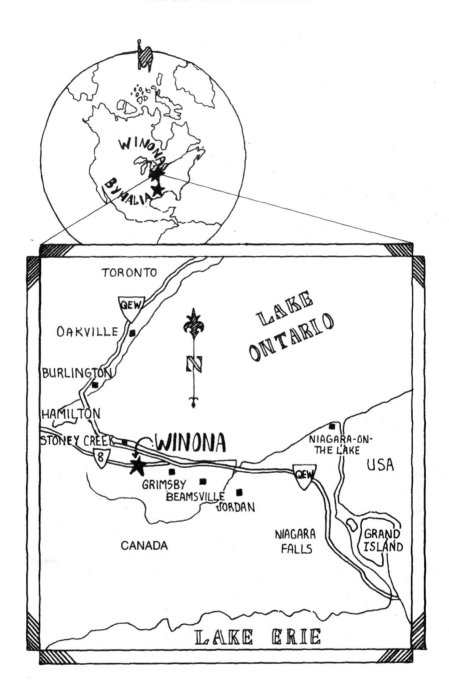

Winona and Byhalia

Winona, Ontario, circa 1972

Byhalia, Mississippi, circa 1969

of E.D. Smith efforts. Every week there are visitors from our Canadian operation to assist the American management. We share computer software, production techniques, product development and attitude. Our standards of operation are getting closer by the day.

The north-south connection allows us to serve North American customers and take advantage of various duty and non-duty trade barriers. To maximize the effectiveness of our two operations, I am pleased that our staff both at Winona and Byhalia are working well together and this cooperation benefits both sides of the border.

E.D. would be flattered but not surprised to know that there is a company in the south-central United States where they answer the telephone by saying, "Good morning. E.D. Smith."

Winona, Ontario

E.D. Smith & Sons Limited and the hamlet of Winona have had a long history together. I have heard it said, that "E.D. would be pleased." He was aware of the pitfalls and dangers and successes of business and it would be no surprise to him that we continue to have some of each. My generation too has been asked why we chose to remain in Winona, in the country, isolated at times from the excitement of the city and its appeal. Perhaps living as we do even today, high on a hill, overlooking Lake Ontario, we are blessed with an overview, a perspective, an ability to view life, business and our place in history.

As I gaze out from my doorway, I know I should have become narrow minded if I had not had my past to live on and my hope of an opening someday, for myself and family to see out to the water beyond.

Damaris McGee Smith 1893

Llewellyn Sifton Smith

Times change. The war to be fought now was an economic one and there weren't a lot of rules and guidelines. Like E.D., I sailed in uncharted waters and by virtue of the fact that the company is still alive and healthy helps to prove I mapped the way reasonably well. The biggest question is how did I know it would work? My background is full of people who had tenacious ideas, courage to see them through and strength in their convictions. I took strength from them.

The toughest part was how to deal with the downside. The people side. In the past no one was ever laid off and here we were letting people go left right and centre. What happened?

The real, modern world touched Winona. Computers, global competition and a recession compounded the problems of multinationals trying to take us over and dissension in the ranks of the family.

The annual picnic has been replaced with profit sharing; the people we work with are no longer our neighbours; the fruit we process is grown around the world.

The values I inherited are intact. My interest in the well-being of the company is perhaps deeper entrenched than any Smith, other than the founder, as ownership and management ride solely on my shoulders.

I am sorry that the last 15 years have seen so much disruption at E.D. Smith but as stated earlier in the book, the story of the company parallels the pattern of Canadian business with all its ups and downs... but, the story is not over yet.

THE EIGHTH GENERATION

A CANADIAN SURVIVOR

THE STONE HOUSE

The Eighth Generation

The Smith Family	World Events
1995 Llewellyn Smith returns company "back-to-basis"; combined Winona/Byhalia management team established; E.D. Smith brands reach record levels of market share; new customers push U.S. sales fourfold; *The House That Jam Built* published	1995 Canada-Spain fish dispute; Canadian federal government finally tackles deficit; O.J. Simpson trial
• • • •	• • • •
2000	2000

THE EIGHTH GENERATION

A CANADIAN SURVIVOR

I don't want to be tagged as the guy who just sold it all. I
have a purpose. I intend to leave a legacy.

Llewellyn S. Smith

I spoke these words over two years ago. They have even
more meaning today. In fact, putting this book together made
me understand just how much I want to help make this world
a better place. Ultimately isn't that what it is all about?

As We Approach the Millennium

*Our mission for E.D. Smith is to be the best, independent,
family-owned, food company in North America.*

We are off to a good start. Let me explain.

Best Dealing with superior people and superlative products
puts us well on the way to being the best. To be the best is a
measurement to ourselves rather than a comparison to others.
It is an internal drive to do the best at all times. It is a term
when applied to a "family enterprise" that perhaps requires
further explanation. At E.D. Smith we have been successful by
applying family values to a corporate or business setting for
most of our 113 years. Values such as Honesty, Trust, Fairness,
Teamwork, Persistence, Recognition and Personal
Development are what have attracted people to join and stay
with our company.

Independent We aim to become less dependent on the bank,
or on one particular customer, or on the actions of competitors.
Independence will give us the freedom to choose direction and

goals. We will be changing the mix of our business such that more production will be in products and brands that we control and/or have greater security of retaining. By having a stronger balance sheet, we will be able to run the business in a more proactive way making more decisions that positively impact the long term.

Canadian Owned   Has there ever been a better time to be proud to be a Canadian? Canada has become the source of the break-through in the food industry. E.D. Smith has helped people like David Nichol put us on the leading edge of many innovations. We are looked upon as a very clean, orderly society and this is particularly valuable in the food business. Just as we admire Americans, we know they are looking to Canada for innovation within our industry.

In retaining ownership, we also inherit responsibilities. We must continue to strive to rise to the occasion of accepting them and protecting them. Steps have been taken to not only reach the millennium but to create the opportunity for the company to enter its fifth generation under Smith ownership. These steps include adequate insurance in case something happens to me; the transfer of shares into a trust until my children Gerard, Graham and Claire are of age; and the creation of a first class Advisory Board.

Family   A family company takes on a life of its own, a personality which needs nurturing. All people in the company belong to the same family and work on the same team, all with the same goals. These goals are the desire for happiness, both on and off the job; the thrill of success, to feel good about their efforts and to ensure that the job is still there tomorrow; and a desire to help improve the world around them.

Food   Our emphasis more than ever will be on our jam and sauce products both of which are foods that the consumer wants, not just needs. Just as E.D. wanted to find a more remunerative way of farming, we want to find even more remunerative ways of adding value to these products from the soil to create or fulfill consumer demand. Let's use strawberries to illustrate this point. We could sell a basket of berries to someone who came to the fields and picked them. But, if we picked them, and then sold them, we would charge a bit more. We would have added value. Further still, if we hull the strawberries and put them in a pretty little basket, they are worth even more. Ultimately, we could process the berries and make a delicious, pure fruit jam and charge yet even more. Value added. Time added. Costs added. The more that is put into a product, assuming someone wants it, the more the consumer will happily pay.

Company   This company had a consistency of direction for over 100 years. Namely, to continually improve and enhance products to achieve better quality, to fill a changing market need and to promote the well-being of everyone involved from owners, to staff, to retail customers, to the public. At no time did we operate with anything less than the highest of integrity.

North America   We have answered the challenge of Free Trade with sales in both Canada and the U.S. when many a pundit thought we couldn't survive. As we look to the year 2000, the company will have solidified its North American position.

Looking Back

During the past 15 years, our direction did not change but the implication of it did, much to the chagrin of many. I was overly pre-occupied with the well-being of the company at the expense of the well-being of the people. This is probably typical of young successors.

*Judy Elliott, Donna Murakami and Judy Evans
in mixing area at Winona plant*

234

The Eighth Generation

The scary thing is, had I been mature enough to return this mutual loyalty to every person instead of my exclusive loyalty to the company, we might no longer be in business.

It was rather like driving in white-out conditions during a terrible storm. You are so intent on keeping the car on the road you cannot sing along with the radio or talk with your passengers. If you stop the car to wait out the storm, other cars will pass you and get ahead.

I feel the storm is over. I have also learned to drive better. The big thing though is that I have learned to care. My experiences at the plant in Mississippi have taught me a lot. It's ironic that I had to go to the United States to learn how to feel about people in my own country.

The staff in Byhalia had been working for many years in a company with marginal direction or focus. Very little money had been invested in the operation and they were ready for a new owner and a new business. With our acquisition, we gave it the commitment it needed. Following in no one's footsteps, having no one with pre-conceived ideas about what I should do, I like to think I've made a difference. Here in Canada, the shoes I am supposed to fill were so big I didn't even want to try them on. I wanted my own pair. Well, I've learned that is not necessary. My father's shoes fit just fine.

We are not the giants in this industry. We are the David to several Goliaths. Coming from a position of strength however, we have our customers' trust, loyalty and dedication to a strong name and quality product. Not all Goliaths can say that.

Bringing out a new line of jams costs the same amount for the E.D. Smith company as it does for a multinational, but the Smiths put their future on the line to do it, while another company can often afford a failure.

Clare Proctor 1983

What Clare means is that as a company, we are often putting our future on the line. Something we have to believe is that we are special. Each individual is special and needs to be treated that way. As a company we are special too. There are few family-owned, fourth generation food companies of our size in Canada. So far, we have beaten the odds. My father takes great delight in knowing he proved the old adage of "shirt-sleeves to shirt-sleeves in three generations," to be wrong.

Now

While it is my hope that one or more of the children will be interested in the business, I have also set up a holding company, such that if this isn't the case, they can pursue other interests without jeopardizing the company's future. My primary interest is that the children find a career that best fits their skills and interests. Although I am keeping them abreast of company events, every opportunity is being taken to expose them to a wider perspective in life.

At an early age they were proud to have their own roadside stand selling jam. Along with other children in the neighbourhood, they have an appreciation of the soil, the land and realize that the business that supports them is dependent on the fruits of the earth. They are beginning to learn what work is all about.

*Olivia Jones has been at the controls of a
Byhalia filling line for over 24 years*

The Eighth Generation

A child who has all its wants supplied and whims gratified, is like a ship at sea without rudder or sails, drifting at the mercy of wind and wave.

Damaris Smith

They have travelled and seen some interesting parts of the world; they are great skiers; they enjoy healthy competition. Gerard has a real knack mechanically, loves engines and cars. Graham is a people person and not afraid to speak his mind even in a crowd. Claire is quick and loves games and puzzles. As all parents know, it is rewarding and exciting to watch them grow and learn.

We have been lucky to have my wife Susan join our family. She handles this new situation exceptionally well. While recognizing our children's natural mother, she participates in every way to insure the kids are raised with ambitions, pride, respect, self confidence and plenty of love. Her parents in turn are wonderful role models and enjoy their marvelous new grandchildren.

I am fortunate that Susan is taking such a positive stance towards the company and its future. She is very proud of what E.D. Smith represents and plans to take a more active role in the years to come. Historically, the Smith women have had a great influence in the success of the company and the happiness of the family. Susan has brought to our family a stability and a smile that people around us see reflected in our positive attitude and concern for the well-being of others.

Susan is a highly-skilled operating room nurse who works very hard, often under a great deal of pressure. I am daily amazed at how she manages to always have time for family and friends. She is an inspiration to us all.

This quiet, stable balance at home has allowed me to focus more clearly on the business. We have a definite direction. Our focus in order of priority is on People, Products and Profits.

People   My belief is that E.D. Smith people are our #1 strength. As we realize on the potential of our existing staff and work as a team in a challenging and cohesive environment, it will ultimately show on the bottom line.

E.D. Smith Labels

The Eighth Generation

The strategy for bringing out the best in our people is consistently operating within our values. It all starts with a proper hiring process and orientation program. By proper I mean meeting every new member of the E.D. Smith family. Helping him or her understand our values, culture, policies and procedures before making a commitment and diving into the job. By welcoming the newcomer into the company as an individual and not a number; insuring there are occasions available to get to know one another, to understand what skills and personality are being brought to the firm. It should encourage a "home grown" attitude because everyone will feel welcome.

We have set targets for employment retention and growth. We are spending double the industry average on skills training and personnel development because too many North American jobs are shifting to low-paying service industries.

At the end of the day, we are going to be proud to say that we have one of the higher paid work forces. Why? Because consumers value the quality of our products and are willing to pay for it.

We are a free enterpriser. We have computers all over the place, but our dealings with people are old-fashioned and I'm all for that.

E. Llewellyn G. Smith 1982

Every person becomes a member of a team. Each individual and team identifies who their internal customers and suppliers are. Performance appraisals are conducted to provide feedback on how well requirements are being met. This transforms the organization into a customer service mentality. It is a rewarding atmosphere.

Sharron Johnston believes in the value of these teams and has been a great support to the company for the past 24 years. As well as her office contributions, she helps my parents with their computer and fax machine and keeps track of family records and board meetings. It is Sharron, along with Edith Beitz, who has been instrumental in putting the E.D. Smith archives together.

Now

Every person has been encouraged to upgrade themselves. In fact the company is a perpetual learning organization. A place where there is a known culture and an opportunity to get ahead in one's own educational and professional agenda and to contribute on a wider spectrum of issues.

Life is one great struggle, brain against brain and the one best equipped stands the best chance to win.

E.D. Smith 1904

Finally, we have an organization that recognizes individuals and teams in a meaningful way. The same way a family recognizes its own members. Part of this comes from trust. It is never easy. It is something that is earned every day. It takes time.

Products Our market strategy will continue to develop quality blended fruit and sauce products. We have already resurrected our jam business such that we are once again Canada's largest producer. Our distribution channels will widen to encompass more segments of the U.S. market. This will include health and natural foods, and specialty direct store distribution.

Packaging and distribution will become more important than food itself. The explosion in the number of households, the reduction of people per household, the lack of time and the lack of food preparation knowledge will all contribute to portable, smaller servings of food that are fresher and ready to consume.

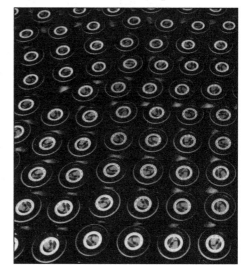

The E.D. Smith of the year 2000 will see a significant swing in sales mix towards our own branded items, less custom contract packing work for other food firms

The Eighth Generation

and a more comprehensive share of the North American retail-controlled or private-label markets. We want to see E.D. Smith brand being sold in every state of the union, in addition to every province of Canada.

As a company we will continue to offer choice to our customers, especially those adults who are trying to lead healthier lifestyles by consuming less fat and sugar and who value the benefits of wholesome, unique, quality food products made from fruits, vegetables and grains.

Fruit growers do more to bankrupt the gravediggers than doctors.

E.D. Smith 1889

"Eat Right, Live Right" with E.D. Smith was a promotion we launched in 1986. This was almost 10 years ago. Recently the Canada Food Guide came out with a new emphasis in exactly this direction. As my dad said, "The innovator gets ahead." We could be accused once again of being "ahead of our time."

Recent studies in the U.S. predict that 80% of the population will be hypoglycemic (having low blood sugar) by the year 2000. Surprisingly enough, it is usually caused by poor diet including excessive ingestion of refined foods, particularly white sugar and white flour products. In the face of this knowledge, it is probably the most neglected, least treated condition in medicine. It is not a disease and does not need to occur at this rate. As many of our products today contain a considerable amount of processed sweetener, we see it as our responsibility to raise the awareness of this concern and offer consumers a choice of products today and healthier products tomorrow.

Profits This is our third area of focus, which I see as necessary to retain our independence and finance our growth. In our ever-changing dynamic marketplace, we will determine the products and distribution niches we need to maintain profitability. This will be especially true in the U.S., where I believe we will see greater specialization.

Now

On the matter of profit and loss. I can say that without profits business is no good to you or to anyone else. Profit is the lifeblood. If we cannot make profits in this business we cannot do the things we would like to do by our employees.

Armand Smith 1950

Recently profits have been hard to come by. I believe we are not alone, as many surviving companies today have had to go through painful restructuring. The cost of innovation and change has been high. That is basically behind us now, so as business improves, our profits should rebound. All of this could not have been accomplished without the dedication of our people. Through thick and thin, our staff has done what it took at every occasion to make our outcome a success. I am surrounded by a work force that is extremely proud of our products and quality. As a team we believe in our future.

These are not just platitudes. I am not saying this because it sounds nice and because it is something most people like to hear. I am saying this because it is true.

So, what are we going to do with these profits? After paying fair and equitable taxes, after re-investing in the business, my aim is to invest in the young people of today, our "Farm Team". When we were in the seasonal fruit packing business, we hired many teenagers during the summer. This first employment experience taught them about our values and provided them with some much-needed income. With our seasonal business now gone, my plan is to re-establish this opportunity by hiring students during the summer. Part of their work will include the restoration of our Homestead buildings to turn them into a retail store, eating areas and museum, that will encourage visitors to the area and give yet another focus to the business. This initiative will also help to create our workforce of tomorrow.

IN 1995, SALES WILL REACH $120 MILLION

The Eighth Generation

Looking Forward to 2000

We see that our purpose is to bring prosperity to the communities we serve. To do this, we have set a target, a goal for ourselves: to reach $200 million in sales by the year 2000.

To help us achieve our goal, we will commission the Damaris Smith Technology and Training Centre. This facility will enhance the skills of our staff, the quality of our products and the services provided to the community.

Once again, by going back to our roots, we see the way clear to the future.

This is an evolution, not a revolution.

Llewellyn S. Smith 1995

I learned a lot from putting this book together.

I discovered the core values that run through the generations.

I have come to understand the ambition of each generation, to better place my own mark in history.

I now appreciate how well my father handled the business and I have learned from his experience.

I have put a plan in place that has its roots in the past to carry the company forward into the future.

I have come to cherish the past as represented by the solid, Old Stone House at the front of the plant; to appreciate the importance of creating a written history of my family, to see where we came from and where we are going—for my children.

Epilogue

As I wrote this book, the path I am taking became clearer. I yearn for a simpler time, a less complicated life. I have come to realize that life is what you make it.

The values that give me comfort, that allow me to sleep at night are those that are the real me—not someone I am trying to be. It is no small surprise that they are the same values that transcend generations.

I do not wish to compare myself with my predecessors as each has made his or her own mark in an independent and unique way. To do so is not a winner's game. It is more important to set my own goals and work diligently and honestly to achieve them.

Having said that, I find it difficult to ignore the uncanny similarities between E.D. and me. Some are coincidental, some are not. If you believe that life is lived in circles, that history can repeat itself, that one generation in turn affects the next, then these similarities are notable. He was a giant of a man and if I can achieve even half as much as he did, I will be pleased.

E.D. and	Me
• born in 1853	• born in 1953
• had two sons and a daughter	• have two sons and a daughter
• company founded in 1882	• I took over in 1982
• the sole owner	• the sole owner
• had the asset of the family farm to "bankroll" him	• have the assets of the family business to back me
• made several bad investments where he trusted people to be as honest as he was and they weren't	• made several investments that went wrong because I chose the wrong people to help and did not check them out well enough
• had a true desire to help local farmers and neighbours	• have a true desire to provide meaningful employment
• criticized by some for changing direction	• criticized for brash moves

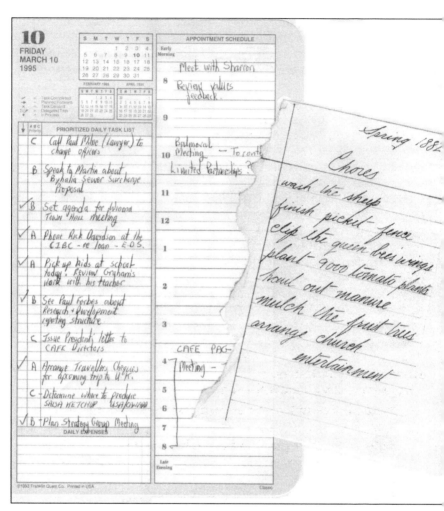

THEN and NOW
My "To Do" list and that of E.D.

E.D. and Me

• took a calculated risk with fruit investment	• taking a calculated risk with Byhalia investment
• turned away from traditional crops to plant fruit trees	• turned from local to global crops
• experimented and studied soil, trees and fruit	• experiment with fruit and recipes in test kitchen
• incredible energy and worked very hard	• same
• became President of various organizations to help promote his business	• President of CAFE National to help promote the well-being of families in business in Canada

We do not mirror one another completely. There are some interesting differences. I am lucky enough to be able to study and read for long hours at a time without hurting my eyes. E.D. was put on a pedestal and admired as an M.P. and then as a Senator but I have not been involved in politics—it no longer seems quite as noble as it did. E.D. was very alone with no mentor, no board of advisors, whereas I feel very honoured to be surrounded by CAFE friends and business associates who help me a great deal. I enjoy spending every spare moment possible with my wife Susan, Gerard, Graham and Claire and we do a lot together, whereas in E.D.'s day children really were "seen and not heard" and did not interact with parents much, especially as youngsters.

However, I feel I know the man.

We both live in the same town and we did not fight in a war.

Both of us had grandfathers who fought in significant wars and we have very intelligent, strong, visionary mothers.

Religion is important although not flaunted.

We are traditionalists at heart drawing insight from our past histories.

I consider we are both visionaries and we both talk a lot about the future.

We both travelled the world as much as we could in our time, to get the big picture.

E.D. lived through the Depression and we survived the Recession.

He started E.D. Smith, Winona and I started E.D. Smith, Byhalia.

He made the first pure jam in Canada, and today we are Canada's largest producer of it.

We both love the thrill of creating and sustaining a family business.

*Llewellyn S. at the portrait of his great-grandfather
Ernest D'Israeli Smith*

During dinner a few months later, the family and I were still enjoying the stories of the Smith family. We are pleased **Silas** decided to move to Canada; we admire **Ananias** for establishing his roadhouse; we feel sorry for **Sylvester** that he had to suffer so much illness; it is an honour to come to know **E.D.** because there are not many like him; we are touched by **Armand**'s gallantry; our appreciation for **Llewellyn** my dad, the children's grandfather, has grown immensely and finally, the rest is up to us.

Recipes

Take a step back into the past and try some of these recipes from the Women's Institute Cookbook published in 1930 and funded by E.D. Smith & Sons, Limited.

The thirties were difficult years and the women, helped by the education and information received from the Women's Institute, became very thrifty in the kitchen. By using readily available foods and a bit of ingenuity, they prepared delicious meals economically. We have suggested how to substitute current E.D. Smith products.

Mrs. Green's Apple Charlotte

Line a mould with rounds or fingers of bread, dipped in melted butter; then pour in some apple pulp, sweetened with brown sugar *(or a can of E.D. Smith Apple Pie Filling)* and enriched with a good-sized bit of butter and flavoured with the grated rind of a lemon. A round of bread also dipped in butter is laid on the top and the whole cooked for about half an hour. Let it get cold, then turn out and serve with cream and sugar.

Genevieve House's Apple Betty

2 cups cooked oatmeal
1/2 cup raisins
1/4 teaspoon cinnamon
3 cups apple cut fine
1/2 cup sugar

Mix all together and bake in a moderate oven 1/2 hour. Serve with cream.

(Try leaving out the apples and sugar and replacing them with one tin of E.D. Smith's Apple Pie filling. What a find!)

Mrs. W. Ptolemy's Lemon Layer Cake

1 small cup of granulated sugar, 1 tablespoon butter, 2 eggs, 1 1/2 cups flour, 2 teaspoons baking powder, 1/2 cup milk. Cream the butter adding sugar gradually. Then add eggs, well-beaten, flour and baking powder, alternately with the milk. Beat until well mixed. Bake in layers in a moderate oven. Put lemon filling between layers and cover with almond icing (use almond extract) and chopped nuts.

Lemon Filling

1/2 cup sugar, 1 tablespoon butter, 1 teaspoon cornstarch. All beaten smooth, add 1/4 cup boiling water and cook till clear. Flavour with lemon juice or extract.

(Today, a jar of E.D. Smith's Lemon Filling does the trick but still gives that old-fashioned look and flavour! Even good with a store-bought cake or cake mix.)

The following recipes are collected from the E.D. Smith test kitchens of today.

Montmorency Chicken

4 to 6 chicken pieces
2 tbsp. (30 ml) vegetable oil
1/2 cup (125 ml) chicken broth
1/4 cup (60 ml) soya sauce
2 tbsp. (30 ml) vinegar
1 clove garlic minced
1 tsp. (5 ml) ground ginger
1 can (19 oz./540 ml) Lite'n Fruity Cherry Fruit Filling

Brown chicken pieces on both sides in oil in frying pan.
Combine chicken broth, soya sauce, vinegar, garlic and ginger.
Add to pan and bring to a boil.
Cover and simmer for about 35 minutes or until chicken is tender.
Remove chicken from pan and keep warm. Stir cherry fruit filling into liquid in pan; bring to a boil, stirring constantly.
Spoon over chicken.
Makes four to six servings.

Quick and Easy Polynesian Pork (or Chicken)

1–2 tablespoons (15–30 ml) butter
1 medium onion, chopped
1 green pepper cut in strips
2 cups (500 ml) COOKED pork or chicken, cubed
1 can (19 oz./540 ml) E.D. Smith Apple Pie Filling
2 tbsp. (30 ml) soya sauce
4 cups (1 litre) hot cooked rice

Melt butter in a skillet or dutch oven and cook onion just until tender. Stir in soya sauce.
Add green pepper, meat and Apple Pie Filling. Simmer, covered over low heat for 5 or 10 minutes until heated through. Serve over hot cooked rice. Serves 4.

Sweet and Sour Ham Sauce

1/2 cup (125 ml) E.D. Smith ketchup
1 tsp. (5 ml) HP Sauce
1 cup (250 ml) E.D. Smith Raisin Pie Filling
1/2 cup (125 ml) orange juice
1/4 cup (60 ml) brown sugar
1 tsp. (5 ml) prepared mustard

Combine all the ingredients in a saucepan. Heat to boiling point and serve hot over ham.

Jam Frosting

1 cup (250 ml) E.D. Smith jam, raspberry, strawberry or apricot
2 egg whites
1 tsp. (5 ml) lemon juice

Beat the egg whites until stiff but not dry. Heat the jam over low heat until it bubbles; add the lemon juice. Pour the jam very slowly into the egg whites, while beating, until the frosting stands in peaks.

Ice Cream Pie

Set out one litre of vanilla ice cream to soften. Blend into it 3/4 of one can of ANY flavour E.D. Smith Pie Filling. Pile it into a baked pie shell, heaping it slightly in the centre. Garnish with remaining 1/4 can of pie filling. Refreeze.

Pumpkin Custard

1 1/2 (310 ml) cups hot milk
2/3 cup (165 ml) E.D. Smith Pumpkin Pie Filling
2 eggs
6 large marshmallows

Mix the hot milk and Pumpkin Pie Filling with a rotary beater until thoroughly blended. Add the eggs and beat just to blend. Pour into 6 custard cups and top each with a marshmallow. Place the cups in a pan of hot water and bake at 350 degrees for 30 minutes. Refrigerate when cool.

The following recipe is so popular you have probably had a taste of it already at somebody's party. Did you ever wonder how to make it? Well here is:

Canterbury Cheese Ball

1 pkg. (250 g.) cream cheese, at room temperature
1/4 cup (50 g.) blue cheese (about 2 oz)
2 tbsp. (30 ml) butter, at room temperature
5 tsp. (25 ml) Lea & Perrins Worcestershire Sauce
1 large clove garlic, minced
1/4 cup (60 ml) chopped parsley
1/4 cup (60 ml) chopped walnuts or pecans

1. Combine cheeses, butter, Lea & Perrins and garlic; beat until smooth. Spoon mixture onto a piece of plastic wrap. Shape into a ball, using plastic wrap to assist. Chill, wrapped, until firm.
2. Unwrap ball, smooth surface and roll in parsley or chopped nuts or a combination of both. Serve surrounded by crackers.

Makes 1 cheese ball.

Party Dip: Beat 2 tbsp. (30 ml) milk into cheese mixture. Serve at room temperature surrounded with assorted crisp vegetables.

Stuffed Tomatoes: Spoon or pipe cheese mixture into 30-35 Tiny Tim tomatoes, hollowed and drained. Chill.

Ham Pinwheels: Spread cheese mixture evenly over six 4 x 6 inch (10 x 15 cm.) ham slices. Roll each, beginning along the 4 inch (10 cm) side. Chill. At serving time, cut each roll into 5 or 6 slices.

Stuffed Snow Peas: Spoon or pipe cheese mixture into about 60 snow peas, blanched, chilled and slit open along the straight side. Chill.

Mini Cheese Balls: Form chilled mixture into about 40 small balls, about 3/4 inch (2 cm) in diameter. Roll in chopped parsley or nuts. Chill.

Lea & Perrins Magic Salad Dressing

1 clove garlic, minced
3 tbsp. (45 ml) freshly grated Parmesan cheese
2 tbsp. (30 ml) lemon juice
1 tbsp. (15 ml) red wine vinegar
1 tsp. (5 ml) Lea & Perrins Worcestershire Sauce
1/2 tsp. (2 ml) salt
1/2 cup (125 ml) olive oil
Salad greens

Combine all ingredients; whisk to blend. Serve with assorted cold salad greens or pour over hot potatoes or other vegetables.

As of February 24, 1995, the following people were working at the E.D. Smith & Sons company in Winona, Ontario.

Donald Aasman
Mary A. Agard
Jill A. Albano
Raymond J. Albert
Sue Ann Albert
Karen Allingham
Donna-Lee Allison
Jemal B. Anderson
Karen M. Andrews
Michelle R. Antonik
John J. Arsenault
Paul J. Barker
Victoria A. Barre
Brad A. Beaudoin
Clarence J. Becker
Frank Bene
Arie Bergshoeff
Henrietta Bergshoeff
Blanche M. Bernard
Joseph Bernard
Paul V. Berti
Charlie Bianco
David Bittarello
Donald A. Black
John C. Blanchard
Randall H. Bodman
Roberta J.C. Bollard
Renata L. Bollito
Neil S. Bosdet
Robyn Bouskill
Michael C. Bowker
Patricia Bowman
Robert J. Bowman
Cheryl I. Bozich
Paul D. Bozich
Tina Bozzo
Frank I. Brajer
Mark I. Brajer
Edward Bruinenberg
Diane Buchanan
Sandor K. Budgay
Sandra E. Budgay
David T. Burke
Tom Burke
Stephen Cadogan
Maria Caiazzo
William Campbell
Joanne D. Capone
Scott J. Carpenter
Gary J. Carruthers
Karen E. Catling

Darcy E. Chaisson
J. Robert Chaisson
Jeanette Chaisson
Mildred Chaisson
Richard H. Chaisson
Jean-Mar Chatelain
Stacy Cheaney
Steven J. Chemerys
Shashi Chhabra
Mario Cognigni
Michael Comeau
James A. Cook
Ross T. Cossett
Paul Creechan
Richard F. Crepeau
Alison Cross-Nicholl
Rosa Cuda
Michael Cunningham
Patricia Cutler
M. Kim Davis
Michelle L. Dejonghe
Marty Delcourt
Ella J. Deluca
Charles R. Dent
Christine Derks
Everett F. Desroche
Charles E. Dewar
Glen Dewar
Michael Dewyk
Dan D. Divjak
Eric Doucette
Patrick Doucette
Jeff W. Dreger
Julie A. Dubber
Simon Dubber
Troy Durham
Peter Dykstra
Lynn L. Eagles
Karen E. Edwards
Belinda Eggleton
Larry Eggleton
Nancy V. Eggleton
Judith Elliott
Richard C. Ellis
Luann Embleton
Dean A. Epifano
Judith D. Evans
Cy J. Eybel
Helen Eybel
James E. Eybel
Joseph Fazzari

Jason Fedorowich
Phyllis J. Ferry
Norman Floro
Kevin Folk
Paul S. Forbes
John Foster
Mark Francois
Margoth A. Galdamez
Dennis C. Gale
Eva M. Gallant
John J. Gallant
Michael J. Gallant
Frances A.C. Gamache
Jeff C. Gardner
Millicent J. Garlow
Donald R. Gaudet
Maurice J.E. Gaudet
Maynard C. Gilbey
Loredana Girardi
Brian T. Goodale
James G. Gowland
Jovanka Grkinic
Sandra G. Habros
Brian J. Hachey
Carole A. Hall
Jeanette M. Halper
Brian D. Hardyman
Lynn M. Hardyman
Robert W. Haylock
Donna M. Head
Terry M. Head
Darryl Q. Heimbecker
Maryke H. Henstra
Valerie Jo Heron
Elizabeth M. Hickey
Norma G. Hishmeh
Robert Hoogendoorn
Ronald Hoogendoorn
Gary Hurst
Ria L. Islamovic
John R. Jackson
Michael P. Jakimczuk
George Janzen
Jason G. Janzen
Sharron Johnston
Craig W. Jones
Marvin D. Jones
Andrew F. Jordan
Anthony J. Jordan
Fred Jordan
Daniel Joseph

Nick Karstoff
Michael Kearse
Leaford G. Kelly
Paula Klassen
Robert Konkle
Todd M. Kostal
J. Murray Koval
Linda K. Kurpe
Douglas R. Ladoucer
Eugene G. Lambert
Elizabeth Lane
Audrey L. Lanigan
Rheal A. Lavallee
Sharon L. Law
Mark A. Lazzarato
Jennifer D. Leblanc
Gaetan Lemay
Edmund Lesner
Deborah Lewis
Maureen A. Lilly
Beverly Lindstrom
Andrew Lister
Donna M. Lyon
Mary Lyon
Peter Lyon
Wayne Mableson
Iain MacGillivray
Sandra MacPhee
Scott Magee
Damir J. Marinic
Madeline A. Martin
Daniel Todd Masche
John Mattina
Nick Mattina
Thomas Matychuk
Dina Mauro
Jeff McDonald
Carrie McElroy
Paul J. McGowan
Allan McIlveen
Lori-Ann McIntosh
Deanna McKay
Brian J. McLoughlin
Silvana Miljanovic
Sofija Mirceta
Antonio Misiti
Vanda Monaco
Bruce Moor
Tony Morabito
Pat Moriarity
Kathleen Morris
John W. Moss
Donna L. Murakami
Alma Nicholls

Vince J. Nicoletti
Duayne E. Nuttall
Sandra L. Oldfield
Jeff S. Orosz
Fred Osborne
Kimberley A. Osmond
C.M. Ottman-Poore
Michelle C. Paquin
Jacqueline Pare
Jerry Parkes
John Penney
Dorothy A. Pethick
Tim Pettigrew
Nancy Pitton
Cynthia L. Poirier
Nick A.J. Pollice
Cheryl Pollington
John W. Pollington
Warren Porchina
Harold Power
Robert Pretto
Patricia Proietti
Luciano A. Quarin
Edwin J. Reekie
Anne E. Rehner
Frank S. Rice
Beverly Ridgers
Jody J. Ridgers
Joanne R. Ridley
Maryanne Roy
Darryl Rubletz
Beverly R. Russell
Joseph Sanseverino
Steven J. Scott
Nenad Sekulic
Nadine Sertic
Leon Y. Seto
Richard Sexton
Dana L. Shanner
Madhu Sharma
Tim Sherratt
Roseanne Shortt
Harold Shrimer
David E. Sidney
David A. Simon
Karen Skarja
Warren R. Skuse
Tod Slabosz
Allan R. Smith
Catherine Smith
E. Llewellyn G. Smith
Llewellyn S. Smith
Paul Smith
Renata D.J. Smith

Stanley H. Smith
Richard J. Sparks
Sheila D. Spencer
Joseph G. Spiler
Jeff G. Stanley
Kim J. Stansall
Ross M. Swim
James F. Szumilas
Jeffrey J. Taylor
Martin Taylor
Sandra J. Teetzel
John Termorshuizen
Brenda Tillman
Patrick R. Todd
Bronek Roy Tomchuk
Boris Topic
Peter L. Toth
Michael R. Troup
Michael J. Urban
Janet E. Vachon
Julien E. Vachon
Nancy L. Vachon
Rene G. Vachon
Brenda E. Valliant
Vicki Vandenbeukel
Clarence Vanderheide
Ilona J. Vanderveen
Jan Vanderveen
Ronald J. Vanroon
Kelvin B. Verge
Charlie Vitello
Michael Walker
Terry L. Walters
Phyllis R. Warren
Scott G. Warrener
Lenora M. Watson
Cynthia M. Webb
Reta Weber
Florence M. Wheeler
Brenda K. Whittaker
Patricia Wilkinson
Brian Wilson
Michelle L. Wilson
Sheryl L. Wira
Darlene R. Wlazlak
Eric S. Wlazlak
Shon Y.S. Wong
Donna I. Wood
James W. Yaneff
Wayne A. Yardley
James C. Zellers
Michael Zimmer

As of April 3, 1995, the following people were working at the E.D. Smith-Gem company, in Byhalia, Mississippi.

Lachelle C. Agnew
James T. Aldrige
Cheryl M. Alexander
Mary L. Allen
James R. Anderson
Jimmy W. Austin
Marlene L. Balfour
Carolyn A. Barksdale
Gitta Beesinger
Troy W. Bennett
Sammie Ella Benson
Kerry D. Blackmon
Travis Blackmon
Barry L. Bobo
Shirley D. Boggan
Annie L. Bougard
Sandra C. Bowen
Cheryl L. Brandon
John W. Bridges
Joe C. Bronson
Janice C. Brown
Jasper Brown
William D. Brown
Annie M. Brownlee
Junior L. Brownlee
Corniece A. Butler
Thomas A. Butler
Freddie J. Bynum
Catha M. Calhoun
Ella P. Campbell
Erma J. Campbell
Arnetta Caradine
Brenda K. Carpenter
Rivina L. Cathey
Ellen E. Childers
Susie M. Churchill
Mary L. Clark
Ricardo D. Clayborn
Bruce E. Cocke
Travis C. Coleman
Patricia L. Collins
Jessie Cooper
May Rose Cooper
Paul K. Creekmore
Wade Crook
Harry L. Crutcher
Ronnie L. Culp
Jennifer F. Dancy
Brenda Davis
Gracie M. Davis
Larry W. Davis

Jack W. Davison
Earnestine Deberry
Jarrod T. Dixon
Mary L. Dotson
Jacquelyn D. Dowdy
Bobbie H. Dunlap
Lensie H. Dunlap
David B. Echols
Cedric Sims Elliott
Jacqueline D. Ellis
Nancy F. Emerson
Thomas M. Ewing
David R. Finley
Pranati L. Penny Finley
William Ford Jr.
Arthur L. Foster
Bettye S. Frans
Latoya L. Galloway
Frank A. Garavelli
Mae F. Gatewood
Terry W. Glaze
Betty L. Glover
Terry L. Glover
Willie C. Glover
Ronnie W. Goode
William M. Grant
David E. Green
Sabrina L. Greer
Kevin L. Griffin
John W. Grimes Jr.
Berlin Lynn Gullick
William J. Gurley
Angela L. Guy
Cheryl R. Guy
Mary W. Guy
Victor C. Hageman
Luther Haire Jr.
Carl B. Hall
Christine Hall
Curtis M. Hall
Clara M. Hardaway
Gwen Harden
Karen L. Harris
Peggy R. Hearn
Valmae V. Hendrickson
Doleana M. Holloway
Gretchen A. Hope
Laverne Hope
Tracy D. Hope
Vincent C. Housley

Jackie L. Hubbard
Carrie A. Humphreys
Frankie L. Ingram
Angela L. Jackson
Joseph A. James
David L. Jarrett
Mattie M. Jeffries
Tamara L. Jeffries
Connie L. Johnson
Loretta Johnson
Barbara E. Jones
Cora L. Jones
Gerald J. Jones
Ira S. Jones
Letitia R. Jones
Nancy M. Jones
Olivia Jones
Shirley A. Jones
Victor L. Jones
Alice M. Joyner
Bradford R. Kelly
Ivy L. King
John L. Lawrence
Matthew Lawrence
Michelle R. Lesueur
Antonino Lo Conte
Annette Lucas
Helen Y. Lucas
Robert D. Maness
Joseph R. Marion
Mary A. Marshall
Janita D. Martin
Willie C. Martin
Shirley A. Mathis
Sam Matlock
Isaac L. Mayfield
Mabel A. Mays
Rodney O. Mays
Arthur Lee McGowan
James McKinney
Mary V. McKinney
Clara M. McNeil
Edward McNeil
Gloria J. McNeil
Mattie M. McNeil
Patricia A. Meredith
Willie A. Milam
Dwight Moats
Andre D. Moore
Merlene Moore
Perniece S. Moore

Duane Eddie Morris
Camilla Moton
Edna M. Myers
Cathrine Newsom
Demarcus A. Newsom
Chris D. Newson
Howard Newson
Roberta R. Newson
William E. Newson
Joyce Norman
Laura T. Norman
Pearl R. Norman
Mark Nunnally
Stanley Parish
M. L. Phillips
Oscar L. Phillips
Terry W. Phillips
Susan F. Prince
Cecil B. Rankin
Bradley D. Rankin
Evelyn Rayford
Fredrick Rayford
Jo Ann Rayford
Joseph Rayford
Leatrice Rayford
Robert L. Redding
Kenneth A. Redmond
Delia J. Reid
Thomas L. Richardson
Doris Richmond
Marvin J. Richmond
Shirley Y. Richmond
Tammy R. Richmond
Mary L. Riley
Laverne Robinson
Davis Rodgers
Connel Sanders
Connie Bernard
Saulsberry
William D. Sconiers
Billie H. Sharp
Charlean Sharp
Jerry A. Shettles
Barry W. Shipp
Kenneth T. Shipp
Charles A. Sims
Betty J. Smith
Deborah M. Smith
William H. Smith
Willie R. Smith
Howard M. Sowell
George Kenneth Stacy
Stella J. Stephens
Orlando M. Stinson

Brenda K. Street
Tanya B. Street
Laura J. Sullivan
Thomas W. Tacker Jr.
Brenda L. Tate
Erich F. Taylor
Dinier R. Thompson
Joseph L. Tidwell
Romulo B. Tolentino
Annette J. Tucker
Chandra D. Tucker
Marius D. Tucker
Mae H. Tunstall
Mary B. Tunstall
Dorothy J. Turnage
Raymond M. Turnage
Basil M. Tysz
Tamra L. Upchurch
Sharon R. Vickers
Joann Walls
Christine Webb
Deanda Webster
Maggie J. Wells
Tracy West
Susan A. Wheeler
Annie P. White
Renardo Wicks
James A. Wilkins
Ahart Wilson
Linda F. Wilson
Lora A. Wilson
Robert E. Wilson
Seggretta M. Wilson
Charles A. Wiseman
Jimmie L. Wiseman
Jarvis S. Wolfe
Edna E. Woods
Patricia A. Woods
Timothy D. Wooten
Veronica K. Yeager
James L. Young
Quincy D. Young
Wade Young
George E. Zinn
Johnny E. Zinn
Linda Zinn

260

The following are members of the famous E.D. Smith,
Winona, Quarter Century Club which held its first meeting on
November 17, 1982. The date indicates the year they started.

1882	Ernest D'Israeli Smith	1942	Beatrice Meehan
1890	Jack Harper	1943	Gerald R. Wilbur
1894	W. (Billy) Nicholson	1944	William B. Heinbecker
1897	Thomas Davey		Masaki Murakami
1901	W.C. (Billy) Dawe		Shigeo Murakami
	Levi MacDougall		Toshio Murakami
1902	Milo Wilbur		Katsuyuki Nakashima
	George Winchester	1945	Alastair A.G. Smith
1904	Frank Millen	1946	D.G. Hardyman
1909	Armand A. Smith		Frank Rakowski
1911	Albert Swick	1948	Arthur L. Parker
1912	Samuel Cameron		Jesse Smith
	James Cook Sr.	1949	Gord Carpenter
	George Honey	1950	I. Maxwell Prentiss
	James Law		J.A. Wamsteeker
1913	John P. Davies	1951	Mario Cognini
	Isobel Swick		Ken Foster
1914	Anne Davies		Rose Gray
1915	Fred Rogers		Carrie Hallett
1916	George Hardyman		Robert A. Hallett
	William Langdon		Abe Knegt
	John A. Wilbur		Bella Legere
1919	Charles Shaw	1952	Arie G. Bergshoeff
1920	William Jacobs		Corneills A. Bergshoeff
1921	Elizabeth Getrick		Olga Markowiak
	Leon L. Smith		Harry J. Payne
1923	Irl Butner	1953	Renata Bollito
1924	Sydney A. Jones		Alma Geitz
	Marjorie Woodford		John Hoogendoorn
1925	Nora M. Langdon		Helen Janicki
	Alice Lymer		Mary LeBlanc
1926	Arthur E. Parker		Rosalia Rosati
1928	Julia Carpenter		Fred Sigurdson
1929	William Fowler		Sarah Snell
	James P. Reekie		David B. Wilson
	Joseph Winchester	1954	Harriet Franklin
1932	Alice Crooks		Bill Newcombe
1934	W. Gordon Grant	1955	Jessie Buckingham
1935	Margaret Armstrong		Joe Fazzari
1936	A.C. Gilbey		Phyllis M. Toohey
1937	Nettie I. Bell		Adrianus Van Dyk
	Eric Durber	1956	Luciano Quarin
1939	Muriel MacLean		J.R. Winchester
	J.M. Woodley	1957	Virgi Bassi
1940	W.B. Reekie		J.B. Carruthers
	E. Llewellyn G. Smith		

1957	J.M. Polson	1962	Nick Mattina
	Leon Radziwon		Roger Randle
	D.R. Running		Phyllis Warren
	Alex Seregelyi	1963	Henrietta Bergshoeff
1958	Judy Evans		Lorenz Bittner
	Maria Golini		Beatrice Del Fiacco
	Carmela Spagnoli		Roelof Oegema
	Mervyn Turner		Anna Perotta
1959	Teresa Fazzari		Stan Smith
	Maynard Gilbey	1964	Everette Desroche
	Leverne Smith		Cy Eybel
	Jack Turner		Fred Jordan
	George A. Wood	1965	John Gallant
1960	John Aplin		Rene Vachon
	Ross Swim		Julian Vachon
1961	Philippe Michaud	1966	Lynn Hardyman
	Vanda Monaco	1967	Bob Chaisson
	Donald Walker		Robert Cunliffe
	Leigh Winchester		Peter Lyon
1962	Nina Di Genova		Flo Wheeler
	Eric Doucette	1969	Robert Konkle
	Maurice Gaudet		Madeline Martin
	Lilian Lucas		

The following have had twenty-five years or more of service at E.D. Smith-Gem, Byhalia. Some were even members of the original "Potato House Gang." The date indicates the year they started.

1952	Cooper Adams (founder of	1958	Kate Bourland
	Gem, Incorporated)		Jessie Hanna
	Ray Tillinghast	1959	Dorothy Boren
	Frances Johnston	1960	Ahart Wilson
	Wardie Reagh	1961	Howard Sowell
	Cornelia Rikard		Billy Hue Sharp
	Alfa Mae Harris		Mary Waldrop
1953	Mary Virginia McKinney		Robert Skarbovick
	Liz Kizer	1962	Leo Butler
	Sarah Y. Bunn	1966	Mary Lou Allen
1954	Lanier Ferguson	1967	Wade Crook
	Berniece Roland		Bessie Anthony
1955	Sadie Anglin	1968	Cora L. Jones
	Hazel Cooper	1969	Carrie Humphreys
1956	Gladys Algee		Joseph Marion
	Jeanette Stallings		
1958	Bobbie Dunlap		
	Sarah Battle		
	Marjorie Brooks		
	Lillie St. John		